BEDTIME STORIES
FOR ADULTS

2 BOOKS IN 1:

RELAXING SLEEP STORIES TO REDUCE INSOMNIA &

STRESS RELIEF. A Complete Compendium to Help Adults Fall

Asleep and Overcome Anxiety Through Deep Sleep Meditation.

Table of Contents

RELAXING SLEEP STORIES TO REDUCE INSOMNIA

How to Fall Asleep Faster and Heal Your Body During the Night. Guided Tales for a Deep Meditation to Reduce Stress, Prevent Panic, and Overcome Anxiety.

INTRODUCTION

─Relaxing sleep stories to reduce insomnia‖ is a self-help book that helps adults who have difficulty sleeping. This book will answer questions such as how do I unwind and calm down at night. How do I fall asleep in 5 minutes? Can meditation help me fall asleep? What is the surest solution to insomnia? These and many more questions will be answered in this book. Lets take a cursory overview on some of these questions here before delving in-depth later on – follow me, shall we?

If you're like me, your night should probably go like this: after an exhausting day, you get undressed, eat some takeout, or sometimes a healthy dinner. Head to the bathroom; have a warm bath, quickly brush your teeth, then stare at the mirror for no reason, put on your fluffy, cozy pajamas, snuggle up in bed, turn off the lights, and boom! Nothing happens.

Not the good type of nothing. The literal ten seconds ago, ─I will collapse on the floor with my sleepy eyes if I don't get to bed as soon as possible‖ (you know that kind, right?) and now the awake kind of nothing. Then you make a second attempt at sleeping again, but then you keep staring at the ceiling, as your eyes gently navigate to the ever clicking clock, an image of what happened in the office flashes in your mind. Then you begin to analyze the image, all of a sudden you hear a noise and then you peep through your window, and you see nothing. You go back to bed again and make another attempt at sleeping again, you close your eyes and use your blanket to cover your face. It's barely a second, and you roll the blanket off your face, and you open your eyes. You failed again! You begin to panic as you become more aware of how close you are from hearing the cock crow or your alarm ring. And you just wish you had slept when you had the chance to, while reading that boring document at work or working on the computer. I mean, it was definitely easier to sleep then. Now all you have are your deepest and darkest thought and worries as the clock ticks endlessly.

If this story sounds familiar to you, then we are on the same track.

There was a time in my life when insomnia was one of the biggest challenge I faced. I woke up every morning feeling devastated. I was so worried about my condition. I never had the opportunity to tell someone how terrible my nights were. I felt I wasn't the only one going through it, and I thought most people at work went through the same challenge. I became less concerned about insomnia until one faithful day when one of my favorite friends at the office invited me for a sleepover at his place. I couldn't say no, I mean it was Friday. TGIF! I definitely had a nice time: we ate some nice meal and chatted for a while, and of course, it was getting late. My worst enemy was here. The Night!

Bedtime had arrived.

His room wasn't so big, and there was no way his little bed would have accommodated us. So he offered to sleep on the floor while I had the entire room to myself. He reached out for some blanket from his wardrobe and laid it on the cold tiles. In less than a minute, he was already fast asleep. I laid on the bed, watching my friend enjoy his sleep.

I was so restless, I tried so hard to sleep, but sleep seemed so far away. I couldn't fail to notice how peaceful my friend slept. I kept trying to understand why it was easy for him to sleep, and it was a hell of war for me to even doze off for a second. I could see why he was more excited about each day than I was. He slept for at least 5hours, and I could barely sleep for up to 30mins. And he was clearly more organized and productive than I was. That was when the urge for a more fulfilling life was created. After that night, I was determined to change my life for good. I didn't know how it was going to happen.

I just knew that things were about to change for good!

Then I thought to myself, —you deserve a good night rest.‖

And you too, my dear reader deserves a sound night rest also.

Not being able to sleep is extensively frightening. We panic with our inability to cope with all the demands of the next day. We even panic just because we are panicking; anxiety becomes the order of the day. The possibility of falling asleep seems unattainable as the clock counts down to another exhausted, irritable dawn. And even when we manage to fall asleep, we wake up debilitated, frustrated, and unsure about the day. We've all experienced sleepless nights at least once or multiple times in our lives. Our sleeplessness may cause all manner of emotional outbursts, which tends to ruin our entire day. And the cycle goes on and on.

Insomnia is a sleep disorder where a person experiences difficulty in falling asleep. It happens to be one of the world's most common sleep disorders. This restlessness, which occurs during bedtime could be caused by almost anything: ranging from a snoring partner, to an event happening the next day, or an activity that occurred in the day, fears of uncertainty, our goals, pains, insecurity.

When suffering from insomnia, we may find it difficult to fall asleep. We tend to stay alert for an extended period of time at night. We may seem to wake up multiple times at night too. Even when we eventually sleep, we wake up not feeling refreshed. Occasional experience of insomnia may come and go without causing serious problems, but can last for some months or even years in some cases.

In most cases, sleep deprivation is short term. Eventually, exhaustion catches up with us. However, some long term conditions like gastrointestinal problems, respiratory disorders, and many others can overpower fatigue. As sleepless night piles up, the bedroom can begin to form an association of anxiety and restlessness. During this period, we become so stressed that the stress response system is hijacked by our brain, flooding the body with flight, fight, or freeze chemicals through the bloodstream. This process increases the heart rate and blood pressure and jilts the body into hyperarousal. When the body is in this condition, the body begins to hunt for potential threats, which leads to the body's inability to ignore any slight discomfort or bedtime noise.

So even when we fall asleep, the quality of our rest is compromised.

Our body automatically goes through an automatic chemical change due to the alternation of our normal sleeping condition.

Our brains' primary source of energy is cerebral glucose. When we have a healthy sleeping routine, our metabolism slows down in order to conserve this glucose for waking hours. But Positron Emission Tomography (PET) studies show that the adrenaline that prevents us from sleeping, also speeds up our metabolism. So while we are asleep, our bodies are working overtime, burning through our brains' supply of energy giving glucose. This symptom of poor sleep causes us to wake up exhausted, confused, and stressed because we have used up the glucose while sleeping. And when this cycle of restlessness and stress last several months, we are diagnosed as Chronic Insomniac. If your sleeplessness and restlessness last from one night to a few weeks, it can be said to be Acute Insomnia.

And while insomnia rarely leads to death, its chemical mechanism is similar to anxiety attacks found in people experiencing depression and anxiety. Suffering from any of these conditions could eventually raise our risk of experiencing the other two. Fortunately, there are ways to break the cycle of sleeplessness. Controlling the stress that causes hyperarousal is one of the best-understood treatment for insomnia. A good sleep ritual can help rebuild our relationship with bedtime.

A few years ago, I was diagnosed with a chronic insomniac. I was worried all day long. I felt hopeless and wanted to settle for sleeping pills, but deep down in my heart, I knew that wasn't going to be the best solution. I knew it would only help temporary, and in the long run, it will cause me more harm. So I began a research on how to help myself fall asleep in less than five minutes.

And after much evaluation of different techniques, these are some of the routines that has helped me beat insomnia.

I always make sure my bedroom has little light coming in, and it's very comfortable. I make sure I don't use my phone or e-books before bed, their light can make you less sleepy at night. Before I leave for work, I always make sure my room is well arranged: my bed is laid to perfection, there are no clothes littered around the room, and all the window blinds are closed. I ensure the room is cool to help minimize threats during hyperarousal. I make sure I avoid caffeine and nicotine; they act as stimulant and can stop me from falling asleep. Most of this caffeine is consumed in coffee, it is also ingested in some sodas, chocolate, or caffeine pills. Caffeine helps us stay alert and awake, even when we haven't had enough sleep. It increases our blood pressure and makes us feel anxious. In the human body, caffeine acts as a stimulant for the central system. An insomniac must stay away from all forms of coffee, caffeine drinks, etc. Since we always wake up tired and stressed, we most times need to seek for alertness, and we resolve to take a cup of coffee. It will only make us feel more terrible at night. So our best option is to avoid any drink that contains caffeine until we are free from insomnia. It is also important that we avoid alcohol, it can affect our sleep quality. Sometimes I engage myself with relaxing activities like reading or meditating. Reading stories and meditating is, by far, my favorite technique, they have proven efficient in the long run. I also regulated my metabolism by setting consistent resting and waking time to help orient my body's biological clock. This clock or Circadian Rhythm is also sensitive to light, so I avoid bright light at night to help inform my body that it is time for sleep. In addition to this practice, some doctors prescribe medications to aid sleep. Honestly, this method is not really safe because most of the drugs lead to addiction.

Most people have learned to treat insomnia with the usual and common solution given to any health challenges, medicine, especially with pills strong enough to subdue consciousness to submission. But instead of immediately trying to wrestle insomnia with drugs medically, how about we make some effort to understand how it originates from human nature. And what in its own confused way has been trying to tell us.

Let's start by giving insomnia an identity, or let's say a personality to help us relate better with it. Let's say insomnia is the mind's revenge for something very important that we forgot to do during the day. Of course, during the day we have lots of important stuff on our mind. So we seem to ignore those vital thoughts, questions, actions that help form our core values and give us a sense of fulfillment and purpose. So when our mind is supposed to be at rest, all those nuggets of information's that we refused to pay attention to during the day come back to haunt us, and of course, we become restless because that's not what our mind wants to do at that moment. So we should form a habit of taking a brief pause during the day and reflect by giving way to some thinking.

It can be very appealing to think of philosophy as a specialized discipline of relevance to only a few academic minded type. But what philosophy actually wants from us is to live an examined self-awareness life. It is indeed a basic necessity for every human being. Self-awareness is as vital as water, food, or exercise, so much so that if we don't do it regularly, it will tell on our mental health.

If we do not constantly and consciously make out time to interrogate ourselves, question our plans, explore our talents, and think over our relationships, we will pay a very heavy price. We will be stripped of the capacity to carry out our life with enough rest in our bodies.

Some important questions we need to tackle is something within us, we might call it our inner guardian or our conscience that constantly reminds us that we are doing something wrong and we are living some stone unturned. This leads to a way of an important, long-lasting solution for insomnia, which has nothing to with any medication or soothing tea but principally more time in the reasonable hours of the day for thinking. More time in which there are no demands on us. We can then meditate philosophically: that is systematically examining everything we are concerned about, thinking through our regrets, discussing our work with our inner critic and paying attention to our inner relationship.

In short, reacquainting ourselves with ourselves.

Insomnia is seldom a physical disease, it's a healthy plague released by our core self that we should confront the excuses, we have put on for too long. Insomnia is beyond not really being able to sleep. Not being to sleep is a symptom of our action: which is, being unable to give yourself a chance to think. How about we spend more time meditating, and thinking through our day and reflecting on all the activities of the day, it would save our mind the stress of doing that during bedtime.

Meditation and reading of stories is one of the most efficient ways of overcoming insomnia. More emphasis would be made on these techniques in the rest of the book because this method has proven to be one of the most effective way in helping insomniac overcome insomnia. The deep relaxation method has proven to improve sleep quality, increase sleep time, and make it easier to stay asleep.

There are some key facts about this routine that makes it outstanding.

Mindful meditation involves focusing on your breathing and getting your mind's attention to present happenings or activities without being distracted about the past or future. This kind of meditation helps us break down those everyday thoughts to evoke the relaxation response.

This kind of meditation is very safe to carry out, it is definitely your best bet if you are looking for an all-natural way of treating insomnia. This routine, if done keenly, improves insomnia symptoms by reducing the measure of arousal in the brain, And the beautiful thing about this method is that there is no side effects when performing this technique. Another reason why it's loves by all is because of its easy accessibility, and it's inexpensive to practice. You should give it a try.

The first thing I always do before I start my meditation routine is to look for a very comfortable place or location to sit or lie down, after choosing a comfortable position, I close my eyes and begin to breathe slowly and deeply. I direct my undivided attention to my breath as I inhale and exhale. Most times, my mind will start to wander and deviate, (it's okay if you experience that, as you practice more you will get better), then I would shift my attention back to my breath. Initially, I would do it for like five minutes and get tired, but as time went on, I could go hours meditating without losing concentration. And after every routine, I will feel better. Feel alive, active, and more connected to my world. So when bedtime comes, my mind wouldn't be restless. It noticed I became more focused and effective during the day. Meditation really helped me get rid of much stress, and I'm so sure it will do the same for you if you remain consistent. And when you become consistent, you would be a few steps away from having a stable mind and getting rid of insomnia for good. Months into my routine, I had friends walk up to me and ask me questions about my mental health, the changes were so visible that it got people talking. I went from being so irritated to being one of the most exciting person in the block. I have been asked by friends and family how I conquered insomnia, and I never get to give lots of details. But in this book, I poured out my entire heart, putting down these life-changing techniques that changed my life for good.

Another life-changing technique that saved my life was reading stories—the power of a well-written book. Amazing stories has the ability to calm your nerves.

I remember days when I would pick a story about amazing creatures like a woodpecker. It was a very soothing experience. Whether it's a story of the blue ocean, or the stories of the tropical savannah, etc, beautiful stories would definitely help you fight Insomnia. Ever wondered why kids are so fascinated about bedtime stories? Or how they never make it to the last paragraph of the story before they fall asleep. That's the power of a beautiful story. It's soothing in the ear, and relaxes our mind and keeps us in touch with our mind.

Over the years, this technique has been used on adults and has proven to be very effective in fighting insomnia. In the other chapters of this book, I will be sharing amazing stories that will transform your life. You will no longer have issues falling asleep.

I genuinely hope that this book opens up your mind to an entirely new world. Because my intent is to effectively communicate all that I have learned in the last few years through experience and research. To also introduce you to a world free from restlessness, insomnia, and anxiety. And also bring you to a self-mindfulness, where you'll become aware and come in contact with your true self. I can assure you that a life free of insomnia is not a mirage. Mindfulness meditation involves focusing on your breathing and then bringing your mind's attention to the present without drifting into concerns about the past or future. It helps you break the train of your everyday thoughts to evoke the relaxation response, using whatever technique you feel is right for you.

So get ready, as I take you on a journey that will change your life forever.

CHAPTER ONE
A GUIDE

What is self-hypnosis?

You can define hypnosis as a state of consciousness, in which a person's focus is detached from his or her immediate surroundings and is totally absorbed by inner experiences such as feelings, cognition, and imaination. You have experienced a hypnotic induction when you focus your attention and totally involve your imagination to the point where what is being imagined feels real.

Have you ever wondered if you've ever been in a hypnotic state before? Everyday ˌtrance' states are part of our common human experience, such as getting lost in a movie, getting engrossed in a good book, driving down a familiar road with no conscious recollection, or when undertaking an interesting activity. When in these states, your focus is predominantly internal, but you do not necessarily lose all outer awareness. You can use this technique to reduce stress and anxiety by accessing calmness and relaxation, or help ease pain.

Hypnosis does not make the impossible possible, but can help you believe and experience what might be possible for you to achieve.

The brain works with patterns and imagery. To communicate effectively, we need more than words; we need to use words that evoke imagery. It is no surprise, therefore, that all the greatest teachers use metaphors, parables, and stories to convey their teachings. The brain has two cerebral hemispheres, and while in our normal waking state, the left brain tends to be more dominant and could be likened to our ˌconscious mind'. This communicates verbally and is the more intellectual, conscious part of ourselves. When we relax or become deeply involved in some activity, our right brain becomes more dominant. The right brain could be seen to be the more emotional, creative part of ourselves that communicates with symbols and images, and could be seen as our ‚unconscious mind'. There is always a difficulty in telling ourselves not to be upset or anxious because words are not the language of the right brain. But one can paint a word picture using guided imagery or metaphor.

When one is very anxious, they are operating at an emotional rather than cognitive level. Anxious people are using their imagination to create possible disastrous scenarios, which generates even more anxiety and hence more adrenaline, which can then turn into panic. They may feel that they are being overpowered emotionally, but if they can engage their focus and imagination to feel calm or to re-experience some positive past experience and give positive suggestions, then they will start to feel calmer and will have reduced chances of having a panic attack.

To enter hypnosis, one will have to be focused, and there are so many ways to achieve this. A low burning lamp or a phone screen could be a visual focus. An auditory focus could be music, chanting, or using repetitions. One of the simplest methods is to engage one's imagination using –Deja vu‖ (or re-experiencing) of an experience, a daydream, or fantasy.

Self-hypnosis or hypnotherapy can be a successful way of reducing stress and opening the mind to new ideas or thought processes, especially when dealing with problem behavior such as certain addictions.

How self-hypnosis works

Based on the work of Sigmund Freud - the human mind can be split into three different areas of consciousness; the conscious, subconscious, and unconscious. These different areas can be seen as different depths of the mind. Freud believed that the conscious mind is the shallowest part of the mind and is in charge of making sense of the things we are directly aware of.

The subconscious mind is below consciousness, a deeper level – hence it is not so easily accessible and controls how we feel or react to certain conditions or incidents, based on what we have learned through experience in the past. It also controls and regulates our essential bodily functions, such as breathing.

The unconscious mind is the deepest part of our mind and is the most difficult to reach – it can include subdued memories of traumatic events.

Hypnotism works by reaching a relaxed state whereby it is possible to sink deeper into our minds and rewrite or reprogram our subconscious.

Through physical and mental relaxation, self-hypnosis can allow people to go around their conscious minds and introduce positive thoughts and beliefs into their unconscious. Upon ‚awakening' from the hypnotic state, the new thoughts and beliefs in the subconscious will, in time, affect the conscious mind and can, in turn, lead to changed behaviors.

Hypnotherapy is not a ‚quick fix'; such methods require persistence and consistency for the subconscious mind to pick up and apply the new messages.

Now that you have an idea of what self-hypnosis is, do you want to be self-hypnotized?

For self-hypnosis to be effective, it is important to approach the process with an open mind. To do this, you need to meet the following conditions:

You need to really want to be hypnotized.

You need not be overly skeptical.

You need not be frightened of being hypnotized.

You need not over-analyze the processes involved

It is essential to think about why you are going to use self-hypnosis and what messages you want to plant deep into your subconscious. Work on some short statements that you are going to use when you reach a hypnotic state. Your statements should also pass the following grade:

Genuine and honest – you will not be successful in planting ideas of things you really do not want to do or achieve into your subconscious.

Positive – your statements need to be of a positive nature.

Simple – your statements need to be very direct and no more than a few words long.

Some examples of personal hypnotic statements include:

To relieve stress at work, you may use: ‚I am relaxed at work.'

To help with an addictive habit, like smoking, you may use: 'I don't smoke.'

To calm your nerves before a public-speaking event, you may choose: 'I am a confident speaker.'

Remember, these statements are messages to your own subconscious – use 'I,' focus on specific actions, and always prepare your statements as present-tense facts. Concentrate on one or two statements to start with – commit these to memory and focus on them in your mind.

Steps to enable self-hypnosis

Now before you attempt self-hypnosis, it is important to tell someone around you what you are doing. Self-hypnosis is almost like falling asleep, so it would make sense to tell the person around you that you are going to take a nap. Nobody appreciates being disturbed when they are trying to sleep. So by telling someone, you make it less likely for you to be disturbed.

To start the process of self-hypnosis, you need to be physically relaxed and comfortable. You can achieve this by sitting in a comfortable chair with your back straight and or lie down on your back while facing upward. Take deep breaths slowly. Breathe in through your nose and exhale through your mouth. As you breathe, ensure that your stomach rises and falls, while your chest makes little movement. Why breathe from your stomach? Belly breathing stimulates the vague nerve, which runs from the head down the neck, through the chest, and to the colon. This activates your relaxation response, reducing your heart rate and blood pressure, and lowering stress levels.

Find an object that you can focus all your attention on- this object should involve you looking upwards to the ceiling or the high parts of your wall.

The next step is to clear your mind of all thoughts and just focus on the object- this can be a little hard to achieve but take your time until all your attention is channeled to that one object.

Now become aware of your eyes, think about your eyelids getting really heavy, and slowly closing- at this point, focus on your breathing. Continue taking deep breaths as your eyes slowly close.

Now use your mind's eye to visualize the rhythmic movements of an object- the hand of a pendulum- anything regular, slow, and steady movement. Visualize the object swing back and forth or upward and downward in your mind's eye.

Softly and slowly count down from ten in your head, telling yourself that you are relaxing after each number. '10, I am relaxing', etc. Believe and remind yourself that when you are done counting, you will have reached your hypnotic state.

Now you're in your hypnotic state. It is time to focus on those personal statements that you prepared. Focus on each statement- visualize it in your mind's eye as you repeat the statements to yourself in your thoughts.

Relax and clear your mind once more before bringing yourself out of your hypnotic state. Slowly and increasingly forcibly count up to 10. Reverse the process you used before when you counted down into your hypnotic state. Use some positive messages between each number, as you count. '1, when I awake, I will feel awesome... etc.

When you reach 10 you will feel fully awake and revived! Slowly let your conscious mind become aware of the events of the day and continue feeling refreshed.

The more you practice and practice self-hypnosis, the more successful it will become for you, and the easier it will get for you to reach the hypnotic state.

What is Mindfulness?

Do you want to be able to clear your mind and focus on one thing? Mindfulness. It seems like a straightforward word. It suggests that the mind is fully aware and attentive to what's happening, to what you're doing, to your movements, and the space around you. That might seem ordinary, except for the disturbing fact that we so often veer from the matter at hand. Our mind loses touch with our body, and soon we're engaged in unavoidable thoughts about something that just happened or sweating about the future. And that makes us anxious.

Mindfulness is the basic human ability to be fully present, aware of where we are and what we're doing, and not excessively reactive or emotionally overpowered by what's going on around us.

Mindfulness is a quality that every human being is born with, it's not something you have to –download‖ from the outside, and you just have to learn how to access it.

While mindfulness is innate, it can be accessed through proven techniques, particularly seated, walking, standing, and moving meditation (it's also possible lying down but often leads to sleep).

When you meditate, it doesn't help to put all your attention on the benefits, but rather to just do the practice, there is no denying the benefits, or no one would do it. When we're mindful, we reduce stress, improve performance, gain insight and awareness through observing our own mind, and increase our attention well-being.

Mindfulness meditation gifts us time, when we can set aside judgment and let loose of our natural curiosity about the workings of the mind, approaching our experience with warmth and kindness—to ourselves and others.

Mindfulness improves well-being. Increases your capacity for mindfulness back up many behaviors that contribute to a satisfying life. Being mindful makes it easier to appreciate the pleasures in life as they occur, helps you become fully immersed in activities, and creates a heightened capacity to deal with adverse events. By focusing on what is happening here and now, many people who practice mindfulness find that they are less likely to get caught up in anxieties, the future, or regrets over the past, are less obsessed with concerns about success and self-esteem and are better able to form deep connections with others.

Mindfulness improves physical health. If improved well-being isn't enough of a benefit, scientists have discovered that mindfulness techniques help improve physical health in a number of ways. Mindfulness can: help relieve stress, treat heart disease, lower blood pressure, reduce chronic pain, improve sleep, and alleviate gastrointestinal difficulties.

Mindfulness improves mental health. In recent years, psychotherapists have used mindfulness meditation as an important element in the treatment of several problems, including depression, substance abuse, eating disorders, couples' conflicts, anxiety disorders, and obsessive-compulsive disorder.

Mindfulness doesn't wipe out stress or life difficulties; instead, by becoming aware of displeasing thoughts and emotions that arise because of difficult situations, we have more choice on how to handle them at the moment — and a better chance of reacting calmly and sympathetically when faced with stress or challenges. Of course, practicing mindfulness does not mean you never get angry. In essence, rather, it allows us to be more thoughtful about how you want to respond, whether that's calmly and sympathetically or perhaps, occasionally with measured anger.

Mindfulness techniques

There are many ways to practice mindfulness, but the endpoint of any mindfulness technique is to achieve a state of lively, focused relaxation by deliberately paying attention to thoughts and sensations without judgment. This allows our mind to refocus on the present moment. All mindfulness techniques are a form of meditation.

Basic mindfulness meditation - Sit quietly and focus on your natural breathing or on a word or ‒mantra‖ that you repeat silently. Allow your thoughts to come and let them go without judgment and return to your focus on breath or mantra. Your mantra should be something positive.

Loving Kindness - Instead of focusing on the breath, this technique rather focuses on the image of different people: people we know, people we don't; people we like, people we don't. We direct well-wishes first to ourselves, and then, as a ripple effect, to others, which frees us of displeasing feelings we may be experiencing.

Body sensations - Notice subtle body sensations such as an itch or tingling without judgment and let them pass. Focus on one part of the body at a time until you have accessed your whole body.

Sensory - In this mindfulness technique, your senses come into play. Notice sights, sounds, smells, tastes, and touches. Name them ‒sight,‖ ‒sound,‖ ‒smell,‖ ‒taste,‖ or ‒touch‖ without judgment and let them go.

Emotions - Allow emotions to be present without judgment. Practice a steady and relaxed naming of emotions: ‒joy,‖ ‒anger,‖ ‒frustration.‖ Accept the presence of the emotions without judgment and let them go.

Urge surfing – Access your cravings (for addictive substances or behaviors) and allow them to pass. Notice how your body feels as the craving enters. Replace the wish for the craving to go away with the certain knowledge that it will wane.

Practicing mindfulness post-meditation

Whichever technique you choose to engage in, know that experiencing moments of mindfulness during meditation is a great first step. After meditation, while our minds will likely experience distractions throughout the day, the more our mindfulness practice is developed, the more we can catch ourselves being distracted, and the more we can bring our focus back to the present moment. After all, that's the whole point of practicing mindfulness meditation — to make us more mindful and less distracted throughout the day.

So how do you remember to be mindful when you're not meditating? At the end of your meditation, recognize how your mind feels and then take a deliberate step to carry that feeling into the rest of your day. You may find it helpful to form a clear idea of what you are going to do next — maybe take a shower or get a cup of coffee — and perform that next task with the same level of awareness that you experienced during meditation. It doesn't matter what you do after meditation, as long as you look for opportunities throughout your day in which to recognize the space and mindfulness you experienced during your practice

What is Guided Meditation?

Guided meditation is when you are guided, by a narrator, to arouse a particular change in your life. Because the mind tends to wander off where it will, many of us find it easier to focus and relax when our minds aren't completely left to their own control. This form of meditation is often guided another person's voice - a narrator in group settings, or by recordings presented on apps, podcasts, videos, CDs, etc.

First, the narrator guides you to relax your body and mind, to help you reach a deep meditative state before going on a journey, in your mind, to reach that goal.

As the brain does not differentiate between an imagined event and a real one, the experience you have with a guided meditation is just like having a real experience. This affects your life in amazing ways due to the way the brain works.

How Guided Meditation works

You can produce change in your life through the practice of guided meditation. This is as result of how the brain works. When you experience something in life, it forms a neural pathway in your brain and the information will be passed to the subconscious mind to store for future use.

For instance, if you're wanted to learn a new skill, your brain has already stored previous experience of you trying to learn a new skill. If your experience was good, you will be good at learning the skill. If your experience was bad, chances are it will be difficult for you to learn the new skill. Through guided meditation, you can reprogram your brain by reaching your subconscious mind and planting new and better experiences in it.

Since the brain does not distinguish real experiences and imagined experiences. When you plant new experiences in your mind through meditation, your brain takes it that you have actually experienced what you are imagining and forms new neural pathways to be stored for future use.

Sports experts even suggest that when you are trying to get better at sports, and you imagine practicing that sport in your mind, the muscles in your body are actually being activated and strengthened as a result.

Most guided meditation routines involve three sections:

Relaxing Meditative Session - In this first session, you will be given a complete mind and body relaxation. This will help you to reach the meditative state required to access your subconscious mind.

Visualization Deepener Session - In this session, you will be guided through a beautiful imaginary scene to strengthen your visualization skills. This will also allow you to sink deeper into the meditative state in preparation for the next session.

Life Goal Session - This last session is where you will be guided through a specific scene to plant a new experience in your subconscious that will produce desired outcomes in your life. It is in this session that the magic of guided meditation really happens, and depending on your goal, you will start to see results within a few days.

Want to understand bathe science of guided meditation? Pat attention here.

Think of your mind as a video player with hundreds of videos uploaded. These videos represent a program that affects the way you think, act, and behave in certain situations. These programs are installed in your brain as you have experience and become stronger every time you have that experience.

If you always had an experience where you failed Math and you were told that you are not good at Math, this experience forms a program in your mind that affects the way you react whenever the subject Math comes up. If someone ever asks you to help with a math calculation, you will simply say, —I'm not good at Math‖ Your brain will not even try to access the calculation because of the program already installed.

The captivating part about all of this is that the programs have not only been written and stored in the brain, but stored in the very cells of your body. The brain has only created a pathway to coordinate your actions based on external factors, which speaks to the cells in your body.

If you stop to think about the implication of this, you will realize that it is not our genes that determine who we are but the images we create in our minds that determine who we are.

The problem is that it is very difficult to change these programs without a way to access the subconscious mind and rewrite these programs by imagination, and create new neural pathways in our mind that will communicate effectively, what we desire with the cells of our body.

Guided meditation gives you the power to reach your subconscious mind by feeding it images, sounds, and guiding your imagination to experience all your senses, thereby giving your brain an experience of what feels like a real experience. So when you go through a guided meditation, you give yourself an experience that creates new neural pathways that affect your whole body and prepares you for future success.

Guided meditation for stress reduction

Stress is a modern epidemic! And you've probably heard (you even read about it a few paragraphs ago) about how mindfulness practice can relieve stress. But if you sit down to practice and your mind continually wanders off and engages in the very thoughts you are trying to let go of, you might feel like meditation is increasing your stress! That's why guided meditations are very useful: they mildly introduce you to the stress-relieving practice.

In general, guided meditation for stress relief, relaxation, and sleep consists of a pleasant, soothing meditation- directed by a guide (a real human or a recording) - geared towards helping the listener let go of anxieties and tensions as they relax in bed or a comfortable chair.

Often, guided relaxation meditations involve calming sounds, comforting melodies, and the likes. These may invite listeners to imagine themselves in pleasant, peaceful environments—under a beautiful tree by a calm mountain or lake, for example, with a gradually rising sun and comforting sounds of gentle waves produced by the lake. The purpose is to encourage people to unwind or relax and sleep. Some individuals discover that to enjoy their deepest sleep, meditations of this kind are invaluable.

There is no telling how much we can achieve when we make use of these relaxation techniques. By learning to calm your body and mind, your physical and emotional stress and anxieties will be relieved. This leaves you feeling refreshed and better, ready to face whatever challenges the day throws at you. With persistent and consistent practice, you can reap even greater benefits.

HOW CAN I CALM DOWN AT NIGHT?

Sleep is precious because it is how the body heals and repairs broken tissues. The thief of sleep is insomnia, and it can be caused by a myriad of reasons which one of them is anxiety. The questions would be, now we know the diagnosis, what is the solution? How can I calm down at night and have at least six hours of uninterrupted sleep and wake up refreshed? Some people sleep alright but wake up tired and unsatisfied. They wake up without that spark that most people who sleep well have. What could be the solution to this? How can I calm down at night? Here are a few tips.

Unwind

Nothing works magic like unwinding; that is preparing your mind to sleep. You know, the mind is like a muscle and can be trained to do amazing things. One of it is, it can be trained to sleep—and by that I mean, prepare itself to sleep before it gets to sleep time. If you set your mind that by a certain time, you would be asleep, your body would be ready for it. So, conclude all your day's activities, and begin the process to your bed. Declutter, eat early, have a bath, and just tuck in as you prepare to sleep.

Be grateful

It helps you relax if you can focus your mind on all the things you were able to achieve than the things you sucked at doing. Failure has a way of creating panic in you, while gratitude—that feeling of contentment and peace, helps you relax. So, count your blessings before you close your eyes to sleep, it helps you relax.

The bed space is for sleep alone

People fall into the trap of doing other work around the space where they are meant to be sleeping. Memories work with place and time; this means, your brain would remember something either because you are at a certain place with certain memory landmarks, or you see things around you that can trigger that memory. If you consistently work in your sleeping space, your brain would recognize that space as work, and you might not be able to tuck yourself to sleep, it might be a tad difficult. So, restrict your bed space for sleep alone and not for any other activity.

Make sure you are in something comfortable

You do not want to be turning around your bed and itching; make sure you are in something comfortable. Buy pajamas that doesn't itch you, let it be comfortable. Use clean bedspreads and duvets. If they are dirty and sandy, it can be really uncomfortable. You want to ensure that these materials you are using are giving you maximum comfort and not the other way round.

Turn off the lights and turn on some soft sound

Soft music can ease you into your dreamland. It can serve as your chauffeur into the dream world. Let it not be loud, let It be moderate and at a moderate volume that would not wake you up at any time and let it be at a certain volume that it would not interfere with your alarm if it rings. You want to be sure it is soft and an enjoyable music. Then turn off the lights. When light the light is on, your brain is active, and sleep can be hard, so turn off the lights and let there be absolute darkness, it can make you relax so fast that you would fall asleep before you even know it.

Organize your schedule before you sleep

We normally have a bad habit of taking our plans and schedules with us to our bed and try to organize them there. It can be very distracting, especially when you need to sleep, and you are always getting off the bed to update a new list or something. Make sure you have all the work for the next day all sorted ou; before you go to bed. Please ensure that your cell-phones are turned off, to avoid any distractions as we begin to fly into our dreamland. If you want to get that sleep your desire, turn off your cell-phones or keep them far away from your reach that when it rings, it won't disturb you. It is smarter and safer for you because you do not want to be woken from sleep only to find out that your mom lost her toothbrush and thinks you are with it.

<u>Seek help</u>

No one is an island, if you have any issue, you can turn to people who can help you for help. Especially if you have issues with anxiety or your stress levels are over the top, it is not wrong to seek the help of a therapist or a doctor to handle your issues. You do not want these things to affect your mind negatively, you want to be on top of the issue and regulate it so that it doesn't affect important things in your life. You do not want to slip into depression and other unhealthy things that come with it.

The bulk of your day might have been filled with different forms or hustling and bustling – your mind has been alert and awake to take care of various levels of businesses in the day, now, its nighttime, you have to intentionally unwind and be calm for a good sleep experience. When it comes to good sleep, tension can be a major barrier; that frustrating moment when you desire to get a shut-eye, but your mind is racing from one point to another, how can I calm down at night? Here are some steps you can take to relax your nerves and get yourself to sleep better:

Practice gratitude at night time: a lot of people do not know, but at night, when you are done with the hustles of the day, calming down to be thankful for all you have, grateful for what you do not have yet, but somehow you are surviving without them, being grateful for the opportunities you have can really help you calm down. Instead of focusing on negative stuff, intentionally take a posture of seeing the best and be thankful for them – do you know why? Your body, many times can not differentiate exactly when your mind is processing something real and something that is not real, for instance; when you imagine a very scary or traumatizing incident, though it is not real or happening at the moment, your body would begin to respond as if it is real, your heart rate increases, your stomach tightens, your pupil dilates et cetera. In the same way, when you practice gratitude, you will make your body calm and begin to ease into sleep mode.

Get a brownout: The hormone -melatonin‖ is the guy in charge of your daily rhythm – simply put; sleeplessness and sleep. The major controller of melatonin in your body is –sunlight‖ or the –day and night balance,‖ now, when you come back from the day's activity, you begin to ease into a calm mode by reducing light intensity. That way, your body begins to have a sense of retirement. So, reducing light intensity can help you calm down and unwind after the day's hustle.

Use an anxiety journal: This would help you write out all the things you have not done, all your to-do list for the next day and whatever stresses you at all, this will help free your mind and get it clear for a good sleep. You can never unwind if your mind is carrying all the cares, worries, and anxiousness of the day; therefore, by keeping an anxiety journal, you can set your mind free.

Reduce movement as much as possible: too much motion in our muscles tells our brain there is still work to do. When you reduce your motion generally and try to be as still as your routine can permit, you will begin to calm down. Your mind would begin to be lulled into a rest mode. So another major way to calm down and unwind is to reduce your movement as much as possible.

Meditate: meditation will put you in a relaxation mode. In a fast-paced world, meditation to an average young person seems to be unimportant or for the overtly religious. In fact, many people see slowing down to meditate as a drag. You can easily practice meditation by taking a comfortable position, focus on the rhythm of your breath; you can even use a breath ball if possible, to follow your breathing rhythm. Breathing in as the ball expands and breathing out when the ball contracts. Inevitably, your attention will leave the rhythm and roam to other thoughts. When you get around to noticing that your mind has deviated—in a few seconds, a minute, five minutes—simply return your attention to the rhythm of your breath.

Focus on a white noise: personally, I cannot trade the squeaky sound of my old fan for anything, as the day drowns into the darkness of night; one of the ways you can calm yourself down and unwind is by focusing on low white noise. If you do not love a squeaky old fan as I do, you can simply get a sleep app and select a sound you like, keep it low so that it will blend into the background. Focusing on the white noise from my fan, an app, or a cricket can help your mind detach from the whole activities of the day and begin to settle down.

WHAT IS THE BEST SOLUTION FOR INSOMNIA

Insomnia is a thief of sleep; it is a situation where a person cannot get the required sleep. This affects sick people, the middle and upper class, and people who have bad eating and drinking habits. Statistics show that Insomnia affects over sixty million Americans yearly, and can range from acute to chronic. The effect of insomnia can be devastating and frustrating; There are also adverse consequences of starving your body of sleep like; stroke, asthma, seizures, compromised immune system, increased sensitivity to pain, obesity, diabetes (due to binge eating), heart disease, high blood pressure, affected sense of judgment and awareness, depression, anxiety, confusion, un-satisfaction, and frustration. These consequences can shorten your life span, hurt the people you love and maybe ruin your business. So how do we beat it? How do we give it a run for its money? Even if insomnia is common, there are ways to overcome its influence over you. So let's, explore them;

It all starts in the mind

The part of you that affects your sleep more than the other parts is your mind. Your mind is the control room where all the anti-sleep terrorists go to attack. Anxiety, stress, depression, etc. all attack the mind, and once the mind is befuddled, the body would react according to what the mind is sensing. So you really need to work on your mind and how it functions. You need to focus your energy on getting your mind in good shape so that your body can follow suit.

Wake up the same time every day and sleep at the same time every day

A routine is key here. And it is easy to handle. Just wake up at the same time and sleep at the same time your body would automatically adjust to this routine. The body is a routine machine. It might fight it at first, but with time it would adjust to these routines, and you would be on autopilot from then on.

Diet and drinking

We cannot deny that our diet, eating habits, and drinking habits affect our sleep. It is a proven fact, especially for those who drink a lot. Alcohol can look like a sedative, but it will force you to wake up when you do not want to and give you a hangover of a lifetime. It can be pretty unhealthy. Caffeine in our bloodstream can take hours to wear out, and during that period, we will find it difficult to sleep. The more caffeine we consume, the more difficult it is to eradicate them from the bloodstream. Eating late can also lead to an inability to sleep. Especially if you are overfed, it will be difficult to lie down and sleep because of how uncomfortable you would be. So it is advised to eat early and plan to sleep.

Napping might be culprit here

I know that every once in a while, you might want to grab a nap and just enjoy the bliss of daydreaming, but napping might disrupt your sleep routine. You want to sleep at a certain time and wake at a certain time and engaging in naps can disrupt that. Except napping is part of the plan, if not, it is not advisable to nap indiscriminately. They say, too much of everything is not good, so let's watch it with the napping.

Reduce worry and anxiety

The truth is, if you are not calm, you cannot sleep well. You will be awakened by the thought and worries. You need to sleep, and for that to happen, you need to do away with those thoughts. That means, all through the day, you will expose yourself to content and information that will not cause certain unnecessary anxiety or panic. Keep your information very pure and see your heart relax.

Being in shape can shape your sleep too

Exercising has very good benefits. It puts you in shape, gets your organs working, and clears your body of toxins. This can also help you sleep, because your body will burn off excess energy and keep you exhausted but in a good way, a good way that your body will begin to crave relaxation. So, maybe three or four hours before sleep, have some good work out sessions and prepare to sleep.

Do you have insomnia? Of course, insomnia is a condition where a person cannot sleep and is quite restive. Here we will take a cursory look at steps to take to beat insomnia.

Maintain your daily rhythm: By this, I mean, try to sleep at the same time every day and also wake up at the same time every day. This is very important in beating insomnia because it creates a pattern of sleep. There might be that luring and mouth-watering temptation to sleep later on certain days and maybe wake up a bit later – this temptation is very risky for people suffering from insomnia. By all means, maintain as much as possible your sleeping time and wake up time.

Reduce or eliminate naps in the day: as much as you can, do not sleep in the afternoon, this would raise the chances of insomnia in the night because sleeping in the afternoon might keep you awake in the night. If you must take a nap, it must not be anywhere near bedtime – it will distort your circadian rhythm.

Stay away from stimulants: For someone suffering from insomnia, caffeine, alcohol, and every form of stimulant is bad for you, they will keep you awake, alert, and restless; so do yourself a favor and stay away from stimulants.

Regular exercises: Exercising regularly can improve your sleep experience both in duration and depth. But the downside is, exercising close to your bedtime will keep you awake and alert and so should be avoided. Try to exercise at least 3 – 5 hours before bedtime to maximize the sleep experience.

Make your bed and the bedroom a place to sleep: as much as possible eliminate other activities aside sleeping from your bed and bedroom, if for example you cannot sleep, leave your bed and go to another room or location to sort yourself out, if it is a worry, or whatever the case may be, tell yourself my bed is for sleep and not for worry. In addition to this, make it your personal policy not to read or operate your phones, tablets, and gadgets in bed. What will this do for you? It will make your brain associate strongly with your bed to sleep, so once you get into your room and on your bed, your brain knows it is time to drift off to sleep – stick to this for some time and see the wonder it works.

Make your bed sleep worthy: it is easier to fall asleep in a very comfortable place with nice temperature, good texture of beddings, et cetera than it is to fall asleep in an area that is disorganized, hot, and uncomfortable. Do the math! For you to have a great sleep experience, make your bed and bedroom as comfortable as possible. The reason why you might be having a rough time sleeping is because your room is uncomfortable.

Do not eat just before bedtime: when you eat close to bedtime, you will stimulate your digestive system, the grinding and churning of your digestive system can keep you awake, so for you to eliminate this completely, try to eat at least 3 hours from your bedtime. In addition to this, you should drink a little bit away from your sleep time so that you do not have to keep waking up to use the toilet; this would definitely interrupt your sleep.

Cognitive Behavior Therapy (CBT): This type of therapy can help people with borderline personality disorder identify and change core beliefs and behaviors that underlie inaccurate perceptions of themselves and others, and problems interacting with others. CBT may help reduce a range of mood and anxiety symptoms and reduce the number of suicidal or self-harming behaviors. A person who has insomnia should consider participating in CBT. It would put you through on a lot concerning this sleep disorder.

Learn to unwind and reduce stress: this has been talked about briefly in another section of this book. But I must add, if you have insomnia, you should try as much as possible to reduce stress during the day, practice breathing during traffic, practice being calm, and maintaining poise at all times.

DOES MEDITATION HELP YOU SLEEP?

Oh, the disgruntlement and grievance that comes with making relentless yet futile efforts to sleep. More devastatingly is the fact that it doesn't just end in a night of sleeplessness, but its ripple effect spill into the next day and just make you start a new day miserably with sleepy and dull eyes with a terrible attitude. Well, you are not alone in this; about 35 to 50 percent of adults in the world have insomnia. A lot of adults keep complaining and whining about not being able to sleep and of cause they keep looking for solutions anywhere within their reach; some have found solutions while others keep searching. I've seen what sleeplessness does to people. So I want to provide an effective and unambiguous solution to insomnia in the following lines and pages.

There is hardly anybody that has not come in contact with the word meditation before. Still, it is a thing of regret that a great number of people don't even know what meditation is all about or how powerful meditation is. Meditation is a very reliable technique for sleep and relaxation. Meditation is primarily seen by many people as a thing of the mind; that only affects the mind and inner soul. But you'd be surprised to know how much effect meditation has on your mind and how that it easily enhances the relaxation of the body and sleep. During meditation, different physiological modifications take place, and these modifications instigate sleep by causing several processes to take place in your body. In the year 2015, research results published in JAMA internal medicine showed that after 49 adults were all subjected to a series of mindfulness meditation, they were able to sleep better, their insomnia symptoms and daytime fatigue was reduced drastically. What might easily come to mind with all these meditation and sleep talk is that the reason why meditation aids sleep is because meditation requires you to be quiet and think less and so allows you to just sleep off. Well if that's what you are thinking right now, you are not wrong at all because in the real sense of it, one of the major reasons why people especially adults find it difficult to sleep is because they always harbor a lot of thought which they regurgitate and chew on each minute their mind is not actively engaged in a present or tangible matter or thing. This thought makes their body and mind all tensed up and unable to relax or sleep, but then meditation allows you to quiet your mind and rid yourself of all the disturbing thoughts that won't allow you have a good sleep. So there are chances of even falling asleep in the middle of meditation.

However, there are other reasons why meditation helps you sleep better, because you see, meditation influences several processes in your body.

Meditation helps to decrease blood pressure and consequently helps the body relax more.

When you engage in meditation, the parts of the brain that bring about or control sleep in your body is stimulated.

Meditation also reduces heart rate, which also helps the body to relax and sleep well.

Meditation also stimulates and increases the activity of melatonin which is the sleeping hormone in your body.

It also increases serotonin which highly puts the body in its relaxation mode

As simple and unambiguous as meditation is, it can solve your issue of insomnia very effectively, and it is not expensive either. So why don't you tap into the power of meditation today and be free from insomnia.

HOW TO SLEEP IN FIVE MINUTES

Reduce light intensity: with all lights on, it is difficult for your brain to know it is bedtime. So first, turn the lights off, put the phones, laptops, and tablets away and try to concentrate on sleeping, that way, your brain is informed that it is time to rest. Not just that, putting away your phones, tablets, and laptops reduce the light intensity; these gadgets emit blue rays that prevent sleep and heighten sleeplessness. So, by all means, keep the lights out.

Kill every form of sound and enjoy the serenity that comes right before you doze off.

Just breathe: breathing is one of the surest ways to relax. By just breathing, you are relieved of every form of tension, and a message is immediately sent to your brain, with information that it is bedtime.

Hence, the breathing exercise is actually very easy because it is not mentally engaging, to fall asleep faster you can breathe in for about 6-10 seconds, hold your breath for about 8-10 seconds and then slowly breathe out, as slow as you can, do this until you gradually fall asleep. This surely works, and I am sure it will work for you in about five minutes

Fantasize: This is you intentionally getting your mind away from the real world, letting your mind wander away gets you closer to sleeping fast.

All set to sleep, but sleep seems far from you? Try fantasizing about things you would like to experience. Imagine going on an adventurous trip (make sure not to imagine things that will make you tensed like being chased by Godzilla or even an anaconda, therefore destroying the original plan of making you feel relaxed), imagine achieving your set goal and the feeling of accomplishment that comes with it et cetera.

Although some people say that it is not safe to fantasize about things because it may hurt your feelings, discovering that all the good things that just happened to you were just imaginations. But envisaging will sure make you fall asleep faster than you imagined and leave the next day wondering how you slept off so quickly.

Pretend you are asleep: fake it till you get it. Pretending to be asleep helps you sleep faster. Just when you are ready to sleep and you cannot for some reason, Act as if you are already sleeping. That way, you feel like you are actually sleeping, and you'll discover that you will eventually sleep off.

Remember, while pretending to be sleeping, you must focus on trying to catch some sleep, regardless of what may be happening around you at that time. Also, try as much as you can to shut out every form of conversation that may come up (if any).

Ignore discussions and familiar sounds, by familiar sound, I mean sounds you are sure your roommate made.

While in bed, act it, act like you are asleep until you sleep.

We just took a cursory look into some basic things this book will touch, and I trust they will be of great importance to you and boost your sleep. Follow me on a journey in this book. I will share with you some adult bedtime stories that would help you sleep.

CHAPTER TWO
STORIES OF THE FOREST

You can listen to these stories as they help you relax your muscles as you try to sleep, also try imagining every character you hear, this will help you sleep faster without stress. Before you do that, you will have to get a pen and a note pad and write down everything you think keeps you awake or makes you restless at night, after that, make your bed in the most comfortable way you think because your comfort is the first key to having a good night sleep. Have you laid your bed? Now lie on it, you might want to switch off your lights as you listen to these stories. Darkness helps faster in promoting sleep while listening to bedtime stories.

These stories will put you to sleep. Oh, and if you are a story lover, you probably already know how this works. As your interest and attention are captured, your mind relaxes, as well as your entire body. That does the trick as fast as you can think about the story you are listening to, or reading. So let us begin. Have a good night sleep

Marilyn the Woodpecker and the cute orphan bunny

There was a little orphan bunny who lived in the woods. His name was Idris, and his parents had died three months ago.

Idris was an adorable bunny and a very playful one too.

He would sit very close to a spot that was his mother's favorite.

It was on a big giant sequoia, where sometimes he sat and just smiled at the other bunnies as they played.

Idris was a very playful bunny, no doubt, but he sometimes liked to sit back and watch.

That was when the beautiful Marilyn would fly from her all-view spot at the top of the giant sequoia tree and perch by him.

Even though Idris loved to make friends and welcomed almost everyone that came to him, Idris had a different attitude towards Marilyn.

Today, unlike other days since Idris' mom and dad passed away.

Marilyn was going to ask Idris why he always acted weird around her.

Marilyn had wondered whether he was different from her because she was a woodpecker.

Or because he just didn't like her. She wondered if he told the other bunnies about her and what he said to them about her.

But Marilyn was a very nice girl; she was good to everyone too.

Marilyn, in fact, was good friends with Idris' mom and dad.

She was as young as Idris, but Idris' mom and dad just liked her a lot.

They would let her peck at any wood without shooing her away.

That was unlike most of the others.

Both the bunnies and every other animal.

After a little while of observation and plotting, Marilyn flew down and perched beside him.

Idris didn't need to look in her direction to know she had just flown and perched by him.

It was only normal to find Marilyn beside Idris when he wasn't playing or with the other bunnies.

A minute passed, and no one said anything to another.

Then another minute, then another, until it was about five minutes of silence before one of them finally said something to the other.

—Hi Marilyn,‖ For the first time in like three months, Idris was the first to say something.

He still kept a blank face, but Marilyn had never really cared that she always had to say hi first, or keep their conversation going.

This was a flicker of light for Marilyn, but it was not going to stop her from asking the question she had in mind to ask Idris.

—Hi Idris,‖ she replied, half expecting that he would not say anything else, and she would have to carry on from there as always.

On the other hand, she was also hoping he would say something else. Marilyn was now about to ask how he was today, but he interrupted her.

—You look beautiful today.‖

—Oh, thanks Idris, and you too,‖ Marilyn returned the good compliment.

They both laughed, Idris because Marilyn referred to him as beautiful and Marilyn because Idris had not missed that.

Marilyn had this cute thing she always did with her hand when she is very happy. Or at least Idris thought it was cute.

She brushed her one hand with the other and chuckled.

Idris always found that adorable but had never said it before.

Idris began to talk and talk about many things. He talked about things he liked, and things he didn't like.

He talked about the bunnies he liked and those he didn't like.

Marilyn had been somewhat surprised, but at the same time happy that finally Idris was talking to her without her dragging the words out of his mouth.

She watched Idris talk and talk about almost everything and everyone.

And she laughed all the while.

Idris didn't like Moscow the fat bunny because he reminded him of some of the terrifying stories he used to hear his dad tell his mom at night.

They were always about some fat bunny that got their fatness from feeding on baby bunnies upon delivery.

He also didn't like Bella, probably the most beautiful bunny. Idris said she was too skinny and had bulgy eyes.

Marilyn laughed until she couldn't hold her tummy anymore, and Idris, all the while enjoyed that Marilyn was an excellent listener.

And that she laughed at all his jokes, even the ones he thought were too lame.

—I think you have something you want to say to me,‖ Idris said eventually.

Marilyn looked down at the bushes and did that thing with her hands and chuckled.

—Why do you think so, Idris?‖ Marilyn asked, but she didn't lift her head to look at him.

—Well, I haven't been so nice to you these past months‖

–I think that should definitely mean something to you‖ –Or don't you ever feel like asking why?‖

Marilyn drew patterns on the ground as Idris went on about the whole issue.

Marilyn was already having a great time with him and was not sure if it was necessary to ask why he had been different to her.

All that mattered to her at that moment was that they were good, and Idris made her laugh in a way she hadn't laughed before.

What Marilyn didn't know was that Idris felt the same way too.

He had never been so happy or free to talk about any of the things he talked about with her today.

They didn't even know when the rest of the bunnies went back to their homes.

Idris had mentioned that he didn't really have lots of friends even though he played with everyone.

Marilyn heard beyond those words that, in fact, he didn't have any friends.

But here they were, Idris had talked so freely that she was convinced it was because he saw her as his friend too.

—Oh, it's not important at all, I mean, it's nothing‖ Marilyn lied.

Idris drew closer and brushed Marilyn by the side with his tail.

—If you say so, Marilyn, then I believe you. Maybe we can hang out again tomorrow if you don't mind?‖

Marilyn looked up at him finally in utter amazement and smiled a broad smile.

—Of course, I don't mind if we will out tomorrow.‖

At this point, Marilyn flew off and headed back home.

Right where she had been all along, Idris saw beside him that Marilyn had not only been brushing her hand, she had been making holes each time her face was hidden from his.

Idris remembered the story his mother told him about a friend of hers who was a woodpecker.

The day they had their most intimate moments, she never came back again.

But she had left her something to remember her with, a very beautiful pattern of holes.

This made Idris unsettled, and for most of the night, he wondered if he would see her again tomorrow.

As the stars began to disappear, Idris finally started to give in to the heaviness that settled in his eyes.

Tomorrow perhaps, he would be able to see Marilyn again.

But staying up all night wasn't a confirmation for it happening.

It was almost noon before Idris woke up from his sleep, he realized that he had been asleep for so long.

—Oh, I must have been up all night,‖ he thought to himself.

And indeed he had been, he didn't even remember falling asleep.

As he looked up, Idris found nicely patterned holes on the roof of his shed.

—Marilyn,‖ he whispered, but she was not there.

He hurried to the nearest collection of water to freshen himself for the day.

That was when he ran off to his mother's favorite spot, which had now become his own.

And there he found that Marilyn was perched there and that, in fact, she had been there for quite some time.

—Good morning Mr. Bunny, you must have had a hell of a night there.‖

Idris looked around in pseudo confusion before sitting with her.

—It feels so good to see you again today Mrs. Woodpecker.‖

—You left quite some mark here, didn't you?‖

No matter how hard Idris tried to hide his excitement and surprise, Marilyn immediately knew he must have stayed up thinking about her.

Marilyn tried to conceal her own joy as well, and somehow she did better than Idris.

On a day as this, Idris will not go out and play with the other bunnies, and Marilyn will not hurry off in search of food.

Being by each other, talking, laughing, and making fun of other bunnies and woodpeckers gave them some kind of satisfaction that food could not have given them.

Idris suddenly stopped laughing and stared at Marilyn, long enough for her to ask what he was doing.

Idris drew closer and started to say something.

—Marilyn, since my dad and mom passed, you've been here for me, and you are not even a bunny.‖

—All the bunnies here have been good to me, but you have been the best.‖

—Without you all those days, persistently making sure I was fine, I may have finally run away.‖

Marilyn was shocked; she didn't even know that Idris thought of running away.

So she asked why, and Idris confessed that he had been missing his own family so much that he felt like dying too.

—Marilyn, if anything happens and I never get to see you again, just know that you hold a place most dear in my heart.‖

Marilyn did that cute thing, she understood just what he was talking about, and that made her even happier.

—Like those holes you see right by you, I am here with you always.‖

—Oh, and woodpeckers don't have a habit of abandoning their friends, I'm sure something happened to your mom's friend or something.‖

That night, Idris had better sleep, and a very long one at that.

A Certain Lynx Story

Larry was a bobcat that lived in the wild regions of North America.

He loved hunting, more than anything; Larry loved to be out there in the field.

He was not the stay at home kind of lynx cat, so he was easily found outside than he was found in.

Larry went hunting every early hour of the day and late hours of the evening too.

During the mid-hours of the day, Larry would rest and also hide from predators.

But Larry was a lonely cat who had no friends.

He had a pretty strict routine, and he maintained it through and through.

Every day, Larry would wake up early and go hunting.

Larry met a lot of other bobcats each day but never got the chance to make friends.

Or rather, Larry never gave them the chance to get to know him.

And he never really did care to get to know them.

All Larry cared about was hunting.

As a single bobcat, Larry would definitely not be able to eat all the meat he gets from his daily hunts.

What does Larry do? Larry shares his meat with other bobcats but never stays back to receive their appreciations.

All the bobcats knew Larry, but he didn't know them all.

Larry was known as the kind and generous bobcat and talked about all over their homeland.

But Larry was a weird one too.

He just comes bearing food, drops the food at the feet of any bobcat of his picking for that day, and runs off.

Larry loved to eat rabbits more than any other prey.

But for the other bobcats, he would hunt other prey as well.

Larry would hunt hares, insects, chickens, geese, rodents as well as deer.

Larry was said to have lots of luck with food.

When other bobcats could not get what to eat, not Larry, he always came home with something.

Always ran away from hunting with other bobcats, some of them were very displeased with this and tried every way possible to make people hate him.

Larry didn't care. Other bobcats understood that he was simply a loner, and probably hunted better because he hunted alone.

Stories went round every once in a while about Larry, but most of the cats knew better.

Larry was not a threat; neither was he a troublesome or controversial lynx.

What made it even harder to taint Larry was the simple fact that he pretty much wasn't seen often.

Larry got trailed sometimes by really curios bobcats whenever he went hunting.

Larry displayed no different type of hunting skill; neither did he use any magic, but somehow he always caught his meat.

Most of the lynxes concluded that he must be some kind of god. They wanted to get close to him, but just didn't know how to.

Sometimes when the lynxes had some kind of party or celebration, Larry would be sent for, but he would never show up for the party.

But Larry was always surprised that they brought some food from the party to him.

There were several stories about Larry.

But the most outstanding story about Larry was the one about his family and what happened to them.

The cats thought that he should have at least had a family somewhere, unless they were late.

And there was a story that went viral once about his family.

Here was what they said about them.

Larry was born during a cold season, and his mother had barely made it through.

Larry's father had died very shortly before he was born.

A predator got him.

Actually, Larry hadn't been born alone. He was one of three other bobcats.

But as the story had it, two of them didn't make it.

One died before being born, and the other died about three days afterward.

Larry was the only one that made it through days, weeks, months.

His mother had been scared that Larry would die sooner or later, she had been preparing her heart for that to happen.

Fortunately, Larry made it through the first year, and stayed alive the rest of the years.

Anyways, Larry and his mother had been living apart from other bobcats, after that night when only Larry survived the birth.

Larry's mother had been so sad and depressed. First, she lost her husband, and then she lost two baby bobcats in a night and three days.

She had to fend for her little Larry all by herself.

Not only did she have to provide food, she had to keep him safe as well.

This was how Larry learnt to hunt in the early hours and late hours of the day and stayed back the rest of the hours in between.

It wasn't because those hours were safer to hunt, but because his mother hunted during those hours.

She taught him to live like that. She also taught him to share what he got from hunting with others.

To protect little Larry, his mother made him stay back and away from sight always.

But Larry's mother was unfortunate or was it Larry who was unfortunate.

Because about two years down the line, predators got her too.

When Larry waited and never saw her, he knew it was finally time for him to step out and assume the role his mother played all along.

But luckily for Larry, once or twice, his mother had taken him with her for the hunts.

Larry saw how it was done.

Other than that, his mother had been giving him lessons on how to hunt.

His father had been a great hunter, and he taught her to hunt as well.

Behind her, Larry sometimes followed her into the field to watch her hunt.

She caught him once, and that was the day she told him to prepare for when he would need to hunt by himself.

Larry cried the day that finally happened, and from that day, he became even more solitary than he had ever been.

This story won the hearts of many bobcats, and they were always sympathetic of Larry.

Even though this story was a very touching one, and it made every lynx sympathetic toward Larry, no one knew for sure what the truth was.

But some of the lynxes believed that somewhere in between, the truth was there.

It may not be an entirely truthful story, or it may be.

It would only take Larry to confirm this, especially since Larry's parents had, in fact, just migrated a month before his father's passing to this place, which was now home for Larry.

Larry may have lost everyone that was family to him, but surely, his mother told him stories.

She should have told him some stories about his father, about herself.

How else did he know that he had two brothers out of which one died before he was born, and the other barely three days after he was born?

They were not just imaginations that he spoke to when he was alone, they were products of stories his mother told him before she also died.

One day, there was a party, and Larry received a special invitation to attend, as always.

One of the nicest bobcats had gone to Larry's shed to inform him about the party—Violet was her name.

A gorgeous lynx she was, and by far the softest spoken one too.

Her father was a big admirer of Larry's.

But he did not just admire Larry because he was a great meat hunter; he admired Larry also because he was a very generous cat.

She had carried a gift with her, it was a specially prepared and spiced rabbit—and it was Larry's best food.

Violet had made Larry promise to attend the party, and she promised to make another rabbit for him if he made it to the party.

Larry swore that that was the best-made rabbit he had eaten since his mother's demise.

For the first time, Larry talked to a fellow bobcat. He mentioned that he had almost forgotten how to talk.

He only talked to himself and sometimes to his mother, father, and two brothers. Of course, that was only a product of his imaginations.

But Larry didn't mind.

Violet was a very chatty and fun one. She asked Larry a couple of questions, but the only one he answered was about what inspired his generosity.

Larry told Violet that his parents had moved to this place because their homeland was not a very friendly place.

Most bobcats want to take what was theirs and what wasn't theirs too.

When Larry's mum got pregnant with him and his late brothers, the bobcats there would bully her and take her food.

Unfortunately, his father was not always there to fight them off.

They suffered so much, and there were only a few bobcats who were generous and kind.

But the bad ones were forcing them to turn from their goodness.

Larry's mother and father were unrepentant, and even though he shared the food he got from hunting with as many bobcats as it could reach, they still were not safe.

The cats were impossible to please and satisfy, and they didn't want to give birth in a place like that.

So, it was for the sake of Larry and his late brothers that his family moved and migrated to North America.

Larry's father died before they arrived here, he died defending his family against predators.

But his mother was a very strong one.

She kept on moving, and it was on the night she got into this new land of rather nice bobcats that she gave birth to her three sons.

She was satisfied that at least; they did not have to die in the hands of those cruel cats back home.

Or worse, die before they had a chance to tend to Larry.

But Larry was in a safe place, and that was all that mattered.

Sophia the Deer

Take a lying position in your bed; let me tell you a story about a certain deer who wandered off from home, and almost lost her life.

Sophia was her name, and she was the last of four Deers.

Sophia loved the water, so she was always the last to leave after a drinking trip.

She would stand in front of the water and stare into it for long.

If anyone called her name, she hardly would notice.

Sophia was often called the water deer because of her love for water.

She once asked mother deer and father deer if they knew how far the river ran, and if they knew where it ended.

Mother deer and father deer found this question both strange and disturbing.

They couldn't help but worry about what Sophia had going on in her mind after she asked that question about the water.

Mother deer worried that Sophia might do something that will hurt her, or that she might be hurt by the water.

Although Sophia never asked about the water again, she never stopped staring into it.

One day, Sophia went to drink from the river alone and stood there, as usual, staring into the water.

Mother deer worried for her after some time, and then she sent Sophia's brothers to look for her.

They searched everywhere but didn't find her.

So they returned home to tell their mother.

Mother deer tried to contain herself through the night since it was late already, and there really was nothing they could do that late.

The next day again, Sophia's brothers and father deer went out in search of her.

Her brothers mentioned that they hadn't checked at the river the other day because it was already late.

So father deer went with them to the stream, but they didn't find her.

They returned later that night without Sophia.

Mother deer saw them coming back and ran to meet them.

Sophia is back, she said.

Father deer and Sophia's brothers ran into their shed and found her asleep.

Sophia had come back home earlier that day, but they couldn't send for father deer and her brothers because they were not sure which part of the forest they would be.

Sophia had stood staring into the water through the night.

It was the early risers that found her sleeping very close to the river and woke her to return home.

She learned that everyone had been looking for her since yesterday.

Sophia got up, shook off the dust from her body, turned to the water, and stared for a little longer before storming back home.

It wasn't strange for Sophia to be found where there is water, but she had never gone to the river on her own, neither had she have to stay so long staring into the water.

Mother deer feared that what she most dreaded was, in fact, closer than she had imagined it.

Now she feared that Sophia was too young to be able to handle herself.

Mother deer had always taken her time to teach Sophia all the things that she needed to know to be able to stand on her own.

And if she came to a place where she had no one to help her out, or if she was caught up in some danger, she could figure things out by herself.

Sophia was so young that she shouldn't be able to catch her own food.

But mother deer made sure she took her out sometimes to teach her hunting.

Mother deer didn't just teach her how to hunt, she also taught her to be conscious and alert for predators.

Your legs are stronger than you know, mother deer would say to Sophia.

Water is also your friend, your very good friend, in fact.

Sometimes you do not need to stand and fight, you need to run.

When you find yourself running for life, water is your friend. Always remember that.

Use your legs as much as you can.

And when you see water, take a mouth full.

Do not be scared of the water because the bucks say it could swallow your tiny body.

You may be a small doe, but if you get in the water, you can swim pretty well.

Your eyes are posited to cover high degrees.

You can survive in any circumstance Sophia, you were made with the ability to.

Sophia wasn't sure what all of those meant, but she loved to learn new things, and since mother deer says they will keep her safe, then they must be very important.

Sophia would recite these words of mother deer's and sleep muttering them.

Sometimes she would wake up with those same words on her lips.

Sophia would ask questions upon questions about the things mother deer said to her.

You may never get it, until you finally do.

So Sophia held those words and lessons in her heart.

Someday, she would need them.

Father deer and her brothers all stayed close to her. They worried for her now more than ever.

Sophia was a lucky deer, she could have died before they found her.

Father deer always warned her against predators, and always teased her about being a small deer.

Anything could happen to you Sophia, he would warn.

But mother deer always came in with better words.

Sophia is a very smart deer, I'm sure she can handle herself.

Sophia would laugh at father deer's ‚jokes' and scream yes, yes to mother deer's good words.

Sophia was very brave and fearless, all thanks to mother deer.

One day at the river, Sophia was going to get bullied by victor the bully.

She turned to the river, took in some water with her mouth, turned to Victor, and spat the water into his eyes.

She laughed at him and sped all the way home.

But Victor never came at her again; he feared that she would have told her brothers.

But Sophia hadn't, she didn't care much, and never even thought of Victor bullying her.

It was almost summer, and Sophia became fonder of staying back at the river and staring into the water.

Mother deer stayed back every once in a while with her.

Although father deer and Sophia's brothers grew into confusion, there was nothing they could do about her.

They would not force Sophia to bend to safety.

And mother deer would always come to her defense.

She would say that Sophia had to be trusted and allowed to live the life that was in her soul.

One day, today, Sophia must remember those words mother deer told her.

On this day was that day, Sophia finally followed the water, and it led her far away from home.

On a hot afternoon, Sophia went to the river for some cool refreshing moment.

Sophia stood as always, staring into the water.

For what seemed like an eternity, Sophia stood there staring.

Other deer came and left, and Sophia hardly even noticed that anyone came to the river.

Victor had been there too, probably the last deer that came to the river that day.

Victor had thought of pushing Sophia into the river, but he feared that since she loved the water so much, it might fight him on her behalf.

Victor was a dumb one, and he believed every story he heard. So when the other fawns told him Sophia and the water was married, he believed them.

Victor stood there today, watching Sophia stare at the water for so long.

Then, Sophia jumped into the river and began to swim.

This very act surprised Victor, because he had always been afraid of the river.

He would never even think of stepping in. But the other fawns didn't know this about Victor.

They would have picked on him for it and teased the bully out of him.

Victor stood there in awe and watched Sophia swim in the river.

Sophia seemed to be enjoying the experience, and her excitement was so evident.

Sophia played around in the water in utter childlikeness.

The thought of not being in the water did not cross her mind at that moment.

All the answers she needed about the water, all her curiosity were being tickled now—more than ever.

Sophia swam farther and farther in the direction that the water flowed to, and away from home.

Victor still stood there, curious about what would happen to Sophia.

He had thought that there was probably something that Sophia and the water did each day she spent alone there.

Victor wanted to see the end of it, but he had become scared as he saw Sophia swim farther away from sight.

If she hadn't been fond of spending most of her days in the river, and sometimes spending her night there, he would have worried more for her.

Victor wasn't sure what to do, but he was too curious to know how she would swim her way back home, especially since it was already getting dark.

But Sophia disappeared with the flowing water and the darkness as well.

Victor stood there still, expecting that Sophia would swim right back, and if she didn't, after a couple of minutes, he would run back to their homeland and narrate the incident to her parents.

About ten to fifteen minutes after Sophia disappeared, Victor called out to her.

Sophia was not seen swimming back, it was dark, but Victor thought he heard her swimming back.

And he did, Sophia emerged again. Victor held his chest with his hands in unbelief.

Sophia got out of the water, and said to Victor, tell my mother I followed the river, and I will be back before she knows it.

Victor stared at her in confusion, but she plunged right back in and headed towards the same direction as she had before.

Now, Victor ran as fast as he could, but he could not possibly meet up in time to bring Sophia's family to come and stop her.

But he did tell mother deer who sat outside waiting; she had received the news as though she had been expecting it.

And this was it; Sophia was going to repeat her great grand mother's life without even knowing it.

Mother deer's grandmother had been just like Sophia, Sophia was, in fact, named after her.

The Big Brown bear

Are you familiar with the name Florence? Of course, you should, he was the biggest brown bear ever. Is it not funny how a male bear is named Florence?

If you don't know anything about Florence, then let me tell you about him.

First and foremost, Florence was a very hefty brown bear. There was no way anyone could not have known Florence, because he was the most outstanding bear there ever was.

Other brown bears his age made so much fun of Florence for many things.

First, they made fun of his hefty size. Then they made fun of his feminine name also.

Before Florence was born, his parents thought he was going to be a female bear, so they promised to name her Florence, after Florence Nightingale.

But it was not a girl; it was a boy, a very fat boy.

He was already being called Florence before he was born, and that remained his name after he was born.

Florence was often bullied, although merely verbally, but he was an adorable bear.

The older bears loved him, especially because he was very good-hearted.

Although Florence was very fat, he was not lazy, and he loved to work.

Florence loved to help people out. He did not like to see older bears working so hard.

Florence would never allow that. Florence would offer to help them out.

Florence was strong, and he loved baby bears so much.

He would never allow any one of them to be bullied as well.

Florence's brothers and sisters loved him so much, and they loved to be with him all the time.

Florence was very fun to be around, and his siblings laughed a whole lot around him.

Of all the things about Florence that his mother loved, it was the fact that he had a very good heart.

But his father loved him the most because he looked like him, and because he was very strong.

One day, Florence was out picking woods with his brothers, and they were going to be scared away by a predator.

Florence's brothers became afraid and were going to drop their woods and run away.

But they had a culture of not leaving anyone behind.

Now, they feared that Florence might be strong, but he might not be able to run from the threat.

But Florence didn't even care, he gathered the woods again and kept them in a bunch beside him.

His brother Jasper was furious and asked if he wanted to die. But Florence ignored him and was picking up the remaining woods so he could bundle them up and carry them with him.

As he carried his own bunch of the woods and began to leave, the predator jumped right at him.

Jasper panicked, screamed, and set out on his heels.

But Florence shook it off with all his strength, that as he turned to pounce back at the predator, he realized that it had already passed out.

The rest of his brothers who witnessed this jumped with joy and relief, bundled up their woods, and left singing victory songs.

This was the beginning of the idolization Florence received by most of the bears.

Florence's father was very proud of him, and won't stop talking about his defeat of the predator everywhere he went.

Because of this, Florence began to have friends. Before that day, Florence didn't have a lot of friends that were his mates.

He had lots of little bears who loved to come around him because of his warmness and playfulness.

But bears who were his mates came around to hear him talk about courage and bravery.

Apparently, Florence had not cared that the predator could have killed him, all he cared about was that they needed the woods and that nothing was going to stop him from carrying those woods home.

When he was asked what he thought about if the predator had killed him instead, Florence laughed so hard that everywhere shook along with his laughter.

Then he answered and said that then he would have bought his brothers enough time to carry the woods back home.

Most of the bears said it was a very crazy thing to think or even do. Others said it was cool, and the younger ones just sat there with their mouths wide open in astonishment.

The next day, news came from the far end of their homeland about a certain earthquake that had taken place.

It was said to have happened the day before that day, and it had killed five predators.

They found the bodies of the predators scattered around the hunting land.

Apparently, the predators had been lying in wait for an unfortunate bear to devour.

Unfortunately, they became their own victims.

As some bears approached, the ground shook so violently that the predators turned on themselves in confusion.

The bears just stood there transfixed for some time, they felt the impact of the quake, but they had not been affected in any way.

These were the same bears who came bearing the story.

It turned out, that when Florence was asked if the predator had taken him down, his laughter caused a quake.

The bears present noticed the quake, but they had been too engrossed listening to him talk about courage and bravery that they had just immediately ignored it.

When the news came, Florence's best friend Edith came to see him.

Edith and Florence were born on the same day, and they had been friends for as long as they both could remember.

Edith knew Florence so well, and Florence knew her as well.

They used to call them husband and wife.

Edith was a portable bear, and she was very loved and admired.

She loved to sing and dance, and when Florence defeated that predator out in the woods, Edith came to see him as well.

Edith often came to see Florence after stories were carried around about him.

The day he defeated the predator, Edith came to warn him about something.

Today, after the news came about the earthquake, she came again.

Some months back, Florence and Edith went into the woods to spend some time alone.

That day, they met a strange brown bear in the woods.

The bear approached them and introduced herself as Florence.

Florence smiled at her and said his name was Florence too, and that his friend was Edith.

But beyond that, Edith and Florence looked at each other in surprise.

It was not just because this strange brown bear bore the same name as Florence, but because she looked so much like Florence.

The only difference was that this female bear was not so fat.

This female brown bear whose name was Florence acknowledged Edith with a broad smile.

She said she knew who they both were. And that she was there to tell Florence about something very important.

She said she should get going very soon, and asked Florence if it was okay for Edith to be there and hear what she wanted to tell him.

Florence said yes, and that Edith was his very good friend.

So the strange brown bear began to talk about Florence.

She said that she and Florence were the same and that he was her reincarnation.

She said that Florence could have been a girl, but that she wanted to be a boy for the first time.

This was why Florence came to be a boy.

Edith and Florence looked at each other again in confusion.

Edith asked whether that meant something for Florence, and the strange bear said yes.

She went ahead to explain that Florence was very different and special.

He had extra abilities which he had not yet realized, and this was what made him so brave and courageous.

She told them about the earthquake and explained to them that whenever they heard about the quake, they should know that it had something to do with Florence.

Florence was a reincarnation of a very special brown bear who was born once in every five decades.

His role in the bear land would be to protect the bears against certain predators.

At some point in the bear land, they would be mercilessly attacked by predators.

The only way to defeat these predators was Florence.

What this female bear did not tell Florence was how he would be able to fight off the predators and save the bear race yet another five decades.

But Florence had it all in him, and Edith knew what it was. She was always there to help him harness all those attributes he had that he needed to be able to defeat the predators.

Today, Edith came to remind Florence that the only way he would not end up causing harm to the same bears he was meant to save was to fight out of love for them, and not simply because he could fight.

Florence kept that in mind, and even though Edith died later on, he was able to do his part.

Olivia the Owl and Insomnia

A story was once told about a certain Owl who had a hard time sleeping, and another owl, who was her friend.

Their names were Olivia and Judith. But Judith told the story.

I once had a friend who suffered from sleeplessness, and her name was Olivia.

I remember when she used to visit me, but I do not remember waking up to her sleeping body.

Olivia stayed up counting the stars, or just lay back while watching me sleep away my life.

Her eyes were bulgy, and they scared me always.

Olivia was a pretty owl, but she was skinny and looked stressed out all the time.

Olivia would count the stars at night so she could sleep, but it often didn't work.

She would blink her eyes rapidly for a couple of minutes unbroken, and it was late I realized she did that so she could sleep too.

Practically all the weird things that I saw Olivia do, she did to be able to sleep.

Olivia liked to do new things—she was brave and highly adventurous.

But I never liked for her to go out and do any of those things on her own.

If there was one thing Olivia was not so fond of, was listening to stories, or even telling them.

—Stories make me yawn like a hungry owlet, they are too boring and tiring.‖ Those were Olivia's favorite lines on listening to stories.

As an adventurous person, she had lots of stories to share, but would never share them.

On this day, my birthday, I would beg her to tell me a story as a wrap-up gift at night.

That I could not sleep was going to be my excuse, and I really wanted to hear a story on my birthday.

Olivia planned to disappear that night, and Judith was bent on finding her where ever she ran to.

Then the night of Judith's birthday drew closer, and Olivia nursed her run away plan along.

Judith went to gather a couple of friends, and upon her return, Olivia was gone.

So Judith set out that night in search of Olivia.

As she searched through the woods, Olivia was nowhere to be found.

Then Judith found a strange-looking owl's house far away from home and into the woods.

Oh, she said, which old owl lives here in this old and lonely house.

So Judith went into the strange and old house to see who was there, and if the person needed some help.

As she approached the house, she heard voices. But as she got closer, she realized it was just a voice, and not voices.

But it seemed like there were more than just one owl in there.

Someone had to be there listening to whoever it was that told the story.

Then Judith was terrified at the next thought that came to her mind.

She had immediately wondered if the old voice she heard was alone, and if she was, then it meant one thing.

The poor old owl was probably insane.

Judith stood in the front of the house for a while, contemplating on whether to go in and see for herself or to just turn around and go find her friend.

But what if the old owl needed help, and why would she be out here all by herself.

Judith noticed for the first time in a couple of minutes that she had been out in the dark alone herself.

The chirping birds drew her attention back to the fact that she was out in the dark and all alone.

But Judith was not going back without her friend Olivia. She didn't actually care so much about hearing stories as she did about getting her friend back.

If Olivia was not anywhere back at home, then she must have come this far into the forest.

Judith thought, maybe this old owl can help her find her friend. She has been here for so long obviously, and she must know how and where to find Olivia.

Judith went right in without a second thought. Guess what she found in there, it surprised her.

The old owl looked like Olivia, so much like her in fact.

Judith knew Olivia's mother, but this was not her.

Olivia's mother was brownish with darker patterns over her brown.

She was not as beautiful as Olivia, but she also didn't look like Olivia.

Oh, Judith exclaimed, she just realized that Olivia's mother was not actually her mother.

She could not remember anything that made them look alike.

She remembered once mentioning the oddness to Olivia, but Olivia had been offended by it.

Olivia use to leave for the forest every day towards the night.

Judith once asked where she always went and if she could come with her, but Olivia had declined.

She said it relieved her of the stress of the day, and she didn't want anyone to be a part of it. Judith let her be.

It all made sense now. The owl she stood before in this old house looked so much like Olivia.

She had her enormously bulgy eyes, and she had that stressed out look as well. But Olivia had it more.

Where is Olivia? Judith finally spoke up.

You must be Judith. The old owl said. Olivia speaks so much about you.

Judith had a couple of questions to ask this old owl, but she needed to find Olivia first.

She wanted to ask why she was out here in the forest all by herself.

She wanted to ask her why she wasn't with Olivia instead.

She wanted to ask her if she even cared that Olivia hardly slept at night.

She wanted to ask about Olivia's father, if Olivia had any siblings.

But right now, she only wanted to find Olivia.

The old owl said she didn't know where Olivia was.

She had been expecting her as well.

She puts me to bed sometimes, the old owl said. Judith could see the sadness in her eyes.

She felt sorry for her and wondered what the problem really was.

But she already understood one thing, and that was that Olivia's mother had a hard time sleeping too.

Then this is a family thing? Judith thought out loud.

Olivia's mother looked at her in remorse but said nothing.

Olivia's mother pointed out towards the farther part of the forest.

Olivia should be there, she said.

It turned out that Olivia went far into the forest by herself sometimes.

So Judith immediately flew off into the forest in search of Olivia.

Olivia's mother followed her behind.

They found her at her spot, she seemed preoccupied with something.

Judith was going to go straight to her and ask her what the matter was.

But Olivia's mother would not let her go any further.

Olivia likes to be left alone sometimes, especially if she came here. The old owl said.

Judith was both confused and worried. So she asked why.

The old owl explained that Olivia's father had died right there when Olivia was just a child.

He took Olivia on a flight around the forest, and they came as far as this.

Judith still didn't understand how he died during a flight.

She grew impatient with the whole story.

What happened to him? She screamed at the old owl. Olivia turned around to find them there.

A weak branch fell on him, Olivia answered, because he pushed me aside.

So the weak branch was going to fall on you? Judith asked.

Olivia nodded in tears. Judith got it all now.

Olivia blamed herself for her father's death, but he had done what any parent who loved their child would do.

Olivia needed to understand this.

Olivia explained that she always came here to remember her father and laugh like she did the day he died saving her.

Judith learned that Olivia's insomnia wasn't really a family thing.

Olivia's mother had always had a hard time sleeping, so Olivia's father always told her stories to help her sleep.

Upon his death, Olivia would tell her mother stories to help her sleep.

Olivia did not always have a hard time sleeping, but her mother needed her to be able to sleep.

Olivia would stay up to make sure that her mother could sleep.

This was how Olivia began to lose sleep.

And every day reminded her that if she hadn't asked to see round the forest that day, her father would still be alive.

And her mother would not have to stay up most nights without getting some sleep.

Olivia took it upon her to play her father's role and ensure that her mother got some sleep.

As Judith listened to Olivia and her narrate this, she perceived that Olivia, in fact, loved stories.

Olivia loved to listen to her father tell her mother stories.

She always slept first when her father started telling her mother stories at night.

They also put her to sleep. But Olivia switched places and roles now, she now told the stories.

But Judith didn't understand why Olivia resisted listening to stories anymore.

Do you feel like you should not be sleeping if your mother is not sleeping? Judith asked.

Olivia looked at her, tears filled her eyes, and all she could mutter was that she really wished her father was still here with them.

Judith understood that that was, in fact, the problem.

Olivia could not stand listening to stories because they made her want to sleep.

But she really didn't want to sleep anymore.

Judith, Olivia, and Olivia's mother had quite a time together.

Later, Judith found out that the woman Olivia lived with had not even adopted her, but she was a good friend of her mother's.

That night, Olivia, her mother, and Judith flew into the main forest.

Judith loved stories, and she was a very good storyteller.

She told Olivia and her mother some stories.

As she told stories after the other, Olivia hugged her mother so tight. On the third story, Olivia slept off first.

Lady Fox and the Hunters

I once heard a story from my father, about a certain fox who lived a double life. I didn't quite understand what he meant, or how a fox could live two lives at a time. But father said it was a lady, who had the soul of a fox in her. Mother said she knew the story also, and that it was a fox, who had the soul of a lady.

Her name was Anika, and she had the ability to live as a fox, and the ability to live as a lady too.

Anika could choose to be a lady in the day, and be a fox at night, or she could choose to be a fox in the day and to be a lady in the night.

Anika was a very beautiful fox, but as a lady, she was beyond what words could describe as beautiful.

Father described her as a very white fox with blazing eyes, and also described her as a tall, slim but voluptuous light-skinned girl. Her eyes as a lady, father told me, were hazel and could be seen through.

Even though Anika was a very lovely and adorable young girl, she was in grave danger as a fox.

The hunters were after her. Father called them the fox hunters; they hunted foxes for many things. They hunted for slavery, for exhibitions, for sports, for rituals, and some of them were hunted simply to be killed.

It all depended on who wanted the foxes. And as for Anika, she was being hunted because of her beauty; no one really knew what they would do to her if they caught her.

I know you may be asking why she didn't just remain a lady, after all, she could choose what and when to be it every day.

Well, this was, in fact, the complication, Anika could choose when to be a fox and when to be a lady each day, but that was only because she had the ability to choose. But she didn't have the ability to remain either a fox or a lady always.

Every day, she must be both a fox and a lady, but she could only choose what time of the day to be a fox or a woman.

Anika loved to be a fox, it was the only way she could truly be free and happy, not judged or controlled. It was the only way she could go wherever she wanted and do whatever she wanted. It was the only way she could look at the world from the angle of an outsider, and also run around naked.

The fox in her made her feel free and very alive. But the hunters were after her, and she had to find a way to save herself.

Anika was a fox the first time her family found her.

Anika could not remember where she came from or what her life was like before that afternoon when the George's family found her.

Mr. and Mrs. George became her family when they took her in to their house to nurse her wound.

The George family liked to go hunting in the woods during the afternoons. And on this day, Anika was found wounded and alone in the woods. Her side had been torn and bleeding out.

Mr. and Mrs. George carried her home and took care of her. They fixed her wound and left her to rest.

But when they got back in to check up on her and her wounds, they found a young girl instead. Her side had the same sewing they gave the very white fox. She looked so beautiful that they immediately knew the fox was her, and she was the fox.

But they could not hide their confusion. When she kept staring at them in confusion as well, they wondered where she had come from, and what happened to her.

Mrs. George spoke up first; she introduced herself and her husband and then asked what her name was.

Luckily, Anika remembered that her name was Anika and that she was both a fox and a lady. But that was all, she could not remember anything else.

Anika pointed at the stitch on her side and asked to know what happened to her.

When she learned that they had found her in the woods, alone and wounded, she began to cry.

Later, the Georges will realize that she cried because she didn't understand why anyone would try to kill her. She was just an innocent fox.

Mr. and Mrs. George tried to help her get her memory back, or at least, to help her remember something. But she could not seem to remember anything at all.

One night when Anika became a fox and wanted to go to the woods. Although Mr. and Mrs. George tried to talk her out of going into the woods, she just could not help it. She longed to run out and into the woods.

So they let her go to the woods on the condition that she would not stay out there beyond an hour, and if she sensed anything strange around, she had to return immediately.

The Georges were very worried she might get hurt again, and they just couldn't stop staring at the wall clock.

It was barely thirty minutes after she left, and Mr. and Mrs. George set out right into the wood to go see if she was okay.

What they found terrified them, and they swore never to let her go out into the woods again, or at least, not by herself.

Anika had been caught by a cage trap, and Mr. and Mrs. George had arrived just in time to save her before the fox hunters got to her.

Anika was taken back wounded again, but this time, it wasn't her side, it was her right leg. The fortunate thing was that she healed fast.

But Anika became so sad and more confused; she still could not understand why anyone would try to kill her. But she remembered something that night.

She had been out in the woods with another fox, a female too. And then suddenly they were attacked by some strange men.

They tried to take them both, but she fought them off. That was how she sustained that wound on her side that night. They could not keep up with her speed, so they left her the moment they saw that she was headed towards the lighted main road.

Anika passed out on her way running, and that was when Mr. and Mrs. George found her the first time.

Anika tried to say something, but she didn't seem to have it all in order in her head. The Georges fixed up her leg and asked her to relax her mind for some time and get some rest first.

That night, Anika remembered everything as she slept, it all came back to her like a dream. Anika had received a heavy blow the night Mr. and Mrs. George found her out in the woods, it was a heavy wood that one of the hunters threw at her as she ran that made her pass out.

It got her head, and that was why she couldn't remember anything.

This was where Anika's double life truly started to be unveiled and understood by her. As for the Georges, they were already trying to figure it all out.

Anika, having remembered who and what she was, had to make a decision of either telling Mr. and Mrs. George, or letting it all go.

Anika was a deity, and not just some girl or some fox out in the woods. Anika actually came from a deity land.

That night she lost her friend, her deity friend, they had found a way out of their land and into the land of humans.

Anika received worship daily from all over the world amongst people who believed in her as a deity.

In the human sculpted representation of her, she was half woman and half fox. She had two faces, one was the face of a fox, and the other was the face of a woman.

It was believed that people who worshipped her when she chose to be a lady would have a beautiful day. And those who worshipped her when she chose to be a fox would have things go according to how they want it to that day. The fox was also said to make one feel like a bird, free.

But Anika wished to be free from her duties. Wherever she was, whether in deity land or human land, so long as she remained able to change from one form to the other, her worshippers would still be served.

Anika knew how to get back to deity land, but she did not want that. She wanted to be free.

The next morning Mr. and Mrs. George came back in to tell her what they found from research about her, but she only cared about staying back.

Mr. and Mrs. George tried to make her see how dangerous that could be for her, but Anika would not have any of it.

That night, Anika went into the woods again. She intended to be sort by the hunters again, so she could try talking to them.

Anika was going to try to be smart, she was going to wait till the hunters got her, after that she would change into a lady.

She would be in the woods as a fox till after 12 midnight, then when the hunters try to get her, she would become a lady right in front of them.

This was Anika's plan, and she believed that it would work out alright.

Mr. and Mrs. George feared for her, so they stayed around in case things began to go south as they had done the first and the last time before.

But Anika was a deity, and what she hadn't remembered was that her wishes were bound to happen.

And that was how Anika made friends with the hunters, and to this day, they no longer hunted foxes.

CHAPTER THREE
STORIES OF THE TROPICAL SAVANNAH

GIRAFFE

A long time ago, in the dark thick African forests, giraffes were hunted down without caution. The lions and hyenas took turns to tear down these tall creatures and feasted on their carcasses without any restraint. It was a meat fit for kings.

But there was one giraffe that gave the entire elite hunting squad trouble. His name was Tao. Tao is not necessarily the tallest giraffe in his tribe, but he was the most distinct. His patches weren't black, and his skin wasn't orange. His patches were green, and his skin was white. He was the easiest to be spotted when the lions came to invade, but he was the fastest to escape.

Whenever the herd came to graze, he would be the one to leave the group and hide. Other giraffes noticed that he was always absent during attacks and started watching out for his movement. Whenever he left the herd, they followed him. He had a special cave where he hid from the attacks. The hid there with him.

They thought that was the only way to hide from the lions, but very soon, the lions found them out and started hunting them inside the caves, but before they always find them, Tao would find a way to escape. This time he escaped back into the fields where the lions used to hunt them out, and the whole herd followed him.

One day, the lions came hunting, and he sat still under the sun without moving a muscle. The rest of his tribe cowered away. He sat still. The lions stopped chasing the rest and started on him, but he sat still, he sat still until it started to rain.

He whispered from the side of his mouth

—Thank you.‖

As it began to rain, he threw a concoction into the air that created a mist that made it hard for the cats to see, and one by one, he knocked them down with his hooves till they lost consciousness. Then he rounded them up and tied them to a tree. The entire clan came out to see the wonders of Tao. They were so amazed that they motioned to crown him king.

Then they asked him,

—How were you able to do it?‖

He smiled and said, ‑Meditation!‖

They wondered what he meant by that, then he explained.

—Meditation helps you calm your mind. It makes it easier for you to be in touch with the rhythms of your soul and really touch the source of your being. It makes it easy for you to unlock great power.

Then they asked him, ‑How did you know this?‖ He said, ‑I watched the sun‖ it was so calm yet powerful. It made no noise, and yet it knew when to rise or set. It knows when to shine and when to hide. The sun knows timing. So I learned this watching the sun. I learned to pay attention to my environment and just feel the breeze slap my face or allow the tides to speak to me.

From there, I started hearing them speak to me. They would always tell me when the lions are coming or when the rains are coming or when there are no rains.

—Wow!‖ They all said, ‑When are you going to teach us?‖ they asked.

He looked up to the sky, paused for a while, and said: —when the full moon comes up.‖

—Why the full moon?‖   They asked,

—Because the earth would be gentle and venerable, then we would tap into its powers.‖   He replied.

Then came the night when the training began. It was a full moon but not like the others. It was red like it bled. The moon bled. They sat still under the canopy of the skies and watched the stars until they became calm. Their worries faded away. Then they breathed in and out until they felt a rhyme in their soul. Their breath was in sync with their souls. They heard every cricket chirp, and every leaf that fell. They heard the clouds roll and mature belly grumble. They heard their heartbeats and that of their neighbors.

They heard the frogs croak, although the frogs were far, far away. They heard the streams flow, and the fishes swim. They heard into the heavens. They even heard light move. They heard it with their ears this time, not with their eyes. Their ears became their eyes, and their eyes was one with their ears.

They were in harmony with themselves and nature. They felt they could control the tides and the winds. They stayed there for hours. The night was hunting time. Although the cats were tied up, their brothers still roamed the forests. The Jaguar was awake. The Tiger growled, the hyena laughed aloud.

Tao awoke from his deep meditation and said: ―it is time.‖ It was like the giraffes knew what to do. They swarm into action like an army that has been informed about the plot long ago before it happened. They swung into their positions and stood in wait for the attack of their predators.

The first to come was the tiger. Its greatest enemy is fire. The giraffes struck out fire from the rocks and shot it at it. The tiger ran with fear in its heart. As though the gods were angry with it. The jaguar came next. They released a swarm of bees towards it. The bees didn't attack anyone else except the Jaguar, and it fled like it had offended the gods.

There was great calm in the forest, and the giraffes weren't fooled by it. The hyenas had not struck, and they too were on their way. The giraffes began to make sounds of big cats from leaves and tree barks they carved around. The sound was so loud, and the wind was on their side. It took the roars and sounded it around the Hyenas. They thought they were being attacked by the cats. So, they ran because it seemed like the cats surrounded them. And like that, they chased the cats away, and the awe of the giraffes filled the forest.

ELEPHANT

There was a distant tribe in the deep tropical forest, the tribe was made up of a few elephants that roamed the ridges and ate the grasses. They were led by their great leader Makhila. She was very bold and courageous. She was the idea of a strong and powerful leader, but there was something that Makhila couldn't do; she couldn't control the rains and that meant her people would have to leave the place of their heritage in search for food. Foraging wasn't their best sport. They had to walk miles and miles and miles unending in search of water and fresh grass. In the bid to find water, a lot of things happen to some of the calves. They are either lost on the way, or are too tired to walk. They always move around to find water, and when they are done, to return back to the lands, their ancestors gave them is difficult. Sometimes, when they return, they meet enemies, and they have to ward them off and purify the land.

Makhila, a skilled warrior, has formed an elite group of twenty strong elephants that are skilled both in war and intellect. An elephant never forgets, they say.

This season was not dry enough, so they had enough grass to go by. Makhila, their great leader, was washed all over with grey skin, the skin wrinkle around the neck and the feet. Her trunk was long and agile, and her tusks went around her face to hug her. She had a king, but he was not the leader, he was just a mate. His name was Mphosa. Mphosa, which in their tribe means ―the father of all,‖ was a large elephant. But he was not as big as Makhila.

The clan was made up of fifty elephants and their calves. The stream was just a stroll by. The clan worshiped the river goddess. It was said that the goddess brought good fortune and strength to fight. As the stream flowed in its ever calm speed, it was not perturbed by any obstacle which is how they ought to be. Whenever they had a problem, they would walk to the stream, drink and bathe, and as they did so, the wisdom to maneuver their obstacle would come, and they would be energized by their encounter with the river to do the best they can.

One quiet evening, Makhila went to the stream to find solutions to her problems, as she bathed and drank in the stream, she saw a little light that was not so obvious. The light was calm and quiet. She thought it was the reflection of the moon on the stream. So she kept on bathing. The light became omnius. It began to show different rays in the stream, it was like the light was alive but yet calm. Makhila walked towards it to be sure of what she was looking at; as she got close to the light, it sprang up!!

It was the river goddess! She had no frame, but her voice calmly pulsated out of the light rays. The light rays were a mix of bright blue, white, green, red, and orange. She spoke with such peace.

–Makhila, the great one,‖ she said.

–I presume you must be the goddess Atal-wahweh‖

–Yes Makhila‖

—I have seen into your heart, and I know your problems, I bring you solutions. You would have the wisdom of the elders and the strength of the ancient warriors.‖

—But you must settle your mind and calm your nerves. Take a deep breath Makhila and see into your heart. Take a deep breath Makhila and see into your past. The spirits are with you.‖

Makhila shut her eyes and took deep breaths and suddenly, she was shot back in time where her ancestors had the same problem and the solutions that they implied to solve it. She saw the great Matuweh, her grandfather, and how he dug earth and planted. She saw how the river helped them water the land and kept the plants wet. She saw her father do the same. She saw how they waited for the harvest. She saw how they made huts for storing the harvests. She thought to herself, —so this is what those ancient huts are for‖ then she saw how a calf got missing—it was her brother, and it forced the clan to move out in search of him. As they searched and searched, the days turn to months and the months turned to years, and until the land they once left, started to leave them. Before her father died, he told her to protect the heritage and the land they once lived in. he told her to protect it. He told her to find it.

Her vision stopped abruptly and she was transported back to her body. As she gained awareness of her environment, she looked up to the ray of light and said, —thank you great and kind spirit. For I know what to do‖ .

She thought of the food they had for now and how they could store it until the dry season went away, and they would have had enough food that lasted them that period, but first, she had to teach her people to plant and watch for the harvest. She was so excited about her discovery that she ran home, trumpeting and waking the clan. Everyone came out, and she showed them what the spirits had taught her.

They began to practice, and with time they perfected the art of farming and harvesting. The earth and the river were with them. The harvest was faster than normal, and they had enough food to last them through the dry season. Not just that, she also thought of a way to save water too. She didn't want the drought to be so fierce that they would not have water. She planted trees across the streams on each side. The streams formed shades and protected the stream from the sunlight and preserved the water. That year was fruitful for the clan, thanks to their great leader Makhila.

GAZELLE

It was a glorious season for the tribe because the tribe of Nkala, had just won its first spring games. The star of the moment was their fastest gazelle Itiya, the talk of the town. The way she outran the other deer from across the river was amazing.

She was placed behind the line, but she outran them still. Her speed was as the wind, and her poise was royalty. She was the deer to look forward to. The tribe boasted about her victory until one day she was running home and stumbled on a stone that threw her off balance, and she landed on the ground. She thought it was business as usual, but it wasn't, she couldn't move her legs. It seemed she had broken her leg and she couldn't move. She cried for help until the other gazelles took her away to the clinic.

The physician checked her hoofs and her hind legs and saw that they were broken. He couldn't find it in himself to inform her, so he called the village chief and informed him that their star gazelle would not be able to run again. The chief disappointed called for a meeting of the deer and spoke with so much grief.

—We thank the spirits that we won the last competition. We thank the spirits that our village has not been put to shame. But we have bad news now, our star gazelle is not in the best shape. In fact, she broke her legs and can't walk again...‖

–Huh!‖ The crowd said.

—Yes, my people, she can't walk again.‖   —The physician advises that we find another runner to train before the time for the competitions come around.‖

—How do we train someone in sprinting in just a few months? It took Taya lots of years to perfect her art.‖

—Yes, I understand your fears. I have these fears myself. Let us wait on the gods for a sign. Meanwhile, we need to inform Taya of these things. And seek her counsel on what to do from now on.‖

As they left the meeting place, they left to inform Taya of it. When she found out about her legs, she was really sad. She refused to speak to anyone for weeks, no matter how much they tried, she just didn't want to talk.

The tribe went ahead to select the other fast gazelles like Taya, to train them to be as good as Taya was. The more they trained, the more they became frustrated. They weren't hitting the mark, and it was frustrating the racers.

—How can we be as good as she is if we never knew what she did to be that good?‖ One of the racers asked.

—Hmmm, that is a true question. But how do we find out from her how she trained? She refused to talk to anyone?‖ Someone answered.

—Well, we have to try.‖

—Yes we have to try.‖

Back in her hut where she stayed, she was crying nonstop. She felt her life had ended, and there was nothing she would ever do to amount to anything good. She felt she had lost the thing that made her relevant. As she cried, she shouted the names of the spirits. She was so bitter that she said harsh things to the spirits. She told them how they promised to be with her, yet they allowed her to lose her limbs. She told them how she would never trust them again. As she was screaming at them, the room was full of smoke.

She stopped to know what was happening, but the smoke did not stop. The smoke got her dizzy and she fell into some sort of trance. In the trance, she saw the spirit Gazelle, and she asked her a question, she asked, —When the Caterpillar is turning to a butterfly, does it not think the spirits are wicked? The wings would hurt, it would lose its cocoon. It would lose everything dear to it. Right?‖

She answered the spirit —yes.‖

Then the spirit asked her, —why do you worry over change? It was an accident but look at the benefits of it. You can still be great and relevant. If you could run, others can because of you. You have become an inspiration, use it to build an army of sprinters just like you.‖

The smoke faded, and she woke from her trance.

Just as she woke from it, she heard footsteps from a distance. It was the footsteps of the village chief and the other gazelles that were coming to convince her to train them.

As they arrived at her doorstep, she opened the door and said, —I will train you.‖

They were stunned. They asked her how she knew they were coming to ask her to train them, and she said the spirits spoke to her. The spirits showed her how it would be beneficial to the tribe if everyone knew how to run like she did.

So, they set out the next morning to begin the training. She took a deep breath and said to them, —training is hard, you will have to be focused and deliberate with your training. You will have to stay on course. Once we start, there is no turning back. Get ready to be the fastest gazelle that ever walked these plains.‖

They nodded in unison, and the training began.

She couldn‘t walk properly, so she was always with a cane. She did her best to train them and prepare them for the competition. She taught them how she trained against the water currents to build her hind legs and front legs. She said water helps you with your grip and stamina.

She took them to the mountains and trained them in high altitudes. She said it would teach them endurance and stamina. They would learn to breathe properly in those high altitudes and learn to maneuver any terrain they ran in.

She took them to the steamy rocks to train them. She said it would work on their agility and their vision. How they will be focused. The steam bursting from underneath the rocks was so hot, you needed to be focused and have maneuvering skills to avoid being burnt.

Then she taught them to be calm, and think deep. She called it meditation. She said it allowed the gazelle to be in tune with its inner rhythms, and with this, the gazelle can surmount any inner turmoil like fear and uncertainty that cripple the confidence of the athlete.

With this, she prepared her clan for the coming competition before it came. The training went beyond just preparing for a competition, it prepared them for everything. Soon, news spread across that the training was special, and Taya had other athletes from other tribes begging to be trained by her. Even gazelles from her tribe that were not runners before wanted to be part of the process.

She thought she lost something, but she gained even more than she lost. She became the greatest teacher the gazelle tribes had ever had.

HIPPOPOTAMUS

Hippopotamus

Far away in the land of Kazulu, rose a king who was savage. He disregarded all the customs of his ancestors. Unlike his father, Malik was cruel and arrogant. He was always ready to get rid of anyone who stood against him. The people of Kazulu lived in great fear. Not certain about what tomorrow held for them, they lived every day like it was their last.

King Malik wasn't contented with the lifestyle of eating grass. He felt the hippopotamus deserved better. He thought to himself, —how is it, that I Malik Pativa, The king of Kazulu will feed on grasses trampled by my subjects.‖ He walked to and fro his palace, breathing so fast. —I know what to do,‖ he said aloud.

He gathered all the hippopotamus in the land for a meeting. All the hippopotamus in the land assembled at the king's palace. They all waited patiently for the king's arrival. It didn't seem like he was coming anytime soon. They began to become irritated as the sun rays hit their bare skin, they had little or no hair protecting them. As they spent more time under the sun. They could see their body becoming orange. They became so uncomfortable but dared not to complain as they all feared king Malik.

After many hours King Malik showed up. He took his seat and began to speak. —My fellow hippos, I can see a lot of you are turning orange,‖ he said, laughing sarcastically. —I feel your pain. I know exactly how you feel, that is why I have created a solution for us,‖ he said with so much conviction. All the hippopotamus were amazed at how much of their pain Malik understood. They kept their fingers crossed, while waiting to hear all that King Malik had to say.

King Malik began to decree, —We would no longer seek refuge on land alone, we can now go into the rivers and cool off whenever the sun becomes harsh. And we don't have to eat grass if we don't want to. We can now have the fresh fishes in the sea for breakfast, or maybe some grasshoppers for lunch and a sprinkle of butterflies and probably have fresh rabbits for dinner. It's going to be up to us to eat whatever we want, no more monotonous food!‖ he said firmly.

All the hippopotamus made merry. They loved the idea except one. Her name was Olla.

She didn't welcome the idea. She loved how Kazulu was: A peaceful and beautiful land where every animal of different species lived together in harmony. Peace seemed to be a birthright of the animals in Kazulu until King Radar (Malik's father) died. He had left the fate of the entire kingdom in the hands of his savage son. As Olla walked away from the meeting, she began to panic. She knew things in Kazulu were about to change for the bad. Most of the hippopotamus thought it was a great decision, —finally! We can now put our large sharp teeth to use,‖ one of the hippopotamus said rudely as he rolled his eye.

The new decree made by King Kazulu spread round the entire land like wildfire. Every other animal went into hiding. Their greatest nightmare had turned into a reality. The kids were warned not to be found around any of their hippopotamus friends.

This new changes made Olla sad, most of her friends weren't hippopotamus. She loved being around other animals. She enjoyed being a part of the other animal's life.

She knew she had to put an end to this. But she didn't know how she was going to do it. She only had faith that change will come and everything will go back to normal.

Olla took a walk up the hill. This was one of her favorite activities. Because up the hills were where are best friend lived. Kari was a very smart and intelligent rabbit. Despite his small size, he was a very confident animal. That was one of the reasons Ohio had a soft spot for him. As she approached his hole, she could notice all the other rabbits running into their holes. She wished they could just hear her out. She wasn't a savage and would never be. She would never intimidate other animals with her size. When she got to Kari's hole, she made a sound, a sound familiar to just Kari and her. In a twinkle of an eye, Kari was by her side. As she looked into his eyes, she could see worry and fear in his eye. —Have you come to eat me?‖ Kari said, hoping to get on her nerves, and it sure worked. Ohio responded, —How can you say that! I love you, and I will never do anything to harm you or anyone,‖ she said swiftly, trying so hard to fight her tears from rolling down. -It's okay, I believe you. Cheer up Ohio‖ . She obeyed Kari. -I have an idea,‖ she said. -So, what's the idea?‖ Kari asked spontaneously as he cracked open the groundnut he had stolen from his mom's farm. —I think we should have another meeting with the hippopotamus and change their thought, —she said. —So what makes you think they will listen to you? —Kari asked sarcastically. —Look, it took just words to make them change their minds, I could use the same word to change their mind, but this time it's going to be positive words,‖ Ohio said. She didn't even let Kari say one more word as she took off, as fast as her legs could carry her.

The day of the meeting had reached, and Ohio was a bit nervous, —what's the worst that can happen?‖ she asked herself as she walked into the mist of the entire hippopotamus in the land.

She looked boldly into their eyes and began to speak, -imagine going to look for food for your family, and you become a meal to another animal. Knowing that you're going to live in fear. Knowing that today might just be your last day. Have we all paused to put ourselves in their shoes? They are wallowing in fear. —Tell me, don't you miss your friends? I'm sure you do. Let's put an end to this madness,‖ she said as tears rolled down her cheek. The entire crowd went dead silent. And they depart one after the other, feeling sober.

It was a beautiful morning, and everyone went about their activities happily. The land was back to normal. King Malik was found dead in his palace. No one seem to know what happened to him. Everyone called Ohio their hero. She had restored people to the land with her words. Indeed she was fit to rule them. A Queen who understands that peace was the greatest!

ZEBRA

In the Dry Sahara region in Africa, Zebras walked in their black and white skin-tight uniforms.

The young nursing mothers in the Sahara are known for their constant gossiping.

They are nicknamed the Harem.

They would take long strolls with their little foals to the oasis.

They could stay there all day talking about strong stallions and family issues.

They spoke more of the leader of the Hunter stallions.

Every Mare's sensation.

Rougher strips, stronger hooves, and faster strides.

He had the loudest bark but the brightest smile.

Rough-stripes

A Single Stallion.

He cared of nothing else but to Fight and Eat.

There are rumors the Homo sapiens had made him a castrate last season.

They had come in their numbers to the Sahara with flying copters and fast desert rides.

They aimed at them.

Shouting Game! As each hunter stallion dropped.

The harem was long gone and weaker stallions too.

Rough Stripes charged on Barking louder.

It worked perfectly until she fell.

His right-hand mare.

Fierce as a Stallion, built for the work.

The ridicule to all stallions.

The Only Mare that stood back.

Feminist!

Feminist dropped, and again Homo-sapiens shouted game!

Rough-stripes was dazed.

He dropped a tear, he couldn't fight anymore.

He turned, snorting to the rest.

The War was over.

At first, they did not understand, but immediately, they did.

He barked once more disorienting the Homo-sapiens, and he fled to Zouma.

Their safest zone.

That was the only time they saw him run.

He got a hit below the belt right before he fled.

He never loved again.

Castrate or not? They deliberated this evening after noticing how big he grow in such a short time.

And how their advances didn't matter to him at all.

‚Let's do a mare contest' Glow; the fairest Mare suggested.

Let's see who he picks.

Hey, that's selfish.

Well, we can argue he won't pick you over us, I mean look us you.

You are the thinnest in the harem; Flesh countered.

Arguments. Silence.

The zebra who wore the latest leaf-shades motioned to speak.

How about we flip the coin.

Let's have a Stallion contest, winner picks his favorite mate.

Runners up decide which one they want too.

That way, the other stallions would not accuse us of not including them.

Besides, we know who will win.

Just that we don't know who he would choose.

Why put the stress on ourselves when we can just put it on him.'

Hoofs come together as everyone loves the idea.

Everyone except What if.

What if he does not win?'

Marriage meant almost nothing to this clan.

They did mate with the nearest available Stallion and strolled with him till they were bored.

Some had foals for them.

Male foals were looked after till they were big enough to choose a stallion group while the female stayed with their mothers until they wander off with stallions on the _Heat year'.

This ritual is highly esteemed in all of the zebra community.

It is the reason they all have foals.

The reason they had not gone instinct.

Today in the zebra Court.

The Harlem was about to make another ritual.

The Stallion Contest.

Everyone is in court Harlem and foals, Stallions alike, and Rough Stripes.

He stood by the Cave's exit as the proceeding continued.

Should we tell him?

Next deliberation!

Harlem's!

The Harlem leader steps forward.

Her zebra-walks across the Zebra crossing and make a gesture to the head of the Court.

The Chief Executive Stallion (CES); Chelsey as he is fondly called.

His real name is Zip it! But who cares.

Chelsey works perfectly.

State your case; Chelsey brays.

‗The heat year has been a measure taken by our fathers for procreation and social interaction.'

Mating if you will. She smiles.

This has led to poor decisions by Foals, male and female alike, as they end up like fools- Pun intended.

Picking the wrong available match.

Everyone deserves the best.

‚Interesting! So what is the solution Harlem?'

I believe I speak for all when I say we should have a contest that will allow the males to choose their choice Mare.

Okay?

The winners get to choose first in that order till the last mare is taken.

Murmurs.

Any objections?

Weak the head of the minority Stallion government had something to say.

Everyone is laughing already.

This is unfair, I would surely get the worst Mare. Let's be considerate here.

Any other objections?

None.

He doubles taps his hoofs on the wooden platform.

—Natural Selection is something that I have avoided a lot using the heat year policy.‖

My father told me this would happen, and I should not fight it.

With or without the policy, things would still go that way.

Insecurities aside. There is no way around it. Find a way to win it, and you will have the best too.

The strongest may win, the Smart too.

We would call this the feast of natural Selection.

Cheers!

The stallion at the door smirks.

Snorts twice, whatever.

The Oasis kept them from the heat of the sun.

It is the day of the feast, there is food a week in display.

The Scavenger Stallion had brought a little from the supplies they stored up for the famine period.

There is hay too many for everyone.

Only the ladies thought of food and the weaker stallions.

The Fifty contestants stood in front, ready to battle.

Nay, one is missing.

Oh! He wants to make a grand entrance. The Harlem chuckled as they spoke to one another.

Five more zebra-minutes Chelsey announced.

Five, four, three, two, one.

That is it!

Only the Forty-nine can...

Everyone is in tears right now.

Loud wails! No one seemed to know among the stallions.

Only the mares wept.

This was meant to be a festival, a festival they organized.

A festival of tears?

Just then, the Harlem leader managed to say.

‚Rough-stripes is dead.'

All the stallions wept.

Everyone wept—everyone except Chelsey.

Zip it! He ordered.

How did this happen?

He was poisoned. The hay he ate last night was the ‗grave potion.' She replied.

Just then, everyone stares at the Leader of the minority Stallion.

Weak.

I did it! He bluffed.

He was arrested and taken into the ‗watch caves.'

One question still bugged –Who would keep the dazzle safe.।

Was mating worth his life?

The next day after much proceedings in court.

Weak was banished to a cave where he ate no food nor drank any water.

Chelsey said he would allow nature to take him.

This is what happens when we mess with nature.

He decreed:

—From henceforth mating is only based on mutual agreement, and no stallion should fight another over a Mare.

Anyone can mate a Mare- Father or Son or Brother, or friend.

The aim is Procreation, remember.

We have a new culture.

Ubuntu- All for one, one for all.

—If I succeed, we all succeed.

If I fail, we all fail‖ .

Other members of the minority clan went into mourning for their leader.

This Clan presently lives at the other end of the Sahara, where they feel more.

They hurt more every year, cutting more stripes on their skin.

Till today in the Sahara. Every stallion move in group sharing mates from the Harlem.

Every young Foal knows of Rough-stripes, the one who natural Selection killed or not?

WARTHOG

Jungwe is the biggest and most revered family group of warthogs, they are known for their freehandedness. The Jungwe group is led by Mabika, son of the oldest ever lived sow in the history of time. Mabika is sick, and Mpoju is next to take over the leadership from his father, but the people do not like him.

Mpoju does not want to be a leader, he needed love and attention, he had no friends and have never mated any sow since his entire life, whenever it is mating season, all the boars come out for him, as it is their custom, they push and ram him with their heads and their upper tusks, Mpoju being a weakling gives up even before the fight and the other boars get to mate with the sow.

Mpoju is very lazy, he does nothing for himself, he cannot fight to defend himself, and he cannot go foraging, the commonality of Jungwe made him like that, he gets to eat food from the gatherings of other warthogs. He does only two things, eat, sleep, and repeat.

One day, he was fed up with all the hate around him, he went into a burrow where nobody could find him and thought to himself —Nobody likes me, not the sows, not even the boars, my father is not proud of me, I'm such a failure, I want to die!‖ , he growls, snorts, and squeals all at the same time. He was furious and sets out to do something different, something for himself, like getting his own food.

Over the last years, Jungwe has stopped foraging during the light of the morning and evening; they switched to foraging at night because of the predators that are in the area. Mpoju doesn't know this, for once in his life he sets out to look for food, and it was at the wrong time. He covered quite a distance away from home to an area where he found food, he knelt down on his front leg, using hid muscular snout he dug up hid lunch, shuffling along with the kneeling position because there were plenty of tasty things in the area, he gobbled grass, roots, and berries, —what a nice lunch‖ he thought to himself. Unsuspecting as Mpoju was, he steps into the path of an oncoming lion, the lion leaps out onto him with brute force and pounces on him, he tries to make a break for freedom but the lion is hot on his heels, he wrestles Mpoju to the ground sending dust cloud up in the air trying to recapture it, he couldn't fight back because he has never done that before, now the lion is holding Mpoju between his front paws, almost immediately, another animal approaches with high speed accompanied with a cloud of dust, it was a warthog but a different one, it was yellow in color with a white mane and tail; black cheek whiskers, it ran so fast towards the lion slashing him with her lower tusk, giving way for Mpoju to run, and she runs immediately after him, the lion was furious and bolted behind them, Mpoju ran so fast as he has never done trying to catch up with the other warthog, they dived into a nearby burrow and relaxed.

—Thank you so much for saving my life,‖ Mpoju said amidst panting, then turned to look at his savior, —Tendi!‖ he exclaimed

—Yes Mpoju, You are alive‖ she chuckled shyly

Tendi is the least popular sow in Jungwe, she is not like the rest of the warthogs, she is different, her skin color and prowess, so much different from every regular sow, she has no friends, nobody even talks about her or remembers her existence, she leaves Jungwe most of the times, to find adventure she says.

Tendi looks so beautiful with her black cheek whiskers, the color of her skin matches perfectly with her mane and tail, they didn't talk much, they just laid down enjoying the warmth they got from the burrow.

Mpoju has never felt this relaxed and loved, Tendi, on the other hand, has not been given this much attention, they talked and talked into the night, Tendi prepares to go foraging, and Mpoju pleads to join her, He begged to be taught how to fight, gather food and become a real warthog, the request was funny to Tendi but she didn't laugh, she obliged, and they walked together step by step.

Back in Jungwe, Mpoju's change of attitude and relationship with Tendi is a wonder to all, but Chake is angry, he doesn't like the new development, he was going to be the next leader when the people reject Mpoju, now he is slowly losing the love and attention from the people.

Mpoju and Tendi have been waiting for the end of the raining season to mate and have their son, it is finally here, and they both can't wait, but there came Chake, he rushed in like a wind and attacked Mpoju, he pushes him down with his head, Mpoju fights back, both of them push and ram each other with their heads and their blunt tusk to see who is more powerful, Chake on realizing that Mpoju was not going to give up like before, slashed him with his lower tusk, blood spurted out, Mpoju fell on the ground, Tendi immediately rushed Chake and pounced on him and fought tirelessly till they were both injured. Chake didn't take this lightly; it is a custom in Jungwe that during the mating season boars fight for a sow and if a boar gives up the other boar gets to mate with the sow, he raised his own army to revolt against Mabika and the leadership that rests on his family. They came when Mpoju was not around, they destroyed Mabika's burrow and every other thing that belongs to him, Mabika was too old and sick to fight, he was overpowered and held captive. When Mpoju heard this, he was so angry, he set out to fight Chake, Tendi pleaded to join him, so he took her along.

Jungwe looks deserted, Mpoju saw Tete, one of the warthogs in Jungwe running and looking back, he stopped him and inquired what the problem was —Chake is a monster, he wants to lord over us by force after we all frowned at his action towards your father he got angry and proclaimed himself Lord of Jungwe, he destroyed our burrows and hijacked our foods, I managed to escape, please come and save us‖ he cried.

Mpoju and Tendi got very angry and marched into Jungwe with speed, sending dust clouds in the air, they were so fast Chake didn't see them coming, Tendi struck first, slashing his throat with her lower tusk, Mpoju pounced on him and slashed him through with his warts, Chake finally dies, Mabika and the rest of the people were rescued. Mpoju was declared the king and Tendi, his queen, and continued to live peace and nobility.

CHAPTER FOUR
STORIES OF THE OCEAN

FIFI THE ADVENTUROUS DOLPHIN

Once upon a time in a faraway kingdom called Oceania

There was a little dolphin called Fifi, she was a princess, and her father, the king, ruled over the seven kingdoms in the ocean.

Fifi had three sisters; they were Kaitlin, Angelina, and Imelda.

Fifi was the last of the four girls, even though she was the last, Fifi was a brave girl.

While the other girls were all about princes, pink dresses, and beautiful tiaras, Fifi, on the other hand, was not interested in all of that.

Fifi loved adventures, she has always had one dream, and that dream was to see the world.

She imagined if there was a world apart from Oceania, she was inquisitive, wanting to know more.

Although she was known around the palace and throughout the entire region, as one of the bravest princess in the kingdom, Fifi wasn't satisfied.

One night Fifi, couldn't sleep, she was very restless thinking about what lies beyond.

She asked,‖ what if my kingdom is not the only one there is, what if what our fathers told us were lies? What if what lies beyond is far more special than Oceania‖ , all these thoughts ran through her mind until she slept off.

The next day, Fifi marched straight to the king's chamber, ─Good morning, your majesty, she greeted,‖ and the king replied, ─Good morning, my princess, did you have a good sleep.‖

Fifi replied, —that's why I have come to your chamber, father.‖

What troubles my princess? Asked the king.

Fifi replied, ‐father, I want to go on an adventure.∣

The king replied, —okay, you have always gone on adventures, you have my permission. But father I want to go outside Oceania Fifi said∣

But the king was taken aback, because no one has ever dared to ask what lies beyond, talk more of wanting to step outside Oceania.

I want to see the world, I want to know what the world holds for me Fifi said

Very early in the morning, Fifi sneaked out the palace for fear of being detected by the palace guards.

Now her journey to an unknown world has begun, and she left looking back at the palace

Now is not the time to feel sorry she said, you have a destination to reach

And with determination, Fifi began her journey to an unknown world.

As she swam, she had thoughts running through her mind —what if you fail to find this world you talk about, what if you never come back, what if you break down with regret.‖

 She said to herself, —Fifi, you can't doubt now, you have to be strong, you are not known to be weak, and you can do this,‖   and so she continued.

She stopped by some stores to get food for the journey and set off again.

She had swum far from the palace, now she was on the outskirt of Oceania, she needed to brace herself up for whatever comes.

Now she is responsible for herself, and as she traveled further, she noticed everywhere had become lonely.

Fear ran through her as she began to shiver, then again, she said to herself, —I can do this, just a little further.

She had not traveled further when she saw something that looked like the shadow of a shark.

—Oh, this is creepy,‖ she said, how come I never thought about these giant mammals?

Fifi was terrified, and so she quickly hid behind a rock and waited patiently for the mammals to pass before she came out.

She swam as fast as she could from where it was after the shark had gone.

As she swam, Fifi marveled at the beauty of the ocean, these she had never seen, she was left in admiration of the ocean, she was dazzled by the beautiful colors she saw.

She had never seen anything like it before, not even all the colors in the palace were well arranged as these were.

She wondered who could have made them or where did they come from, she was excited that she had begun to see what she dreamed and thought of, there really is another world from Oceania

But what Fifi did not know was that her journey just began.

As she swam further, suddenly there was a sound that came from afar off, she thought she heard screaming, she panicked.

And as she came closer, she saw two jellyfishes, bullying another fish, she thought to herself, why don't I rescue this little fish

She swam towards the scene, suddenly she felt someone grab her from behind, and it was another jellyfish.

Now she had come face to face with danger, what will happen to her if she doesn't find her way out, what would happen to her dream of seeing the world outside of Oceania?

Fifi knew she had to do something, she had to save herself,‖ what should I do,‖ she thought.

She was taken to the other two guys; Fifi had to think of something

What if I pretend to have a cardiac arrest and die, I am sure they will let go of me

So Fifi went ahead with her plan

What do we do? Asked the first fish

I don't know‖ the second fish replied

—I think we should just throw her body here and pretend like we were not here, —the third fish said

—I agree with him, that's what we should do,‖ the last fish said

They left as quickly as their tales could carry them

Fifi was glad her plan had worked, and she was relieved that the little fish had been left alone too.

Now she could continue her journey

She had traveled far when she saw a reflection; she didn't know what it was so she moved closer.

Fifi went, she moved until she was directly under the reflection.

She wondered what it was, she could feel a little bit of warmth, suddenly she saw a shadow, she got scared, but she dared to go closer, this time she could see shadows that seemed like giants.

What are they she thought, and she pushed her head above the water, and she could breathe what seemed like what she could not explain, but it felt so good.

One of the giants saw her, and reached out to her, Fifi felt her hands on her skin, it felt so good.

Fifi knew she wanted to stay here, but first, she had to return home to tell her parents what she had found.

ANDRE THE UGLY MANATEE AND THE MAGIC FLUTE

Far, far away in the kingdom of bloom, there lived a certain manatee called Andre.

He was the only child of his parents; they loved and showed him so much care.

He was ugly; he did not have friends because the other kids thought he was too ugly and fat.

They never wanted anything to do with him, even if anyone wanted to be his friend, he or she wouldn't because of fear of being bullied also.

Andre was always bullied because of his appearance, and that made him very sad

Sometimes André would be seen crying.

Andre stayed home most of the time, except during school hours, if there is one place he would rather not be in, that would be school.

One day at school, during one of the breaks, Andre opened his launch box and began to eat.

Leon who was a bully and most feared in school, walked to him.

He was the most handsome guy in school, he was also the football team captain, he was from a wealthy home, and all the girls came around him.

The school principal revered him also because of the affluence and influence his family had.

So Leon and his cohorts walked up to Andre, Leon picked up Andre's food and threw it away.

—What did you do that for,‖ Andre asked.

—Because you're fat and ugly,‖ Leon said.

Leon and his friends walked away laughing and calling him names

—Go back to your mummy,‖ Leon said

When it was school over, Andre walked home with tears in his eyes, dejected, and feeling unwanted.

—Hey, how was school today,‖　Andre's mom asked

—The usual mom‖　Andre said

—You will be fine,‖　Andre's mom said.

Andre walked up to his room and sunk in his bed, the picture of what happened in school began to flashback in his head, he growled in anger.

One day, Andre was swimming as he always did, to clear his head

This time he went farther than he usually did, there he came across a small house

He wanted to know what was in it, so he peeked.

—Hello, is anybody here‖　he called out, but there was no response.

—Hello' he called out again, still there was no response.

He walked into the house, and suddenly the door shut behind him.

Although, he was ugly and was usually bullied for it, he wasn't the type to run or shy away from danger.

He stepped a bit further into the room when suddenly a magic globe appear before him

He heard a voice saying, –comes closer, Andre.|

How do you know my name? Andre asked

I know everything that happens in bloom, I see all said the voice from the globe

How do I know you speak the truth? Andre asked.

HA, HA, HA, are you dumb Andre? Where have you seen a globe talk, I am made from magic.

Andre gasped, I thought magic does not exist, how is this possible?

—Well I exist,‖　said the voice from the globe

And I know that you are always bullied because of your looks.

Suddenly Andre's countenance changed, he had a look of worry.

Do not worry Andre, I can help you said the voice from the globe.

─Really, You can?‖ Asked Andre

─Yes I can,‖ said the voice from the globe

Don't you want anything in return? Asked Andre.

Yes, I do, said the globe.

That you promise never to tell anyone that you found me,

I promise.

And so the voice from the globe told him to find in between one of the shelves, there he would find a magic flute, and whenever he plays the flute, he would become handsome.

Andre took the flute and played it, immediately he became handsome.

He was very happy to have found the hut and, more so, the magic globe, and so he went home.

Hiding the flute, Andre step into the house very excited.

His parents saw the glow on his face, they couldn't tell why or what had happened, they were both happy to see their son happy.

The next day, Andre hurried off to school excited, ready to use his magic flute.

Andre played the flute, and immediately his looks changed.

 Everybody began to notice, even the girls spoke to him now, and they all wanted to be with him.

On the other hand, Leon was upset and jealous and wondered how Andre became handsome all of a sudden, and he swore to find out how.

During the games in school, Leon asked Andre to join the team as he has become like one of them.

Are you serious? Andre was surprised,‖ well, of course, I am,‖ Leon said.

And so Andre joined the school team and became popular just like Leon and his cohorts,

Little did he know that Leon was on his tail.

Andre never played the flute at home, because he knew his parents loved him just the way he was.

But if they ever found that he used magic to enhance his look, so that he can have friends

They were going to be very mad at him, and so he kept it a secret.

Because all the while he never had friends and he would stay home, he had learned a lot of things, from playing football to playing different kinds of instruments.

Andre did extremely well in the games, which increased Leon's anger.

Not too long, Andre was made the captain of the football team, and Leon came second place.

This time Leon has had enough and began to stalk Andre.

He began to look out for Andre, wherever he went, what he ate, drank.

Now Andre had already become friends with the magic globe and formed a habit of visiting the house.

One day, on his way to the house on his usual visits, humming and singing, without the knowledge of Leon coming behind him.

And so he swam to the house and as he entered Leon followed suit.

Andre walked excited, talking to the voice from the globe, he narrated how his day went

Hiding behind the door, Leon, heard Andre talking to the magic globe, and with a smirk on his face, he had his plan thought out.

And so Leon thought about stealing the globe, the next day without Andre knowing, Leon went to the house with his friends, he had told them what he saw, their thought was to make money from the globe.

The next day Andre went to the house and to his surprise, the globe was nowhere to be found.

Andre panicked, he feared someone must have found out about the globe, or the globe might have just disappeared like that since it was magic.

But Andre knew that the globe would not leave without first telling him, so his fears became great.

Down at Leon's place, they tried to get the globe to work, but the globe would not speak because he had seen them come to the house and had sensed what their intent was.

Leon was furious and vowed to expose Andre, so he called Andre.

Hey Andre, you looking for something? Leon asked.

Hum, I don't know what you are talking about, Andre replied.

Well, you do know, I have your globe said, Leon.

Andre panicked, this can't be happening

If you want your globe back, you have to come to my place, said Leon.

Andre was at leons, he was asked to make the globe talk, but Andre wouldn't, and so Leon threatened to tell the whole school how he had been lying to everybody about his looks.

But Andre wouldn't do it because he had promised the voice from the globe not to tell anyone about it.

Leon saw that Andre would not give in, so in anger, Leon broke the globe, and all of the magic disappeared including the magic flute.

Andre went back to how he looked. Although he was sad, he was also excited because, with time, he had learned how to be confident in himself.

Even though everyone saw him as ugly, he saw himself as unique, he relied on his ability to do what others couldn't do, he figured he did not need anyone to be happy.

After that, people began to like him just the way he was.

DANNY THE GREEN TURTLE AND THE MERMAID

A long time ago, two kingdoms cohabited together.

They were kingdom mermaidia and kingdom turtulia.

These two kingdoms lived in peace and harmony, for decades.

But the ruling kingdom was mermaidia, and everyone lived in peace.

But there was one who wasn't happy with how the kingdom was ruled.

She was the wife of the king Jon of turtulia, her name was Queen Lucinda.

One night the queen had a discussion with the king.

—Your majesty, can I have a word with you,‖ she said.

Yes, my queen, the king replied.

Why? The king asked.

As a king, you can only be seen as a king only if you have a kingdom of your own she said.

But that's not true, as long as my people love and respect me and I can provide protection and food for them, then I am seen as their ruler said the king.

But the queen would not agree, she saw the mermadia's as a threat and that they made them look weak in the sight of their people.

And so she convinced the king into believing that the mermadia's were actually making them feel inferior, even in the eyes of their people.

And so war broke out, the king of mermaidia charged the king of turtulia with treason.

And so his kingdom was divided, and then a law was given that no mermaids should interact with the turtles.

If the law was broken, it was punishable by death.

Ten years later.

After the war, there lived an orphan turtle named Danny, he was an enthusiastic fellow,

Danny was always excited to do things and help out in the neighborhood.

He would never go a day without helping out, no matter how slow he thought he was, he would always deliver.

He also loved the seashell hunt.

So one day, he went about his day like he always does, trying to get seashells, and as he did, he heard a voice from a distance.

Danny was captivated by the voice, and he decided to find out where the singing was coming from and who had that lovely voice.

As Danny looked closer he saw a mermaid, he looked with astonishment and wondered where she must have come from.

Hello, lady, Danny asked, the little mermaid jumped from trepidation

She asked, who are you, and what are you doing here?

I am Danny, he replied, what's your name?

Fiona, Princess Fiona she answered.

What brings you here to turtulia, Danny asked.

I love to walk, so I decided to take a walk down here said the princess.

You know you are not supposed to be here because there is a boundary separating both kingdoms, right? Danny asked.

Then why did you come, you know you could get killed for treason Danny said.

Goodbye, Danny said the princess.

The princess swam as fast as she could, before Danny could, say goodbye she was gone.

Danny thought about the princess as he walked back home, her beautiful voice, and her radiant beauty.

And so Danny resolved in his heart not to tell anyone about what or who he had met.

First, for her safety and also, he wanted to see her again.

Every day Danny would walk down to the boundary, hoping to see if the princess would come.

He would wait for hours, hoping she would come.

Days went by, weeks went by, and he still had not seen her

One day like he always did, he was waiting as usual, but this time he had decided not to come again if she doesn't show up.

It was almost nightfall when he decided to leave, and as he turned to leave, he heard a voice singing and then he stopped

Danny could not believe, although he was excited, he did not want her to know.

Danny put up a serious face.

Hey, what you are doing here, Fiona asked.

What do you mean what I am doing here, said Danny.

I come to hunt for seashells, what are you doing here? Danny asked hoping to push the attention to her.

I walked down today like I normally do, Fiona said.

And so they began to talk, and they began to know each other better.

They talked for long.

Danny was staring at her, he was mesmerized by her beauty, and Danny didn't want her to leave.

The moment they shared felt like heaven.

It was time for Fiona to leave and Danny didn't want her to go.

I have to leave Danny, she said.

Oh okay, said Danny.

Goodbye Danny.

He left the boundary also, he felt like he had butterflies in his tummy.

What's wrong with me, why am I feeling like this, Danny thought.

And he knew he couldn't talk to anybody about it, what do I do, he said.

But Danny remembered that it wouldn't be possible to have anything to do with her because of the law and consequences.

He had to do something, and so he went back to the boundary, hoping she would be there.

Weeks passed, and she had not showed up, so he said to himself, why don't I look for her.

For once Danny forgot about the law and what might happen if he was ever caught in mermaidia.

And so Danny went in search of the princess, he traveled far, he had not imagined that the journey would be very long, he had thought the princess just strolled to the boundary

He thought to himself why she would come this far just to see the boundary, little did he know that she came because she was searching for a way to reunite the two kingdoms, so they can live as they did in the past.

Danny managed to get to kingdom mermaidia, he was tired because he had traveled very far.

He marveled at the beauty of mermaidia, its giant buildings with beautiful colors and beautiful people.

He had not seen anything like this before; he could see some of the kids playing around.

Somehow it made him remember home, but he was determined to find the princess, and so he continued.

Danny had to walk carefully so he would not be detected because if he was, his mission will be terminated.

Finally, he got to the palace, it was easy to find because it was way different from other homes.

Danny sneaked past the guards, he knew he had to find her.

So he peeked through every door he found open but didn't find her.

And then he heard one of the maids say she was going to attend to the princess, and so he followed, hoping to talk with her.

He had finally gotten to her door when he heard her singing, his heart leaped for joy.

—Finally I found her,‖ he said to himself.

And when the maid went in, Danny immediately followed her in.

—I can see you are excited about your wedding, my princess,‖ said the maid.

Danny was heartbroken when he heard them.

And so he turned to leave.

—Danny is that you,‖ the princess called out.

Oh yes, it's me, Danny replied.

What are you doing here?

I came looking for you, I hadn't seen you in weeks.

Yes, I couldn't come because I was preparing for my wedding.

Oh, that you didn't say, said Danny.

Yes, I didn't tell you I am betrothed to Prince Arthur said the princess.

But I love you, said Danny.

I love the prince, said Fiona.

Then why did you come to the boundary.

And the princess told him everything.

Danny was heartbroken and understood, even though he loved her so much he had to let her go, so she could be happy.

But how are we going to reunite both kingdoms, asked Danny.

I have a plan, now that you are here Danny, we can convince my father the king to evoke the law.

How is that going to happen? Asked Danny.

—We would allow the guards get to you, they will have to arrest you, which would mean a death sentence and then we will go to the king to talk him into letting you go, and if he disagrees, I will kill myself if any harm comes to you, ‖ said Fiona.

Now that's crazy, you want me to die? Danny panicked.

Yes I know it is crazy, but that's the only way out, Fiona said.

Danny was arrested by the guards and taken to the king.

Princess Fiona heard the news and ran to the king, she pleaded with the king.

—Father, you can't do this, —said princess Fiona.

—Keep quiet, don't tell me what I can or cannot do, ‖ said the king furiously.

He is my friend said the princess.

What! The king was shocked.

The princess pleaded, but the king refused and ordered Danny to be taken to the dungeon.

Fiona tried to make her father see why he shouldn't kill Danny.

Father, why do you want to do this, why can't we live together with the other kingdom, I thought we stood for love, peace, and harmony, why is it difficult to extend all that to these people the princess said.

—They betrayed us,‖   said the king

Not Danny, besides, if you claim to love your people and me and you really have love in your heart, you would show it.

If I committed treason, will you kill me dad? She asked.

No, I love you too much to lose you said the king.

Then do this for me, let's live together in peace with kingdom turtulia.

Days passed.

And so the king thought about what the princess had said days back, and he was restless.

After giving it a long thought, the king announced to the entire kingdom and gave a new decree.

People of mermaidia, I king Xeroxes the second, hereby decree that the law which prevents anyone from kingdom turtulia comes into kingdom mermaidia is abolished.

My daughter has made me see that love should not be said, it should be seen in our actions and not just our words

And so the king sent word to kingdom turtulia, and they reconciled.

Danny was released from the dungeon, and was granted permission to go home.

And both Danny and the princess were happy, and because of that, the entire kingdom of turtulia attended the glamorous wedding of the princess, and they lived happily ever after.

BEAUTY THE SEAHORSE AND THE RACE

On a race track

Horses running

Crowd cheering....

And there a winner emerges

Yes, yes, yes was all beauty could scream, while she twirled

She was filled with excitement as one of her favorite parent had won the race, her dad.

She loved him with all her being, although she lost her mom when she was given birth to, her dad was all she had, and now he had her feeling all proud of him.

Her dad and mom named her beauty, because when she was born, she had beautiful stripes and they were colorful, almost everyone that saw her envied her even though she was short-snouted.

Being on a race track was all beauty has ever dreamt of, she wanted to be like her dad, standing in front of the crowd winning championships and waving to the crowd as they waved back.

But all this was just a dream, as she has always been told that she would never become a sprinter, but that didn't get to her, she never saw herself as being too short for the race track.

She had her dad, her coach, her superhero, and he meant everything to her, what could go wrong as long as she had her dad she had all.

Way to go, dad, she screamed.

Beauty never thought about what she would do if ever lost her dad, she just lived in the moment

One night her dad fell ill, and because he knew he wasn't going to make it, he called her to his side

—Beauty —her dad called

-Yes, dad‖ she answered

You look just like your mom, her dad told her

I know, you always tell me I remind you of mom, she said smiling.

Yes I do, her dad struggled to smile

What's wrong dad, are you okay? She asked

—I want you to take care of yourself, don't let anyone tell you what you can or cannot do, always believe in yourself,‖ her dad said

—Why are you saying this? Beauty asked

—Oh I know how strong you are I know you will do well when I am gone,‖ her dad said

Tears flowed from her eyes as she knew where he was going to, she could not afford to lose him now, what would she do, she thoughts

Shah shh, shh, she tried to stop him from saying anything else, but he was dead already.

Beauty could not hold back her tears, she screamed so loud like it was going to ease the pain, but he was gone, what else could she do.

Few years had gone by, and beauty still wasn't on the race track, when her father died her dreams died

Beauty worked as a bartender, she sold tickets to the games.

She worked on different jobs, she had to make ends meet, she figured the world was owned by those who survived its hardship and so did all she could to beat it.

She had lost everything, but not her pride and of course her dad's house, she closed very late, but she didn't care, it almost seemed like she was living a suicidal life.

Beauty would always go home every night and wake up in the morning to repeat to same circle, although she never stopped training.

One day as she went about her work, bartending and selling tickets to games, she met Dave

That guy you bet on will lose said beauty

How would you know that Dave Asked?

I just know she said

After the game Dave lost, she had predicted right, of course, she knew her game well

How did you know, Dave Asked?

My father coached me she said

And why aren't you on the track, Dave asked

Because I am not fit, can't you see? Beauty yelled.

Why do you let your look define who you are Dave said to her

Nobody wants me, I have tried so hard she said with tears in her eyes

Why do you listen to what people say, you can or cannot do, Dave said

Immediately Beauty remembered the words her dad said to her, and she began to cry profusely,

Oh, how she has missed him so much that she forgot who she was and wondered how she got here.

Soon she got up on her feet and decided to that, by all means, she would be on that race track doing her thing just like her dad taught her to, it was time to make him proud

And so she went in search of her dad's old friends, those she thought would help her get what she wanted, she worked harder to impress them not minding how she looked, she wanted to get in by all means

After months of hard work, she finally got in; she had trained like a mad horse, passion-driven, and with her only goal to make her dad proud.

This was the opportunity she was waiting for, now that she had it, she wasn't going to mess it up

Finally, she was on the race track, she heard the crowd cheer she lifted her head up and looked in the crowd, she saw her dad, her coach, her hero standing and cheering

She knew he was proud of her.

FINDING MANDY THE OCTOPUS

—Mandy, Mandy, Mandy‖

Where are you? Mandy's mom called out to her

Mandy was a little octopus girl who loved to play hide and seek, she was a very playful girl.

Everyone loved Mandy, how she would sneak up behind you and scare you, Mandy loved to have fun, no time was boring for her.

If you ever got angry, Mandy was the one to call, the neighbor loved her, her friends at school loved her.

She was free-spirited, but also stubborn, she would play pranks with her friends, and she wasn't going to slow down.

Yes, mom, Mandy ran to her mom

I have been looking all over for you; you are going to be late for school, and your bus is here.

Mandy packed her lunch and left for school, she was excited because it was the beginning of a new session and she couldn't wait to show her friends all of the tricks she had learned during the holiday

Hey Mandy, how are you? Zoey asked

I'm cool, and hey I have something new to show you, and it's going to be fun Mandy said

It better be cool as always, Zoey replied.

After school, Mandy walking back home as usual, but this time she realized she might have walked through a wrong ally.

Mandy was scared, she had just witnessed the killing of a woman, she had screamed, and was on the run

She hoped they had not heard her scream, she hoped they were not after her, she swam as fast as she could.

She couldn't go home because she thought they might find her there, she was terrified.

What will I do, she thought

What will happen to mom, what will she think, Mandy was scared, and it was getting late?

Back at home Mandy's mom was worried, she hoped Mandy was not playing one of those her pranks again, she had called the school authority to find out if Mandy was still in school, she called her friends, but they had not seen her after school.

Her mom was scared, what could have happened to her daughter, where could she be? Mandy's mom was worried.

Mandy had swum deep into the deep blue sea, she couldn't go to the police, she feared

She couldn't go to the police, what if they found her and do to her what they did to the other woman

Back home, Mandy's mom had to call the police, the search for her daughter had begun, she hoped they would find her as quickly as possible.

Mandy saw a restaurant, her stomach rumbled, she had not eaten since lunch in school, and now she was weak and tired from all the running, she just wanted food.

She walked into the restaurant to beg for food, she was lucky to find some food on the table, and now she wanted to rest.

The restaurant was going to be closed, and she had to find a place to lay her head, she finally had to sleep outside.

Back home, the police had searched everywhere looking for Mandy, they got to the ally and found the body of the woman Mandy had seen.

The next morning Mandy woke up with body pains, hoping this was all a bad dream, but no, it wasn't.

So she thought to find a way to reach her mom, she walked down the streets for a while and found a phone booth, she leaped for joy, as she remembered she had some seashells which she could trade with

Mandy dialed her home line

Hello mom? Mandy asked

Mandy, is that you? Her mom asked

—I have been worried sick about you, and the police have been looking all over for you Mandy,‖ she said.

Mandy was in tears, she had missed home.

Where are you darling, so I can come get you? Her mom asked

Mandy told her where she was, and immediately the police drove to where she was

Mandy's mom jumped out of the vehicle, and swam towards her, she gave her a long hug

Mandy cried over her shoulder and began to explain why she couldn't return home.

CHAPTER FIVE:
STORIES OF THE MOUNTAIN

SNOW

Even before any humans walked the planet, a very long winter set in when the world was the land of animals. For three years, the sun didn't come out. The air had always been dark. Thick clouds had hung low, covering the sky. It snowed all the time. This long winter was causing great distress to the animals. Food shortages were worrying enough, and the lack of heat made it nearly unbearable. They became terrified.

The animals had called for the holding of a grand assembly. It welcomed all the beasts, birds, and fishes of all sizes and shapes. When the animals looked around at the grand gathering, they noticed only one thing in the whole animal kingdom was missing: Bear.

Then, they remembered that for three years, no one had seen any bears.

All of the animals were swift to decide that the most important thing to do was to find out what had become of the sun, for their sufferings will not end without food. Yes, they have to find the sun! Then they have to get it out again. They agreed that many prompt and courageous animals should go to the upper world on a search mission. That's where they thought they'd taken the sun. These are the animals chosen for the mission: Lynx, Fox, Wolf, Wolverine, Mouse, Pike (a freshwater fish), and Dogfish. Then, they remembered that for three years, no one had seen any bears.

The group finally found the secret doorway, which opened up to the upper world after much traveling far and wide through the air. Excited, they all ascended to the universe above.

After spending some time exploring the upper world, they saw a waterfall. A campfire burning by the water, with a tipi next to it. There were 2 young bears by the tipi. They asked the cubs where their mother was, and they told them that she was hunting. A number of large, round bags hanged up inside the tipi. Visitors to the animal pointed to the first bag and asked the cubs,

—What's in that package?‖

—This,‖ they asked,

—is where our mother holds the rain.‖

—And what's in this one?‖ said the animals, pointing to the second bag.

—That,‖ the cubs answered, —is the wind.‖

—And this one?‖

—That's where Mother keeps the fog.‖

—And what could be in this next bag?‖ the animals said.

—No, we can't let you know that,‖ said the cubs, —for it was a great secret for our mother to tell us, and if we tell you, she'll be very angry and bop us on our heads when she comes back.‖

—Ah, don't be afraid,‖ said the fox. —You should tell us. She's never going to know.‖

Then the cubs whispered, —This is the bag where she holds the fire.‖

—Aahh—‖ the visitors said. They looked at each other, stammering their good-byes. They hurried to a secret spot outside the tipi and conducted a fast meeting. Their first agreement was to travel quickly, as the mother bear could come back at any time. That they did, and they found a more comfortable place to hide. The next question was a tougher one. How to get the fire from the bag?

—Somehow, we have to scare the old mother bear,‖ Fox said.

—I know!‖ Lynx announced.

—I'm going to turn into a deer on the other side of the lake,‖ Wolverine said,

—Great idea!‖

—Mother bear will see you across the water and will try to kill you.

—Yes, yes!‖ cried the others.

So Lynx went around to the other side of the lake and turned into a deer. Now, as a Deer, he wandered near the edge of the lake to attract the Bear's attention. In the meantime, Mouse scrambled into Bear's canoe and chewed a deep cut in the handle of her paddle close to the blade. The others hid near Bear's tipi.

When one of the bear cubs saw the supposed deer across the lake he cried out, look at the deer on the opposite shore!‖ The old mother Bear immediately jumped into her canoe and paddled toward it. Deer walked slowly along the beach, pretending not to see the canoe, to tempt Bear to paddle up close to him. Then all at once, Deer doubled about and ran the opposite way. Old Bear threw her whole weight on the paddle to make it go faster, and the paddle broke suddenly where Mouse had gnawed it. The force of Bear's weight threw her into the water. The other animals were watching the hunt from the other side, and as soon as they saw the mother Bear floundering in the water, they ran into the tipi and pulled down the bag containing the heat. One at a time, they tugged the bag through the air toward the opening to the lower world from where they had come.

They hurried to get back to the opening as fast as they could, but the bag was very large, and none of them was able to keep up the pace for long. Whenever one tired out, another would take the bag, and in this way, they hastened along as quickly as they could, for they knew that the old mother Bear will soon get ashore and return to her tipi, and that when she did she will discover the missing bag. Then she'd be furious and follow their footprints to catch them! Sure enough, the old mother Bear was soon in hot pursuit and had almost overtaken the animals when they spied just up ahead the opening to the world below. By this time, the stronger animals were all so tired, they could hardly move at all. Now Dogfish (the small shark) took the bag and pulled it along a good way, and finally, Pike (the freshwater fish) managed to inch it along some more.

At that very moment, Bear lurched toward them. All the animals together pushed the bag until it tipped through the hole to the lower world, and they each jumped in after it to safety, just in time. As soon as the bag dropped to the world below, it broke, and all the heat crammed inside the bag rushed out. Warmth spread at once to all parts of the world and quickly thawed the ice and snow. Floodwaters ran high for many weeks, but then the waters subsided. The trees and bushes and flowers which had been covered by ice grew green leaves once more, and springtime bloomed anew. From that time till now, the world has always seen a warm-season returning after a cold one, just as we see today.

THE LITTLE BEAR

An old man living in Alaska was sad. All of his friends and family were long gone. He began to wonder if he should leave the village and start a new life somewhere else. —If I lived someplace new, at least I won't be around all these memories anymore,‖ he thought. But he also worried, —If I paddle away to another village and the people there see that I'm alone, they may think that I had to run away from my home village because I was accused of some disgraceful thing.‖ Instead, he thought that he would just go off and live in the forest by himself.

The poor man was so sad, traveling alone in the woods, it actually occurred to him to go to the bears and just let the bears kill him. The bear village was by a large salmon creek, so he went over to the creek early in the morning until he found a bear trail, and he lay down across the end of it. He thought that when the bears came out along this trail, they would find him, and that would be the end of him.

By and by, as he lay there, he heard the bushes breaking. Then a large number of grizzly bears came along. The largest bear led the rest, and the tips of his hair were white. Then the old man became scared. All of a sudden, he realized that he did not want to die at all, and certainly not by bears. So when the leading bear came up to him, the old man stood up. He announced: —I have come to invite you to a feast.‖

At that, the leading bear's fur stood straight up. The old man thought that he was surely done for, but he spoke again, saying, —I have come to invite you to a feast, but if you are going to kill me, I am willing to die. I am alone. I have lost all of my family and my friends.‖

As soon as he had said this, the leading bear turned around and growled to the bears that were following. Then the group of them turned back the way they had come. After a while, the man turned and walked toward his village very fast. He wondered if the biggest bear had told the bears behind him to go back and get ready because they were invited to a feast.

—Well, in case that's the way it is, I better get ready to make a feast,‖ thought the old man. As soon as he got home, he started to clean up. He took away the old sand around the fireplace and replaced it with clean sand. Then he went for a load of fresh wood. When he told the other people in the village what he was doing and why they were all very much scared. They said to him, —What made you do such a thing? The grizzlies are our enemy. You do not want grizzly bears in your home.‖ When he was back home, the man took off his shirt and painted his chest. He put stripes of red across his upper arm muscles, a red stripe over his heart and another across the upper part of his chest.

Very early in the morning, after he had thus prepared, he stood outside of the door looking for his bears. Finally, he saw them at the mouth of the creek, led by the same big grizzly bear, the one with white hair on its tips. When the other village people saw the bears, however, they were so terrified that they shut themselves in their houses. But the old man stood by his door to receive his guests. He brought them into the house and gave them seats, placing the chief in the middle at the rear of the house, and the rest around him.

First, he served them large trays of cranberries preserved in grease. The large bear seemed to say something to his companions, and as soon as he began to eat, the rest started to eat, too. They watched him and did whatever he did. The host followed that up with a course of salmon, with sprinkles of clover weed and dandelion on top for garnish. Then a course of deer meat with pine nuts. For dessert, raspberries with honey. After they were through, the large bear seemed to talk to his host for a very long time. It was almost as if the leader bear was giving him a speech, for he would look up at the smoke hole every now and then and act as though he were talking. When he finished, he went over to his host and licked the paint from his arm and chest. And so each of the other bears, in turn, did the same. The old man felt as if they were licking his sorrow away.

The day after all this happened, the smallest bear came back to the old man's hut in human form and spoke to the old man. He had been born a human being, he told the old man, but had been captured and adopted by the bears. This bear-man asked the old man if he had understood their chief, and he said, —No.‖

—He was telling you,‖ the bear-man replied, -that he is in the same condition as you. That he, too, is old and has lost all of his friends. He had heard of you before he saw you, he said. He told you to think of him when you are mourning for your lost ones, as he knows how that is, too.‖

When the old man asked this bear-man why he had not told him that day, when the bears were at the feast, he replied that he was not allowed to turn into his human form and speak his native language while the bear chief was around.

After this, whenever the people of the village gave a feast, they would always invite an enemy to the feast. And they would become friends, just as the old man had done with the chief of the bears.

THE SQUIRREL

Two squirrels in a forest worked happily in a coconut plantation. One day a strong gale winds perturbed the entire coconut plantation. It swept the ay coconuts, and the field was helter-skelter with baby coconuts in minutes.

The squirrels were delighted at once but soon discovered that all the baby nuts, along with the flowering bunches, had dropped and that it would take quite a while for the coconut trees to bloom again and for these flowers to become nuts.

What do we do? They ate the coconuts and slept. After three days, eating only the dropped baby coconuts became really difficult, because they tasted differently. They are numerous in numbers, others were really good and ready to eat.

The squirrels tried in vain to peel a coconut husk out, and they were tired. Dr. Dove approached them, seeing them in that condition and inquired about their question.

Yeah, don't worry I will help you solve this problem. All I want you both to do is peel out the husk at the back of the nut so you can drink the water and start working.

With this advice the squirrels got inspired and did as told. They soon found a tender spot in the nut that has to be drilled to get to the surface. So Dr Dove closely grasped the coconut and stabbed it with his beak. The water was gushing out. In addition, the squirrels drank the water, and felt refreshed.

Now you can start scraping the rest of the husk around the nut, so I can help you crack it, Dr. Dove said.

We can't crack the nut, because its shell is really hard: one of the squirrels said. I have an idea for that too, don't worry. Soon the squirrels resumed their work of peeling the husk out in an hour. Dr Dove then asked them to hold the husk intact at one end. They did the same thing, and then they jumped on the nut then rolled it around.

Now we're going to carry a rope, and at the end, we're going to tie it to this nut, which still has some husk. I have an idea: a squirrel yelled. What is it, then? Dr Dove asked.

There is a money plant that has many ropes like branches on the nearby neem tree. I can cut one of them here and carry it over.

Soon the squirrels carried a long rope like a money plant branch and cut their leaves.

The squirrels themselves tied the coconut like money plant branch to the rope and waited for further instructions.

Perching for a while on the nearby banyan tree, Dr. Dove thought, flew down, and picked up the other end of the trimmed plant money branch with his beak and alighted on the same branch.

Come up and join me: Dr. Dove Soon said the squirrels joined with Dr. Dove on the banyan tree branch. They picked up the coconut.

Now let it all down by holding on to the end of the rope at once.

As the squirrels got ready, Dr. Dove was asked them to wait and listen.

We have to drop through it in such a way that it falls precisely on the stone below, and it splits.

They crashed on the first attempt. They untied the nut. Finally, they tied the nut and tried again.

The second attempt was a fantastic success. The nut broke.

You should go down now and dine on....

Dr Dove flew away saying this.

Thank you Dr Dove for helping us learn the trick of breaking and eating these strong coconuts. You helped us survive too. Thank you very much: The squirrels joyfully shouted back.

THE TREE

Elise is a tiny girl. She's 6 and loves animals. A big tree is in her yard. She chose, one day, to climb the tree.

Elise went out and stared up at the huge tree as it was towering over her. She was sad. It was early in the morning; her mother and father were both sleeping. Elise wiped her eyes away that night and took the lowest branch, and started to climb. Elise climbed and ascended and climbed, it seemed for hours. The higher she climbed, the more Elise focused on the oak. Wasn't that high? It seemed like she'd climbed forever! She looked down, and was no longer able to see the ground! She started getting scared. She really was tall!

Elise took a deep breath and looked back up when she noticed a bluebird climbing on.

—Well, hi over there!‖ The bluebird yelled and raised a hand at her. The bluebird had a little bag full of worms on hand. —Can you talk? —Elise asked the beautiful cat. —I can, of course! Want to get some new worms? —The bird was chirping again. —God, thank you, no! I just have to keep going!‖ Elise grinned and climbed the vine. She tried to make it to the very top.

—It has been interesting to talk to you! —The bluebird screamed at Elise. —And you!‖ Elise replied.

She kept on climbing and seeing even stranger things! Elise noticed a bunny wearing a top hat on one branch which she sat on! He kept yelling nonsense and running about, so she left him alone.

She missed home and the ground as she moved on more. She looked down and could not see anything but a branch. Little Elise sighed and started to climb her tall tree. Before meeting a tall monkey wearing a bow tie, she climbed higher and shared some tea with an owl, a cardinal, and a colibris. She marched to the tea party along the branch and said, -Excuse me, Mr. Monkey. I think I'm lost. —The monkey looked up at Elise and howled. — Guy!! Come on! Get some coffee! —That's said. —No, thanks, but I want to go home . Will one of you get me home again? —Asked Elise. Cardinal croaked, —I cannot hold one that is as big as you are! —He shook his head with disbelief. —I'm sorry, deary, but neither can I comfort you.‖ Owl had a wonderful British accent. Elise looked up at Monkey, who had gone over to her. —Where's your house?‖ Elise pointed to her below. —The way down there is a house aaaaallll, Sir. I climbed this tree and lost myself. -Monkey grinned and grabbed Elise's hand as he started swinging branch after branch. —Did you just say it's down there? —The little girl smiled, and Monkey kept running around. Elise was giggling, as the ride was fun, when they reached the field. The Monkey slowed down and helped the little girl softly to the field. —Join us for some tea time, if you wish! —The Monkey said to her, and started to swing back over the tree. Elise sat there in astonishment for a second before saying, —I will! —The little girl went back into her home and up the stairs. Elise smelled the familiar scent of bacon and eggs as soon as she walked in. Her mom was in the kitchen, preparing coffee.

Elise rushed into the kitchen and embraced her mother, who was stunned by the very sudden embrace. —Why hello!‖ Elise's mother said. Elise sat beside the warm breakfast and responded, —You wouldn't have thought! —As she laughed, she slipped into the food.

Elise has never told anyone about the tree adventure and all the tea parties to this day. She's also holding tea parties in the tree with the dumb Monkey and all the others.

THE EAGLE

When an eagle died on earth a long time ago, her soul left her body and floated to the heavens, where she lived as a cloud human, watching over and caring for the eagles and animals on earth. The eagles were referred to as all birds in the animal kingdom.

The eagles and animals were conscious of these people in the air.

There came a time when a whole year had gone without rain. The plant died, the water holes dried up, and the animals starved to death. The eagles and animals came together to discuss what to do about this devastating drought.

—I guess we need to eat the ostrich,‖ Lion said, licking his lips.

—No! —Ostrich sneered.

—I think that we should be looking to move somewhere else,‖ Monkey said.

—Living nowhere else,‖ Wild Dog yelped. —The drought is everywhere.‖ Owl said, —We need to speak to people in the cloud. —They'll know what to do.‖ Eagles and animals decided that the eagles will be going up to the clouds and talking to the clouds. They may be bringing food down to earth to feed the starving eagles and animals.

Tortoise and his wife also attended the conference. Ahem, —he announced. —Do you really think a flock of eagles would receive attention from the cloud people? They need a King to accompany them. To give our quest somebody of value. I am going to be their King. I'm going to talk for us all.‘ The eagles twittered among themselves. The eagles finally decided to take Tortoise as their King along.

Hornbill rubbed his head violently. —How are we taking Tortoise up to the clouds?‖ He was wondering. Hyena smiled and chattered with Monkey. No one had ever thought about this subject. There had been a lot of proposals. Owl eventually suggested the eagles could stick feathers on the legs of Tortoise. If he had enough feathers, he could soar. When all the feathers were sticking to his paws, Tortoise looked ridiculous. Many of the animals tried to laugh, but they knew that their only chance of survival was Tortoise.

Everyone held their breath as Tortoise flapped their wings. He rose slowly from the ground and shot up into the sky. The animals cheered, and the eagles rose higher and higher upward towards the clouds as Tortoise climbed.

When Tortoise and the eagles landed in the clouds, people in the cloud were delighted to see the eagles and proud to have chosen to bring their king with them. The people in the cloud cooked a feast—ripe fruits and tasty vegetables that the eagles had not seen for a long time.

Who is all this food for‖ One of the eagles asked excitedly.

—Why, this is for you all,‖ the people in the cloud said.

No time spent on tortoise. He charged greedily forward and took the last morsel of food as the eagles watched him. The people in the cloud were shocked that the eagles did not eat, but they figured it was the practice of the eagles to allow their king to feed first.

The eagles got really angry and hungry! They charged towards Tortoise and all his feathers were taken out. He then flew back to earth to tell the other animals about the trick that Tortoise was doing.

The feathers of Tortoise fluttered back to earth, and he was stuck in the sky. In desperation, he looked around. He would surely die if he sprung back to earth. Suddenly he heard Parrot running around searching for a morsel of food he had lost.

—Please, Parrot,‖ Tortoise pleaded, —tell my wife to create for me a big pile of leaves so that I can leap from the clouds and not be crushed to death when I land on the hard ground.‖ The parrot was angry with Tortoise for eating all the food. As he returned to earth, he told Tortoise's wife she had been asked by her husband to build a pile of rocks for him to land on.

The wife of Tortoise set up a mound of bricks. From the stars, Tortoise looked down and saw his wife standing by something. It was a pile of leaves, he thought, so he closed his eyes, held his breath, and jumped. His little round body dropped to the ground and heavily landed on the rocks. He cried out as he shattered his shell.

The wife of Tortoise rushed towards his side and stared in horror at the damage to the beautiful shell of her husband. She nursed him and took care of him until he eventually recovered, but the cracks in his shell remained forever like scars—a sign of what he had done to the poor eagles. Elsewhere, people in the cloud were unhappy when they saw how fooled the eagles had been. They were wailing and weeping, and their tears fell from the sky and soaked the earth like rain. The grass and the trees rose again, and the eagles and animals had food again. But the eagles never again trusted either of the tortoises, and tortoises hide their heads inside their shells to this day in fear when they see an eagle.

CHAPTER SIX:
STORIES OF THE MOON, STARS, PLANET AND EARTH

STORIES OF THE MOON

Once upon a time, there lived a man and a woman in a remote place, far from anything. His name was MOON, and Ela was her name. MOON had white skin, and Ela was brown. In the beginning, this didn't matter, but over time there would be tiny little cracks, first in minor ways, and then in ways, they couldn't hide anymore. MOON first saw Ela in a room filled with smoke and decided he wanted her; he wanted to know the taste of her brown skin, he wanted to run his hands over her ample body's soft curves. Ela never believed him. She didn't believe much about fairy tales or herself or any of it. MOON chased her and chased her, and then because she was starving, she let him take her to dine. At her place, Ela let him have a drink because she was lonely. She let him touch her as she was a different kind of hungry. She lay with him and enjoyed his body's meat against her, how sweetly his rough hands kissed her, he brushed her shoulder with his lips. MOON gave her joy, giving him pleasure, and then, lying next to her, breathing heavily. Ela was grateful. She ordered him to go. He did but promised to come back, despite her protests.

MOON sent Ela a beautiful bouquet of scented wildflowers. She called and said thank you, and please don't do that again, but she placed the flowers in her living room on the coffee table and smiled at them every day. He kept calling, and sometimes she answered, and they spoke about all kinds of things. MOON continued in his search, and Ela eventually relented and joined him for more dinners, and sometimes, they had drinks, and sometimes they saw moving pictures, and she still let him spend the night. Indeed, Ela had forgotten that there was ever a time she wouldn't want MOON around.

The guy looked so different. Ela always thought he was too distinctive. MOON worked with his hands and had never been far from something outside the walls of the distant area. He learned about the stars and the Sun's location. In the heart of the deep woods, he knew about hidden waterfalls, and he showed them to her, letting her drink the cold, clean water from his rough, calloused hands. Ela's played with her mind and her heart at times. She was acquainted with words and spent her days writing books. She spoke various languages and had traveled through oceans to countries, and even farther. She longed to be closer to places where she could see bright lights and busy streets, and where she could see someone looking like her once in a while. Yet Ela had to do a job and complete studies. She was biding her time. MOON and Ela knew none of the same things, but he knew how to kiss her and how to press her lips to her neck and how to hold her as she slept, and if the moments shared between them were all that mattered, they could probably have found a happy ever after.

Other things mattered, however. MOON had an evil mother who lived high up on a hill in a grand home. She maintained an impressive garden and enjoyed welcoming guests to a spacious living room lined with big and imposing furniture. More than she grinned, the evil mum scowled. The wicked mother believed her son to be a king and wanted nothing but the best for her eldest child. She didn't think Ela was good enough, and she let this be known all over the World. Ela gave gifts and kind words to the MOON's evil mum. She said thank you, please, and she offered to wash the dishes when invited to dinner. The wicked mother who didn't want MOON to love a woman with such different skin couldn't sway any of her movements. This was something of a scandal, she said. Think about the name of his son, she said. Eventually, Ela started heading up into the hill to the grand home. She and MOON pretended it didn't matter to the evil mum. Her disappointment, they told themselves, was an unfortunate fact. We resisted harsh words and blunt thinking. They believed that nothing could get in the way of their happiness and ever after. However, on festival days, when there was a lot to celebrate, Ela still found herself alone and waiting while MOON paid his respects and was feasting with her kin. Ela wanted MOON to choose in those lonely moments, but she didn't dare inquire, she couldn't bear thinking he would not want her.

A day came when Ela learned that she was carrying the MOON's child. It was a blessing, which was unexpected but welcome. He said his heart was so full it ached when she told MOON. He offered his hand at marriage, and at his side, a place in his kingdom. Ela told him that they'd wait and see. It was she who wanted to say yes. Both began to prepare for a future, and when they saw the doctor and heard their unborn child's pounding heart, they looked at each other and found that they had one thing to share— love. MOON and Ela were so blinded by their happiness that they shared their good news with MOON's wicked mother, who, when she learned the news of a new heir to the kingdom, a bastard heir, she narrowed her eyes into dark, hard slits. She said no such child would ever be remembered or accepted by anyone under her rule, a child from two dreadfully different worlds. Ela put her hands to her stomach and tried to protect her precious unborn child from words of such poison. Ela was exiled from her home by the evil mother, and MOON stood by and said nothing, torn between his mother and would-be wife. Ela was trying to find a way to redeem his silence. She never will forget.

It happened on an average day full of exceptional moments, a day when MOON painted the nursery for the infant, a gentle shade of pink that would be a girl called Emma. He stood in the room admiring his work, picturing his wife holding their child close to the large window, maybe looking up at the stars. Ela stood in the kitchen, preparing an excellent meal for her man, humming her son, sure of her happiness. She was overwhelmed by a sudden grievous pain in her womb's place. It was such a sharp and precise pain that she couldn't make a single sound. The last moment Ela recalled was dropping to her knees and saying, —I can't bear to lose this.‖ MOON found her, on the floor, bleeding painfully, breathing shallowly after the smell of burning meat filled her room. Everyone mourned the child's loss, but instead of breaking them apart, their grief made them love one another more and fiercer.

When she completed her studies, Ela told MOON that she had to leave the distant location, far away from everything. She had been offered a role she had been planning her whole life for. Living with too many reminders of what should have been had been too hard. She did not want to raise children in a position where they would still be treated by their people as more hers than his. He told MOON he understood. He said they'll findi a way to love each other over an unlikely distance. She praised him. She believed in her happiness.

On the eve of her departure, MOON sat on a wooden pier beside Ela. They gazed out on waters illuminated by the stars, their heads dizzy with wine. He asked a woman about the most beautiful things she'd ever heard a man say. He presented her with a ring, a beautiful tear-shaped diamond. He was trying to move the ring on her finger, but it didn't suit. Ela, nervously crying, said it was a bad omen. MOON had said they'd repair the bell. He said it was just a fact, and it didn't matter what specifics were. He said, yes, take this bell, yes live in my kingdom here, with me. Ela stared at the exquisite ring and wondered how she'd never shared her love for him. He was talking of how he made her forget all the tragedies her that had befallen her before he loved. She tried to stop but wept and felt her heart falling apart.

MOON thought the tears indicated that she said yes. Ela handed the ring to MOON, her hands trembling. She said, I can't stay; I can't believe you were asking. She said you know me not; the specifics matter. She said if you could leave this place with me, you should have asked. MOON said he never understood other life types. These were his people, he said, and this was his land. He said he'd spend his life making her love the way he did that land, that his family would grow to embrace her. He became furious; she said it was his; he said he would never let her go. Ela hugged her stomach and recalled the child growing up there once, and how her loss so closely tied them together. They sat in silence together, the night air cooling all in between. He knew all along that he was right about the fairy tales.

STORIES OF THE STARS

The boy who loves counting stars

He sat on his roof with a pad of paper every night, shortly after the Sun went down, and began counting. He enjoyed the twinkles, the distributed shapes, the bright ones, and the dark ones. He would note the sound of crickets and note them over.

Yet he never managed to count them all. The Sun would rise every morning, and he'd become frenzied as he counted the fading stars. He grew up loving the dawn because it took his joy away.

He had wanted to count more quickly. He waited until the months of winter when the nights were the longest. Yet he never managed to count them all: too many stars and too little time.

So, he was talking about a proposal. It had been so easy. He'd have to avoid the Sun coming in.

So, the boy began sewing the World's most giant quilt. He spent years doing it during the daytime while counting the night stars.

He went to the top of the highest hill when the quilt was big enough and spread the quilt over the Sun as it was setting.

The Sun clinked out, and the guy began counting in silence.

It did work. The next morning, the Sun was not coming up. His paper pad packed with numbers, far more than he had ever counted before. He counted and counted until ten years had passed, and he was unable to find another star to add to his ledger.

The boy dropped a small sigh, put his pad down, and felt grateful that he was finally able to count all the stars.

He went back up to the highest slope, took the quilt corner, and pulled it off the light.

But the Sun was just a dark, black ball left to it without even the slightest sign of heat. Over the years, it had gone forward. This will never be back again.

And after all, the boy who loved counting stars knew he skipped one last star.

STORIES OF THE PLANET

Jupiter and Mercury laughed a devilish laugh as Earth passed them. The trouble with gossip is that one feels caught in the act when the subject suddenly appears.

As Earth moved on to talk to Mars, Jupiter and Mercury continued their blabber mouthing.

The Sun had organized a tea party for all the big planets in his galaxy. It was an annual tradition, a philosophical afternoon of talking and debating. However, there was also plenty of time to complain and gossip.

Naturally, the Sun had outdone himself; he liked to give lavish parties; many stars were working until they would fall. Like every year, the party took place beyond the Asteroid Belt, close to Jupiter. That way, not everyone had to travel so far, and their location was almost in the middle of their Solar System.

A screen made of stardust showed a reality show of stars with no discernible talent going at each other, calling each other names. The stars in this galaxy had their own lives, and this was their entertainment. Most of the planets looked down on them. However, some enjoyed their company and were fascinated by the life of the stars.

Earth went up to Mars. The old friends greeted each other heartily. Although, secretly, Mars was growing to dread the conversations with Earth more every year. The inhabitants of Earth were planning on moving to his Planet in the future. Mars was an old and conservative planet, and although he had been waiting for proper lifeforms to evolve on his Planet, they simply had not succeeded to his liking. He had grown lonely, dusting himself off all year, until the Sun's party. However, he did not like the idea of the arrogant inhabitants of Earth roaming around his Planet and changing his natural order, not to mention disturbing his peace of mind!

Pleasantries soon transformed into grudges, as Mars once again urged the Earth to restrain its inhabitants. As Mars raised his voice, the other planets soon gathered around them, not wanting to miss out on something exciting. After all, they had to live off the drama of this party the whole year-round.

Earth was not going to let another planet tell him what to do.

Earth was proud and viewed himself as the center of this Solar System. His Planet was the most evolved of them all. He had a plentitude of multiple species wandering about. Those species all had a shared history in evolution; they had science, stories, brains, emotions, and even religions.

Granted, there were some problems to be dealt with. But he was not about to let Mars tell him off like that.

—Maybe you are just an old jealous stuck-up planet, envious of our evolved life forms, Earth said in a harsh voice. The other planets gasped and exchanged triumphant looks.

—You should be thankful that such a fine species as humankind is curious enough even to visit you. Ever since I met you, you have been complaining about being lonely. About the lack of life and excitement on your Planet. Well, now it is finally coming your way. The Earth said quite convincingly, as the other planets nodded in agreement.

Jupiter looked at Mercury and then to Mars. Should they let Mars in on their plan? Jupiter decided Mars could not be trusted. At least, not yet.

Mars knew the Earth had a good point, but was he ready for such a great disturbance at his age? He decided to leave the subject for now. He still had years to think about this. After all, it would be quite sometime before something like this was about to happen. Besides, if Mars decided Earth's inhabitants were unwelcome, he had enough power to destroy them.

The program for the party never varied; every year, things happened in the same order as the year before, as if set in stone. Luckily, the planets had a lot to catch up on as they were anticipating the official start. The Sun would take the stage for his speech at the same moment every year. It was his moment to shine and to show he was the biggest star in this galaxy. When all the other planets have had enough time to admire the Sun, it was time for tea and the debate.

The Sun enjoyed his moment, and how the other planets were in awe of him, how they feared him. For with one strike, he could obliterate them all. However, they did not know that he would never do that. For who else would he converse with? These tea parties were all he had.

—Welcome, my friends, to our annual tea party. I lost count many years ago about which edition this is. But it does not matter. We are here! The Sun spoke with his rich, deep voice.

The other planets beamed and clapped, the stars in service glimmered.

Stars were swooshing around, setting up a large table, filled with all sorts of sweets and pastries. Tea from a giant teapot was poured into the cups by the Moon, a demeaning gesture, according to Earth. The Moon was not recognized as a planet by the Sun.

Soon, all cups were filled with a steamy treacly liquid. Not precisely the tea Earth was used to.

The Sun spoke again. -As you have all had a chance to catch up with each other, it is now time for the discussion. I chose an interesting topic, if I do say so myself. A topic, both current and ancient. Why are we here?‖ .

The assembly sighed. Earth was already dreading this party and possibly even more now, for his inhabitants were always asking themselves the same question.

The Sun decided to ignore this reaction. —In relation to that question, I want us to explore why we are here and why all of our functions and compositions differ so greatly. Are we the only planets? Is this even the only galaxy?‖ The Sun continued.

—Well, Mercury's composition is the foulest, that I do know!‖ , Uranus joked. The others giggled, Mercury turned dark grey.

—There are ladies present, don't be so rude!‖ Mercury said as he looked over at Venus and Jupiter.

The Sun had a look of a disappointed and impatient teacher. He continued his opening statement and steered the conversation back to the topic he had proposed. —I would like to suggest everyone gets a say in this matter. Everyone who is a planet on its own that is‖ as he looked at the Moon. —Jupiter, my darling, why don't you start?‖

Jupiter blushed and showed more of her orange and red colors. However, she spoke with confidence and poise. —Thank you, my Sun almighty. In our long existence, this remains the unanswerable question. An important question, yes, but there is no one and correct answer. That is why it is so exciting to come back to it every once in a while, as the Sun repeatedly has proposed during our ceremonies. Every time I think about it, I have a different idea of the answer, and I bet most of you do as well. For our existence is ever-changing, and our experience and development help us come closer to a possible answer. In a way, it is the essence of our existence to think about it, but it is also our weight to carry while we survive.

RETURN TO EARTH

Maggie rubbed against the sizeable oval window on her small round face, flattening her tiny nose on the spacecraft's cold glass, and cried out with joy.

She could see a tiny blue line, lying suspended far out in space's blackness.

She knew Earth was this, her house, their home.

She couldn't believe it was close.

With the back of her hand, she wiped the tears from her eyes. She went to the next chamber of the Vanilla spacecraft (named after its favorite ice cream flavor), flying through a round pneumatic door.

While this chamber had been designated as the control room, the spacecraft had barely anything to monitor or function. Vanilla had been fully automatic. She picked up the radio, which had long since been silent. Now that she was so close to Earth, she hoped that she would hear John's familiar voice cracking out of the radio receiver.

—Hello, Maggie. Congratulations on the success of your epic interstellar flight. You made us proud today -But there was no such voice coming out of the microphone. It's been long gone, dead. Maggie hadn't been sure how long. Without giving up, she impatiently flicked several times over the radio switches.

Maggie had lost track of time a long time ago and never tried to test it out on the clock, which blinked the time and number of days like a counting period for the stopwatch, for fear of seeing an extremely large figure on the screen.

She was sleeping most of the time, for that was what she was supposed to do. She would buckle onto her bed so she wouldn't float away, then inject the blood-red substance onto her arm and fall asleep for an uncertainly long time.

When she woke up, she just went to the window to see the space's vast enveloping blankness, sprinkled with tiny white lights of distant stars. They were not twinkling as they did on Earth.

The dosage of the medication she took after lying was very high. The scientists had told her a month before her departure.

The medicine will keep her alive and with youth. She would neither age nor die, or even starve to death, without this. She will be remaining 13 for a very long time with this. Upon waking up each time, Maggie had to send the shots within 15 minutes.

Maggie spent thirteen years of her life locked up in the laboratory until she was sent out into outer space to do her research. They never brought her out to show her the World in the thirteen years she spent in their dark, top-secret laboratory. Not a single one. She was showed only her images and videos of the Planet and the outside World. They allowed her to watch TV in her spare time when she wasn't being taught. Of course, the networks were censored and filtered, and she just saw what they wanted her to see. She didn't pose any concerns about her parents or any related issues.

We told her she had to go on a short trip, and they would take her to all the places she had seen on TV when she came back.

Maggie obeyed. She loved them and trusted them, particularly John, and did whatever they told her to do.

She was able to conduct their project by the age of 13.

She boarded Vanilla spacecraft alone a year later. To their surprise, the scientists found that the girl was strong and optimistic, rather than apprehensive.

With this, they were satisfied. Thirteen years of preparation, thirteen years of lies they had been telling her had paid off. On the other hand, the poor girl only knew she was going on a short trip, and when she came back, she was able to go to all the fantastic places on Earth she had ever seen on TV.

As the spacecraft eventually set off successfully and left the Earth on a freezing night, the scientists cheered and danced with joy. They knew they had done something special, and we're going to become celebrities as the World comes to know. The money will then run.

John was named one of the twelve scientists to be a part of the project. The night Maggie left, John was weeping. He did not weep with joy at their success, nor did he toast with his family.

John loved his daughter Maggie. The others merely regarded her as a model for the laboratory.

John thought he had meanly deceived the little girl. He had promised her that she'd be back in days. He would later wish he hadn't. He realized they wouldn't be here when she comes back. We must have been dead for long. This was a long journey.

Countless experiments have shown that the drug, which was to be regularly injected into the blood, increased a human's longevity by significantly reducing his metabolism. The drawback has been that it only worked at zero gravity. This made the scientists think about long and far-reaching space journeys, beginning with Project Maggie.

Maggie had spent the first day chatting on radio with the only men she met onboard the starship.

Via the radio, the scientist whom she called John asked her, his voice interrupted only by the statics _ my Maggie, how do you feel? Lonely' she was sobbing already' I feel so lonely, John.' John tried to comfort her. He told her to be as confident as she always has been. It was only a matter of a couple of days before she returned.

Another scientist then spoke to her. He was named after Milton. What do you see of sugar outside? From here, I can't tell. Still, I saw the World a short while ago. I moved farther away from it' Later. You're going to be here with us again real soon, —the discussion ended.

John talked to her again when it was time. They exchanged farewells. John told her at the right time to take her medication like a good girl. He has told her that he loves her. She even said she loved him.

She took her medication five minutes later, after strapping herself to her bed because she had to lay down while she was taking it. She then injected her arm with the first bottle of the drug. She fell asleep within seconds. In reality, she was falling into a deep coma.

She found the radio irresponsive after a long time when she woke up.

She had never heard of them anymore.

Maggie spent the fifteen minutes she got after this time waking up, close to the round glass window, watching her homeworld she had been away from for a long time. Her heart was pounding just to look at it. She sounded like she was screaming at the top of her lungs.

He figured once he got there, she and John would go out together and see other places she always wanted to go after seeing them on television. John had offered to take her to entertainment parks. They'd go shopping together... Her mind was full of suggestions and feelings that she'd do with John, Milton, and others.

She figured she'd find them waiting for her when she returns. She'll walk out of the spaceship and run into the outstretched hands of John.

She just started sobbing. She was here, alone. Nobody was there to comfort her or brush her tears away. After some time, she composed herself for being reliable and a good girl by recalling John's words.

She went to the fridge, taking the last RL35 bottle and a sterile syringe. She pushed against the wall and drifted to her pillow, holding onto the ties.

She said it'd been a very long time. They had told her it would only be for a couple of days, but... she was thinking of testing the control room monitor to see the number of days she was in the spacecraft.

No. No. She is asking herself. She didn't want to see it, now that she's close home. What's the sense of being upset when it's time to be happy.

It was also time for her to take the last dose of medication, which she would fall asleep soon after.

She wanted to wake up at Earth and see John first.

CONCLUSION
HOW TO IMPROVE ONESELF

Insomnia is an enemy of time, and strength. The body is naturally wired to sleep as a result of the body using sleep as a mechanism to fix its damaged tissues and cells. The body needs to rest. It exhausts energy, and sleeping is the body's way of fixing itself, now when you deprive the body of this basic quality sleep, you disrupt your body's natural process, which can lead to a couple of complications. Almost everyone at some point in their life has experienced a lack of sleep due to stress, bad dieting, and other factors. It is a fact that nearly sixty million Americans have a taste of insomnia every year, in some it is acute, while others it is chronic.

Another thing that poses an issue here is that there could be medical ways of treating insomnia. By that I mean, using drugs to treat it, but we have decided to explore natural ways to do it, and these methods are known to improve not just sleep but your life in general.

The adverse effects of insomnia could be; stroke, asthma, seizures, compromised immune system, increased sensitivity to pain, obesity, diabetes (due to binge eating), heart disease, high blood pressure, affected sense of judgment and awareness, depression, anxiety, confusion, un-satisfaction, and frustration. But all these can be dealt with, and your life can turn back again to how you want it to be. You need to have control over the things that happen to you, even your sleep.

Let's outline a couple of things that would help you keep tabs of your progress and not lose your sleep unhealthily.

First, have a routine and never break it. You can train your body to adjust to sleeping times. For instance, if you travel to a place that has a different time zone from yours, you will find it difficult to sleep when everyone is sleeping because normally, your time of sleep is during the time they are awake. The time you are awake is the time they are asleep. With time your body eventually adjusts to that time zone. So the trick is, you can train your body and your body can learn. So, fix a certain time that you need to fall asleep every day and a time to wake up. You can't just fall asleep and wake up at any time if you want to build a routine. So, fix a time to fall asleep, and fix a time to wake up.

Secondly, be consistent. Nothing maintains the payload more than consistency, you have to keep on doing it for your body to register it.

Thirdly, leave work at work. If you turn your sleeping space into your workspace, you will find it difficult to fall asleep. Leave everything that has to do with work in your workspace, so that when you are ready to sleep, nothing will stand in the way. Have some cool music, turn off the lights, and go to bed peacefully.

Finally, eat well and exercise well. Your diet greatly affects your sleep and your body's metabolism. If you consume substances with a lot of caffeine in them, you will find it hard to sleep. Rather than eat processed food that might give you indigestion, consume more natural things, like veggies and fruits. Take a lot of healthy drinks too and drink lots of water. Then exercise well. Burn off those excess calories and allow your body to work. Let your body use up the energy it has, and replenish it with clean energy.

With these practices, you would be sleeping like a baby in no time.

HOW TO BUILD CONFIDENCE AND BE HAPPIER THROUGH MINDFULNESS PRACTICE.

Some situations can cause you to feel —less-than‖ and also burden you with beliefs that you are incapable of being, doing, or having what you want. It is important to remember that it's not uncommon to wonder how to be more confident in yourself.

It is also important that you learn how to tap into your inner strength on those days when you do not feel confident because your confidence affects your performance in any area of life and, likewise, your performance affects your confidence. The downside to experiencing low self-esteem can present both negative emotions and limiting beliefs, something that can be easily remedied through applying mindfulness-based lifestyle practices like meditation.

There are ways in which you can build your confidence and be happier through mindfulness, they include;

1. Learning How to Meditate

There is actually no "right" way to meditate.

That being said, basic mindfulness meditation is probably best because of how easy it is to pick up. In a nutshell, mindfulness meditation revolves around being —mindful,‖ i.e., focusing on the physical sensations of the present moment.

Most people still have no idea how to meditate. That's okay. Though it brings ease, it can be kind of complicated. Many meditation techniques originate from the East, including the Judeo-Christian method of meditation, Buddhism, Hinduism, and Taoism. Mindful meditation will help you get in touch with everything good that already exists in your world.

Below are some of the ways to meditate;

Sit comfortably in a quiet place.

Think of a quality or attribute you appreciate about yourself, or something you are proud of, in order to feel positive about yourself, and contemplate on this for a while.

Next, identify some positive intentions for yourself. These could be: ‚ I want tobe happy,‘ or ‚I want to be healthy.‘ Recite whatever phrase comes from your heart and has most meaningful to you. Repeat this phrase a few times.

Once you start feeling the positivity that comes from adopting a kind attitude to yourself, you can then take the good feelings outwards by bringing forth an image of someone you love and offering them the same wishes you have offered yourself.

At the end of the meditation, you will notice how starting this practice with self-love, then directing that love towards others, enhances feelings of kindness, compassion, and connection.

Another way to meditate is to;

Find a comfortable place to sit and minimize distractions.

Close your eyes and begin to take some slow deep breaths, following your inhalation and exhalation, to allow yourself to settle into a peaceful, meditative state.

Begin by bringing a real-life situation to mind where you want to be able to step into a state of confidence. Maybe it is a conversation you need to have or a presentation you've been asked to deliver. Perhaps you are desiring to ask someone on a date or set a meaningful goal.

As you bring this situation to mind, create a picture, and then fire off the anchor you previously created. You should feel yourself shifting to an emotional state of feeling totally confident. (If not, simply repeat the anchoring process and test it to be sure it works.)

Play out the scenario in your mind in the most positive way you would most like to see it unfold. Follow the movie reel all the way through to completion, where you end with the most favorable outcome. Take in everything you see, hear, and feel around you. Notice how much confidence you have and how amazing that feeling is.

When you are ready, open your eyes and journal for a bit about how this process was for you. Repeat as often as necessary.

2. Build the Habit of Meditating

Meditation is not something that you can do just once or twice and instantly reap all of the benefits.

You need to meditate consistently to keep your mind quiet and confident. You'll see a noticeable difference (in terms of your ability to stay out of your head and feel more confident) after about 2 weeks... but you do not expect to meditate today and wake up with superhero-level confidence tomorrow morning.

The most effective way to build the daily habit of meditation is to make it part of your daily routine. You should create a morning routine right now if you do not already have one. Once you are comfortable sitting in silence with your thoughts for 5-10 minutes, it becomes very easy to catch yourself getting anxious and overthinking things at that moment. Then you can quickly practice mindfulness, stop the negative self-talk, and turn on your natural confidence!

3. When Anxious Use Mindful Breathing

By learning how to meditate and successfully building the habit of meditation, you will develop a confidence that will stay with you no matter what you are doing. You will be missing out on **an amazing benefit of meditation if you do not consciously apply mindfulness to your life in times of stress.**

Imagine that you are in a stressful social situation, like when you notice a cute girl you want to approach at the bar. However, instead of then saying hello, you get nervous and start to tense up. You start thinking of a bunch of excuses not to approach her or all the ways you could screw it up, or maybe you are sitting at home all alone, and you start over-analyzing something that is on your mind. Perhaps it is whether or not you should ask for a promotion at work. Or maybe it is why none of your friends has called you lately.

Either ways, you get lost in a whirlwind of negative thoughts, become completely paralyzed, and feel like complete shit about yourself. Here is what you should do instead, focus on your breathing. **This works because when you focus fully on**

breathing (i.e., each inhalation and each exhalation), it is very difficult to simultaneously think about anything else.

Here is a quick and easy way to put this into practice:

You catch yourself getting lost in negative thoughts

Sit down on the floor or in a chair and ensure to maintain a tall and erect posture. Relax your body (especially your shoulders, neck, and chest)

Set a 5-minute timer on your phone

Begin breathing through your nose. Focus on your breathing (like you're doing a mini-meditation)

Feel the cool air enter your nose (and your belly rise) with each inhalation

Feel the warm air exit your nose (and your body relax) with each exhalation

Take action (do what you're thinking about or move on and do something else)

This simple practice is like an instant medication to relieve stress and eliminate anxiety. This is more effective (and works way quicker) if you're used to meditating on a daily basis. **When you catch yourself thinking about anything besides your breathing (and you definitely will), simply re-focus on the next inhalation.**

4. Listening to Music

Another way to exercise mindfulness is by listening to music that soothes you and even singing along. The genre of song that helps you relax does not matter. The mindful way to listen is to concentrate on each note. Maybe even dance along! Music is a great way to release stress.

5. Speaking Your Thoughts

Do you find it hard to focus on a steady stream of thoughts running through your mind? Does trying to push aside these thoughts while meditating just stress you out more?

Instead of fighting the notions in your head, try to observe them objectively. Consider creating an audio journal. You can record yourself during your drive to and from work. Instead of fuming while you are stuck in rush-hour traffic, you can spend the time relaxing your mind. It is an easy way to process what is going on in your head.

Here are four ways mindfulness can make you happier and also enhance your self-confidence:

1. It can help you get out of negative thought loops

Meditation allows you to realize that you do not have to listen to the voice inside your head, especially when it is negative and focusing on –bad‖ things about yourself (e.g., how you look, what people think about you, etc.).By meditating regularly, it becomes easier to –get in the zone,‖ turn your brain off, and stop negative self-talk. Whether it is loops of worry, planning into the future, replaying events from the past, or caught up in self-judgment -- when we develop the skill of mindfulness and bring this quality of awareness to the working of our own mind, we open up a whole new possibility toward greater happiness. We begin to have the power to be the master rather than the slave of our minds. **Meditating can physically alter your brain to be less anxious and more confident**

2. It can make you feel more connected to others

We are social animals that have evolved to be in relationship. To flourish, we need to feel connected to others. Mindfulness can deepen and enrich our relationships as we bring a quality of present-moment attention to the people around us.

3. It can connect you to a sense of inner contentment

Mindfulness is a practice that can help us cultivate a sense of inner wellbeing, which allows us to feel content and well without needing to obtain anything from the outside world. It's a rare feeling in this age of consumerism, but it is available to all of us at any moment.

4. It can enhance your gratitude.

The practice of mindfulness helps us to slow down even if just for a few moments and reconnect with what is happening from moment to moment. This slowing down enables us to notice more of what is present both in our environment and within ourselves. As we notice more of what is happening around us and within us, wonder and gratitude can spontaneously emerge. Whether it is being more present to the tastes of a home-cooked meal, or connecting with something as simple and miraculous as the breath -- mindfulness can infuse our lives with gratitude and enhance our appreciation of the ordinary things which can so often pass by unnoticed.

5. You spend less time worrying about the future

The practice of mindfulness helps to keep the mind focused on the present moment, which means the mind is not constantly worrying about the future. Research shows that 85 percent of what subjects worried about never happened, and with the 15 percent that did happen, 79 percent of subjects discovered either they could handle the difficulty better than expected.

Final Words.

If you feel you are going through a phase of low self-esteem, gently welcome into your life the practice of mindfulness. Even 15 minutes a day is enough. If you sense one of your friends or loved ones is in the same state, advise them to do the same

DEEP SLEEP STORIES
FOR STRESS RELIEF

Bedtime Lullabies for Stressed-Out Adults. How to Improve Your Relaxation and Fall Asleep Faster with Meditation Tales to Revitalize Your Body and Life.

Introduction

Stress has fast become an essential part of our daily lives. A typical stressful day usually involves interactions with children, a spouse, employees, a nagging boss, and other communications. In addition to this stressful mix, there are daily worries that can rob life of peace and harmony. These concerns include paying bills, broken cars, mortgages, health issues, etc.

The outside world too quickly puts us under emotional, mental, and physical pressure. The older we get, the more serious the effects of stress on the mind and body can be, and too much can lead to hormonal imbalances that make a person anxious and overactive. The key to relieving stress and anxiety naturally would be downtime and healthy habits.

If you are looking for stress relief, you may be frustrated with the number of suggestions available. Everyone seems to have a way to reduce these subtle but powerful influences that not only ruin our joie de vivre but can also often cause mental health problems that go far beyond the original cause of the problem.

There are many options available to manage your daily life better. Some of these options include meditation, yoga, hobbies, etc. and while most of the information you receive on stress relief is valid, you should spend time testing the ideas and figuring out what kind of stress reliever is right for you and your situation.

Current scientific studies show that sleep is one of the most critical factors for stress relief. It's an area you cannot cheat. You need to have enough rest every day to live a long, healthy life. It's the best way to have enough energy every day to fight stress, and one prominent way that stress shows up is in sleep schedules. When you are stressed, you usually find it challenging to fall asleep at night. As a rule, 8 hours of sleep should be enough for a healthy adult.

Here are a couple of ways you can calm down at night and get some good sleep.

Choose a schedule and stick to it.

Choose a time to fall asleep and a time to get up. Keep this up every day, including the days when you have the privilege of sleeping. Sleeping only 1-2 days a week can disrupt your sleep schedule for the entire week. If you lie down and are not tired, do not get up. Read a book or listen to music to relax.

Avoid Caffeine - Reduce Caffeine (even if you think it won't affect you) at least 6 hours before going to sleep.

Smoking - If you smoke, avoid smoking an hour before bed. Smoking can cause restless sleep.

Create a relaxing routine - take a bath or shower, read a book, listen to soothing music, or stretch before bed to relax your body and mind.

Avoid snacks until late at night - Reduce snacks after dinner to simple and easily digestible meals. When the body works to digest a lot of food, it can disrupt the sleep process. Avoid snacks with artificial additives or sweeteners and avoid protein.

Prepare for the night - Prepare for the next day as much as possible. Get dressed. Plan your day. Preparation helps you relax and sleep better.

Create a sleep-friendly environment: If you find it difficult to fall asleep at night, take a look at your room. Is it overloaded, ruffled, disorganized, or overly decorated with many items? Being able to fall asleep at night can be as easy as cleaning your room! Our outer environment often reflects our inner state of being. If we keep our spaces organized, we have an area where we can relax and not be disturbed by the chaos of the day or by our mind.

Make the room as dark as possible - use an eye mask if necessary. Use earplugs to block the sound, or use a fan or soft music to mask the sounds that can interfere with sleep. Turn your watch, so you don't see the time. All of these tips will help make a relaxing atmosphere for you to sleep in.

Maintain a consistent bedtime routine - For those of you who have children, you can understand this mantra. A regular bedtime is essential for babies to learn to sleep through the night, but it is also vital for adults. By following a routine, we create a physiological response in our body that prepares us for sleep. If we end our evening the same way every night, our body begins to suspect what will follow, which is ultimately sleep. Routines don't have to be elaborate or complicated to be effective. It should consist of things that calm and relaxes you and leave you with good thoughts and feelings.

Listen to music explicitly made for sleeping - Listening to profoundly soothing and melodic music and inviting your mind to let go of raging thoughts is perfect for relaxing at the end of a busy day. When music is used as part of your bedtime, it puts you in a state where sleep is the next and most natural response. Repeating music can also help you sleep overnight, creating a deep refreshing sleep.

With the push of a button, you can fill your home or office with fantastic music that works behind the scenes to reduce the pressure you feel during the day. Then you can use the same music to put yourself into a sweet and restful sleep. Relaxation music requires very little preparation, is very inexpensive, and offers you a level of anxiety and stress relief that you have never experienced before!

If you have trouble sleeping, you can also follow these additional tips:

Turn off the electronics and turn your watch away from you (don't look at the clock or check your phone if you can't sleep). Don't worry if you can't fall asleep, and remember that your body will eventually take control and help you relax.

If you are awake in bed for more than 20 minutes, move to another part of the house (one without a bright light). Do something relaxing for a while until you feel tired and go back to bed.

HOW TO BEAT STRESS

Here are some stress relief ideas that are simple, cheap, and sometimes even free:

1. Always take time out.

Stressful situations often compound our lives, and we must take a 10-minute break to relax during the day. For example, on a hectic day, take 10 minutes to relieve stress, such as deep breathing and stretching.

2. Go outside to recharge your batteries.

Don't stay locked in the house or office all day, as this will make you darker and more anxious. You need to get enough sunshine every day as this is important to increase serotonin production in the body and thereby increase mood and energy.

3. Exercise regularly.

Movement is essential for the human body to function effectively. It eliminates toxins from the body (such as lactic acid and uric acid, which are partly responsible for stress). It is a natural remedy to relieve stress and anxiety as it increases endorphins, reduces stress, optimizes physical performance, and sharpens the mind. You don't have to do any strenuous activities. Something as simple as a 30-minute brisk walk paired with deep breathing every day will work wonders to relieve stress.

4. Have a favorite relaxation ritual.

A fun way to relieve stress is to wait for something relaxing and rewarding at the beginning or end of the day. Here are some suggestions for natural relief from stress and anxiety:

Have a soothing drink. Herbal or green tea and hot milk with cinnamon and honey are popular favorites.

Stretch yourself while using the shower to release tension.

Write in a diary to relax before bed. Knowing your thoughts, problems, and arousal can clear and calm your mind so you can fall asleep fairly quickly.

5. Another approach to relieving anxiety is to join an organized group that can help you relax. This group activity allows you to make contacts and reduce anxiety and stress. The downside,

however, is that you have to take the time to attend classes. All good intentions in the world are useless if you don't find the time to introduce yourself!

One of the best ways to relieve anxiety and stress is to integrate all of these approaches into your current lifestyle seamlessly. These activities provide a soothing and relaxing sensory contribution to stress relief and can be done by almost everyone according to their lifestyle and preferences.

It is possible to reduce stress.

To relieve stress, you need to learn to deal with incidents, situations, and stressful people. If you are too busy in the office, you will learn to reject tasks that you think you cannot do. You have to learn to say no because if you accept things that you cannot do, you have a problem that will strain you. If some people bother you too, avoid them.

Calm your mind. Plan time in a day to do something you enjoy. For example, if you like to work in the garden, you can do this for half an hour in the morning before preparing to work. If you want to watch a movie, you can do it before bed. Focus on them during these activities, and do not think about other things that worry you.

Calm your body. You can do this by getting an hour of massage. Use an aroma oil with lavender scent or rose petals to apply it to your body as this will help relieve tension and relax your body. You can also take a hot bath at night before bed, as hot water relieves tense muscles. Take a dip in your bathtub and pour drops of aromatherapy body wash or oil into the water.

Eat well. If you do not eat a balanced diet, your body will weaken, and the need for stress relief will increase. You need a few reserves to deal with the onslaught of stress. Make sure you eat lots of fruits and vegetables and include lean meats and fish in your diet. Avoid sweets and fortified foods with low nutritional value.

MEDITATION

Meditation is a simple technique that, when practiced for only 10 minutes a day, can help you control stress, reduce anxiety, improve cardiovascular health, and achieve a more exceptional ability to relax. Research has shown that meditation, including mindfulness meditation, can offer significant health benefits that have virtually no disadvantages. Not only is it useful for dealing with stress, but studies have also shown that it can also help fight insomnia.

When our body suddenly experiences stress or a threat, we respond with a characteristic —fight or flight| reaction. The —adrenaline rush| we experience is the result of the release of the hormones adrenaline (adrenaline) and noradrenaline. They cause an increase in blood pressure and pulse, faster breathing, and increased blood flow to the muscles. This function gives us the space to find out what our valid energy, attention, and emotions require, which are legitimate and which are not. Think about it: if we could distinguish the two, our experience of stress and anxiety would be very different. We feel pressure when we don't have this space in our thoughts and our life. We feel relieved when meditation gives us space and clarity we need to organize our priorities. One standard vehicle for reflection is breathing exercises.

Deep breathing: One of the easiest ways to relax is to control your breathing. Only ten deep breaths can have a positive effect, and more intensive breathing exercises are available for more relaxation. Close your eyes and notice your breathing. Pay close attention to your natural breathing frequency and feel how the air flows in and out of your nose or mouth. Imagine the flow of air that flows through the mouth, airways, abdomen, and outwards. Examine your body for tension. When you exhale, you feel the stress leave this part of your body. Imagine how your breathing reaches your forehead, neck, shoulders, arms, and then release the tension after the end.

Guided imagery. This exercise helps you to focus your attention on an image or story so that your mind can let go of the worries or thoughts that keep you awake. Get a comfortable position in bed. Close your eyes and relax. Start visualizing a scene, memory, or story that you find comforting. It's very individual - find what works best for you by trying a few options. A few examples are a favorite vacation or a peaceful place outdoors, a relaxing activity like cuddling up with a book in your favorite chair, or something repetitive like remembering steps from an exercise or a dance routine.

The key is to find something to focus your attention on and let go of other thoughts. Create this scenario in your head. Visualize all details of the picture or story as slowly and carefully as possible. Whenever you find that your mind wanders (a worry for the day or a —must‖ for tomorrow), recognize it and let it go. Return to your relaxing story. It doesn't matter if it takes a while before it works. Every time you exercise, you will improve.

Progressive muscle relaxation: This is a technique that stretches and relaxes muscles throughout the body in a specific order. It can help reduce mental and physical stress and can be beneficial before bed.

Find the time to exercise: Daily training can help relieve stress and help you sleep well. This does not mean that you have to run a marathon. Even moderate exercise can be a boon to your mood and sleep, especially if it's constant. Exercise also offers many other benefits to other aspects of your health.

Consult a doctor or psychiatrist

If sleep disorders affect your daily life, it is essential to see a doctor who can make a thorough assessment to identify possible causes. Following the established diagnostic process can determine if there are more serious health problems that need treatment and can help the doctor learn the most appropriate treatment for your needs.

COMBATING STRESS-INDUCED INSOMNIA

There are countless ways to improve your sleep hygiene. Some notable examples are:

Set up a consistent sleep schedule so that your body and your daily rhythm work to your advantage.

Follow the same bedtime every night to relax mentally and physically while sleeping.

Make your bed comfortable and supportive, and your bedroom free from excessive light or outside noise that could be disturbing.

Minimize the use of electronic devices, including cell phones, in the hour before bedtime, as they create mental stimulation and emit blue light that can suppress the body's production of melatonin, a sleep-promoting hormone.

Journaling - If you wake up at night because you can't stop thinking about something that causes you to stress during the day, journaling can be a useful technique for you. It can help you clear your mind, deal with strong emotions that make you lose sleep, think about things, and develop plans that can help you deal with situations that are stressful for you.

Work through your stress - If you lose sleep due to anxiety, you may be able to relax and sleep better by changing your perspective. Anxiety, including the type that keeps you awake at night, is often a natural response to situations that require some kind of action. If you see your status as a challenge rather than a threat, you can switch to an active decision-making mode instead of staying in a passive and anxious state.

It is also a good idea to use your bedroom mainly for sleeping, to connect your bed and bedroom to sleep rather than stress. Consider getting up and reading a book, doing things at home, and doing other non-stimulating activities that can promote sleep when you're ready. If you still find it difficult to fall asleep at night, do the following:

1. Try not to fall asleep when you go to bed.

Focus on relaxing and recuperating, knowing that sleep will follow. This will put less pressure on falling asleep and help you rest sooner rather than later.

2. Enjoy being in bed.

Stop worrying about the speed at which you fall asleep and enjoy the moment in bed, comfortable, calm, and without responsibility.

3. Take a hot bath or shower.

Recent research has shown that a warm bath or shower, preferably one to two hours before bed, can help people fall asleep faster - 36% more quickly, to be precise.

4. Use the hour before bed to meditate and relax.

It will help you take your time to meditate and relax on purpose. If you feel worst in either area, you should use an app or device to help you. Headspace offers endless possibilities for short and long meditations. It gradually helps you to meditate for an hour (or more if you dare).

5. Try to address your concerns.

Whether you're scared or just thinking about what to do the next day, it is sometimes easier to worry after your head hits the pillow than to relax.

6. Read a book.

Relaxing at the end of the day is essential if the goal is to fall asleep quickly. One way to do this is to read well. However, light, engaging non-fiction is probably the best way to relax. Otherwise, you may want to stay awake all night to find the end.

7. Focus on your breathing.

Stressed or anxious people suffer from chronic under-breathing because stressed people breathe shallowly and short and often even hold their breath unconsciously. To relax, work on breathing as you imagine a number in your head. While it sounds a little weird, it almost always helps you slow down and relax.

8. Change your sleeping arrangements.

Have you ever thought that you couldn't fall asleep because your body subconsciously thinks your bed is not comfortable? You may find that adding a pillow-top mattress, soft pillows, and cozy sheets is all you need to get to sleep.

9. Don't be afraid to lower the temperature.

The idea of lowering the temperature in your bedroom can be off-putting. However, according to Sleep Advisor, it is easier to fall asleep in somewhat more relaxed rooms.

Chapter One
What Is Self Hypnosis?

PART 1

Self-hypnosis is easy to learn and can significantly improve your quality of life. The benefits of an excellent hypnosis relaxation session reflect in your daily life and help you feel a lot calmer. Here's how:

Find a comfortable place to relax and sit or lie down and make sure that your arms and legs are not crossed and relaxed.

Concentrate on your breathing, take a deep breath, and let go of it slowly. Sometimes, when you inhale and exhale, it can help you relax.

In either case, you may want to close your eyes now or before. The next step is to relax your body. This step is essential because we know that you do to a relaxed body and an anxious mind at the same time. There are various techniques for body relaxation. I like to imagine a little ball of warm light (maybe the sun) floating in front of your forehead. You can then direct this warm light from your head to the tip of your toes around your body and imagine how it massages, calms, and relieves every part of the body down to every tiny cell during the process. The more specific you are, the more relaxed you become. For example, imagine how even your nails become more comfortable. If you encounter concerns during your relaxation time, acknowledge them, and let them float.

Then you can imagine being at the top of ten levels. You may have already planned what will greet you at the end of the steps. Make sure it's a beautiful place to be, so relaxed when you're there. Take the time to go through every step of your imagination. Give yourself a positive statement for each level, such as —I am relaxing so profoundly now.‖ Use your imagination to make this experience as vivid as possible. Switch on your five senses entirely.

When you have reached the last step, you can relax in the place you have imagined. It can be a lovely garden, a forest or a beautiful beach. Use your senses again to fully appreciate the sounds, feelings, smells, and sights unique to the location you selected.

Finally, return to the process. Imagine you descend each level, making pronouncements as you go. Do this until you are ready to open your eyes and continue your day feeling good.

How does hypnosis work to relieve stress? The hypnosis session consists of two main parts. One is deep relaxation, and the other is the planting of positive messages and images. The subconscious is exceptionally receptive to new programs in a deeply relaxed state. This state is called the —trance‖ state.

Positive words such as —my mind is calm and clear‖ or —my self-esteem is overflowing‖ or —my desire for nicotine is gone‖ can be printed on the subconscious. When the session is over, you leave the state of trance in a conscious state.

Self-hypnosis is easy, and with a little practice, you can let your imagination run wild and try different relaxation methods to see what works for you.

Are you stressed most of the time? If your worrying is a constant habit, you will be relieved of the stress with hypnosis and self-hypnosis. It takes a while to learn this skill, but once you learn it, you can change your life and become calm and confident no matter the circumstances.

You may know that hypnosis can help, but it can bother you a little. Stage hypnotists often give the impression that their subjects are under their control, which can alarm you because you don't want someone to have power over your mind.

While hypnosis is mind control, YOU are still in control, whether someone else hypnotizes you or you do it yourself. Hypnosis is only a moderate state of trance. It's like watching a movie that you're immersed in or dreaming. They don't fall asleep and always know what's going on. You can —wake up‖ at any time, as you do when you imagine.

Anxiety is a bad habit, so hypnosis reprograms your subconscious by planting suggestions. These suggestions will help your psyche, the —automatic‖ part of you, to find other ways to get what you want without causing fear. In a way, you have acquired the bad habit of fear through stress, so hypnosis reprograms your mind so that you can relax more quickly and solve your challenges. After a hypnosis session, you will be completely relaxed and comfortable and experience this comfort in your daily life.

You will feel the effects immediately. For example, if you are worried about work, you will find that you are more relaxed and that the situations that have strained you no longer affect you in this way.

To induce self-hypnosis means to self-induce deep relaxation.

For some people, this may be the first time that they experience deep relaxation. As you relax deeply, you are very impressive, so the suggestions the hypnotherapist gives you have a big impact.

Remember to ask the hypnotherapist for some tips on how to trigger self-hypnosis: Most therapists have CDs and tapes available for you to practice at home.

While hypnosis is beneficial in relieving stress, it can work wonders in all areas of your life, especially those that cause stress - for example, at work and in your relationships.

Once you know what hypnosis looks like, you can create a light trance and make suggestions. Unlike claims that take a long time to produce results or that don't work at all, the recommendations you make with self-hypnosis work because your subconscious mind takes them into account and puts them into action.

Make a list of what you can intentionally and deliberately do to improve your life; to help you achieve your goals. You will be amazed at how quickly you can achieve your goals if you have made suggestions to achieve them.

In addition to reducing stress, the benefits of hypnosis include:

Eliminate self-destructive behaviors

End dependencies

Increase self-esteem

Improved health and well-being

Sharpen the mental focus

Rejuvenation and increased energy

Strengthening relationships

Memory retrieval

But for the effectiveness and speed of results, little can achieve the power of self-hypnosis for coping with and treating stress. Hypnosis can create a pleasant, calm state that is so far removed from the stress that it is called a -state of grace.|

Indeed, self-hypnosis provides a way to relieve stress entirely and, thanks to the post-hypnotic suggestion, provides a valuable means of dealing with stress and anxiety. When done correctly, it can give robust stress relief and treatment that goes well beyond the actual self-hypnosis sessions. And the fantastic thing is that practicing self-hypnosis doesn't have to take forever.

One thing is sure: the time and effort invested in learning and then practicing a form of self-hypnosis bring real rewards in terms of relief and stress management. It is a robust method that helps you deal with stress, and possibly the most effective stress reliever available.

If you are struggling with stress regularly, self-hypnosis - with proper nutrition and moderate exercise - is the best stress management and relief tool you can use.

The first significant advantage of using hypnosis to manage stress is simply the hypnosis itself. Hypnosis is like a mental and spiritual massage.

Another factor, and probably the most significant factor in stress hypnosis, is the ability to give up on things that are beyond our control. As soon as you can give up things that are beyond your control, your stress level will drop. Too often, people let themselves be emotionally invested in situations, and while this is usually not a bad thing, it can sometimes be overwhelming.

Another great advantage of hypnosis for stress is the ability to tolerate others. Sometimes there are negative people in our lives who bother us. When someone has an unbearable boss at work, they can be hypnotized to be comfortable with the way that person is and let go of the things that previously bothered them.

How does hypnosis change your attitude to stress?

The answer is the subconscious which controls how you feel. It is the most primitive and least developed part of our brain. An example of how the subconscious controls our feelings is how we watch scary movies. When we watch scary movies, we are aware that nothing will happen to us, and the events of the film do not affect our lives. But this makes no difference to your subconscious, and that is why your heart pounds and your neck sweats.

But the beautiful thing is that hypnosis can help you change your subconscious mind exactly how you want it. Hypnosis is an experience that enables a hundred people. And from this experience, it makes you feel different at any time of the day.

If you haven't always had the natural ability to get the best out of every good or bad situation, this kind of positive, relaxed attitude doesn't happen by chance. To overcome a tendency towards stress, irritability, anger, or fear, you must train your mind to react positively to every situation and develop a deeply rooted tendency to always see the glass half full and not half empty. This is done through hypnosis, a daily program of relaxation, positive suggestions, and visualization. Your —instinctive‖ response to challenges and problems depends on the type and quality of your conscious thinking.

If you usually think that life in general consists mainly of a series of worries and irritations, you will often be stressed and angry. You will also find that many of the realities of your life seem to confirm this view somehow and that people always seem to give you reasons, intentionally or unintentionally, to get upset.

Your subconscious mind reacts to the harmful nature of these common conscious thoughts and works hard to create and translate your living conditions and their corresponding influences into reality. In other words, if you are still consciously thinking that life is stressful, your subconscious mind will ensure that a stressful life is what you get.

The subconscious mind - which contains or has access to power, wisdom, and skills beyond human understanding - is nevertheless guided by the nature of the thoughts, images, and feelings it receives from consciousness. Your consciousness guides your light, and the entire power of your subconscious is used for any purpose - positive or negative - that your conscious mind suggests typically.

As a result of your conscious mind training to consistently send positive thoughts and mental images into your subconscious mind, you will find that your tendency to stress and negativity will disappear, with all of the resulting benefits for psychological and physical health.

As mentioned above, this can be achieved by sticking to one or two daily sessions of relaxation, positive visualization, and confirmation; in other words, self-hypnosis. Take at least 10 minutes at least once a day to relax mentally and physically and to feel comfortable in a quiet place, preferably on a bed or a large chair. Close your eyes and start breathing deeply and regularly. Then imagine all your muscles, start with your feet and then work your way up to your neck and face, relax and unwind. After a few minutes - with a little practice – you'll have a floating feeling - evoke an image of calm and serenity in your head, or visualize yourself in situations in which you usually are stressed but see yourself calm and positive.

Maintain this visualization - improve yourself again with practice - while breathing relatively slowly and regularly. Then start saying silently or verbally that –I'm calm, relaxed and at peace‖ or –Every day I'm more relaxed in every way.‖ Repeat the confirmation slowly and deliberately for about 20 to 30 times while maintaining your relaxed breathing and visualization.

After about 10 minutes, return to mindfulness and continue with everything you did before. If you do this once or preferably twice a day after just a few days, you will find that the stress will decrease and you will feel healthier and less prone to worry or tension. After a few weeks, you will find that your attitude towards life has changed in general. You will feel much happier, have better relationships with others, and also realize that no problem is more important than you. Self-hypnosis for relaxation also increases mental clarity and allows you to think faster about practical solutions to deal with difficulties that arise.

MINDFULNESS

We have so far established that our perception of and response to situations are essential in dealing with stress. There are often diverse ways to respond to any situation we find ourselves in, and mindfulness gives us more options for our response.

Mindfulness protects us
First of all, attentive practice helps us to pay attention to the present moment, to control the current, repetitive, and unproductive thoughts that lead to stress. Mindfulness enables us to regulate ourselves.

For example, suppose you don't get an instant response to a relevant text you sent to your partner. You could worry about what happened, fear that he's gotten hurt, and then think about all the things that could have gone wrong.

Instead, change your reaction by paying attention to what is going on at the moment. Instead of delving into self-created thoughts and concerns, you may notice a desire for response and the resulting fear. However, you would not react to these thoughts or intensify them, but return to your work.

This practice of paying attention to our experiences is not the standard mode for most people. Instead, we spend much of our time responding to events and producing explanations, implications, and stories that often cause stress. If we pay attention, we can maintain a more direct experience of the action and nothing more.

Mindfulness relieves you of pressure
Another aspect of mindfulness is an attitude of curiosity and acceptance of everything that is going on. In our example, you can accept that there are several reasons for not getting a response to your text. You might be curious if your partner doesn't take the text as important as you do.

Mindfulness and an open attitude leads to a greater acceptance of what is happening, a better ability to tolerate stressful situations, and a decrease in reactivity and repetitive negative thinking

Mindfulness creates a new relationship with experiences
According to some psychologists, the basic conscious practices of intention, attention, and attitude lead to a fundamental change of perspective to ―rethink.‖

Mindfulness enables us to identify with thoughts, emotions, and physical sensations as they arise, and to be with them rather than being controlled or defined by them. We recognize that ―this worry is not me‖ or ―these thoughts are not me,‖ which promotes the ability to see a situation as it is.

This practice increases our confidence in our ability to deal with events so that we are not stressed by events that would previously be perceived as a threat.

Mindfulness Practices
Stopping is an easy way to practice mindfulness in the face of stress. If you find that something has triggered and you want to respond, do the following:

Slow your movements

Breathe

Observe: What do you feel in your body? What do you think? What other options are there?

Continue considering several options.

It helps to put a friendly attitude into practice and to accept your thoughts and feelings as they are. It also helps to arouse curiosity to explore the situation with new eyes and to open up new opportunities. With everything that arises, ask yourself: Is this okay? Can I try this? You can practice this in small moments and develop skills that will serve you well in more difficult ‖crises.‖

What happens in the brain during meditation?

More and more research is investigating what happens in the brain during and after meditation. This evidence continually shows that mindfulness practice changes the structure and function of parts of the brain that are associated with emotional control. This corresponds to the behavioral studies conducted with experienced meditators, with the results showing that the practice of mindfulness improves self-regulation of attention and emotions.

The influence of mindfulness on the brain
Respond to threats

The area of the brain associated with the threat response, the amygdala, is smaller in meditators. In comparison, the area of the brain related to thoughtful reactions - the prefrontal cortex - is larger. These changes indicate that mindfulness reduces reactive and scary results that increase stress.

Regulation of emotions

Another area of the brain that changes after mindfulness training is the hippocampus. This part of the brain involved in regulating emotions.

What is the evidence of mindfulness for stress relief?

New evidence suggests that mindfulness effectively relieves anxiety and stress.

A 2014 review by scientists explicitly addressing the effects of mindfulness on stress relief found that ‖of the 17 studies, 16 were positive changes in psychological or physiological outcomes related to anxiety and stress.‖ Despite the limitations in some studies that included smaller samples or no control group, the authors conclude that ‒mindfulness-based stress reduction is a promising method for stress management.

A recent systematic review of the American Medical Association (JAMA) journal found that ‒meditation programs can result in a small to moderate reduction in several negative dimensions of psychological stress.‖ Mindfulness meditation programs have a similar effect to antidepressants usually prescribed for anxiety. Other magazines published in the past two years have consistently reported that mindfulness meditation has a positive impact on anxiety and stress.

Here are the things mindfulness can do in helping you to deal with stress:

You become more aware of your thoughts. You can then step back and not take them literally. This way, your stress response is not primarily triggered.

You do not react to situations as others would, that is, spontaneously. Rather, you sit back, properly analyze the situation with your -wise mind‖ to find the best solution, and then respond appropriately. Mindfulness helps you with meditation exercises.

Mindfulness activates your ‒being‖ mentality, which is associated with relaxation.

You are more aware and sensitive to your body's needs. You may notice pain earlier and then take the appropriate or necessary actions.

You are more emotionally empathetic. This is because you now have a higher level of emotional intelligence. Hence, as you increase in emotional intelligence, your tendency to react in anger to situations is greatly reduced.

You are more caring to yourself and others as you grow in mindfulness. This compassionate mind calms you down and inhibits your reaction to stress.

Practicing mindfulness reduces brain activity in the amygdala, which is necessary for activating your stress response so that your background stress level is effectively reduced.

You can concentrate better. When you do your work more efficiently, you feel better, which reduces the response to stress. You are more likely to enter -the zone‖ or ‒river‖ as Mihaly Csikszentmihalyi calls it in psychology.

You can change your attitude towards stress. Instead of just seeing the negative effects of stress, mindfulness allows you to think differently about stress itself. Watching the increased pressure helps you recharge your batteries, has a positive impact on your mind and body.

Remember a challenge in your life that causes stress. A situation that you can now work with. Not one of the very big challenges you faced, but not so small that it doesn't cause stress. A 3 on a scale of 1 to 10 is a good guide.

Remember the situation. Imagine yourself in the situation and all of the difficulties involved.

Notice if you can feel the stress in your body. Physical tension, faster heart rate, a little sweat, butterflies in the stomach, tension in the back or the shoulders or in the jaw, maybe. Pay attention to your stress signals.

Prepare yourself for your feelings. Notice how you feel. Label this emotion if you can, and pay close attention to where you feel the emotion in your body. Try to recognize it as much as possible. The more precisely you can localize the emotions, the more you'll notice the sensation, the better. With time and experience, you will continue to improve.

Bring conscious, attentive to emotions. This includes curiosity, friendliness, and acceptance.

Try to put your hand on the site of the sensation - a kind hand that represents kindness. Pretend to put your hand on a child's injured knee with care and affection.

Feel the feeling with your breath. This can promote awareness of the current moment and attitudes that are attentive to your experience.

When you are ready, stop this meditation

GUIDED MEDITATION

Guided meditation (sometimes referred to as guided image-guided meditation) is simply –meditation with the help of a guide. It is one of the easiest ways to get into a state of deep relaxation and inner silence and one of the most effective ways to reduce stress and bring about positive personal changes.

How does it look like?

Guided meditations happen when you let someone or something guide you while meditating. That person can be a meditation teacher or someone really experienced with meditation.

The first thing your meditation guide would do is to ask you to place your self in a comfortable sitting or lying position. You will then listen to your guide as he guides you through a series of relaxing visualizations. When you are relaxed and become calmer, the stress subsides, and your mind becomes clearer.

While in this deeply relaxed state of mind, your subconscious is open to positive suggestions, and your guide will use this time to take you on an inner journey that is meant to improve one or more aspects of your life. For example, guided meditation can be tailored to stress relief and insomnia reduction. It can also aim at healing you emotionally or developing you spiritually. You can join a guided tour to reach your full potential, or you can opt for a guided tour to experience deep relaxation.

As you can see now, guided meditation can be not only a relaxing experience but also one that improves your self-confidence, positively transforms your perspective, and inspires you to live your life to the fullest.

It is an effortless and enjoyable experience that leads to deep relaxation, stress relief, and increased esteem for life.

At the end of your meditation, your guide will gradually bring you back to a normal state of consciousness so that you feel refreshed, rejuvenated, and relaxed. A guided meditation can last from 5 minutes up to an hour, depending on personal preference. In most cases, guided meditation of 20 minutes or more is recommended if you want to experience a really deep state of relaxation and maximize the positive benefits.

What is the difference between guided meditation and traditional personal meditation?

Most traditional meditation techniques require that you take control of your own consciousness by focusing your attention on a single focus point. This focus could be your breathing, it could be a physical act, or more often, it could be a mantra - a tone, word, or phrase that you repeat mentally.

While these powerful meditation techniques are wonderful to achieve inner silence and improve your ability to concentrate, some people find it difficult to know fully.

Guided meditation has become so popularly preferred to traditional personal meditation techniques basically because they do not require prior training or effort to use them. Even if you are someone who finds it extremely hard to let go of your thoughts, even if you are very stressed or overwhelmed with mental activity, you will quickly find peace of mind if you are led rightly.

Because this type of meditation is so simple, it is beneficial for people who are new to meditation. However, guided meditations can also be very useful by people with a lot of meditation experience. Experienced meditators often use image-guided meditations to experience a deeper or more vivid meditation, to dive deeper into their minds than normal, or to address a particular aspect of personal development that they want to address.

Guided meditation is also quite different from traditional meditation in how it uses music and the sounds of nature to improve your meditation experience.

What do nature sounds and other kinds of music do in guided meditation?

Guided image meditation recordings usually include quiet meditation music that helps you relax as you are guided through the meditation. Think about the difference that a good soundtrack makes in a movie. Guided meditations benefit from music in the same way. Music adds another dimension of expression and depth to your guided meditation journey while calming your mind.

It is also not uncommon for CDs and MP3s with a guided meditation to contain sounds of nature. These sounds are very relaxing and can also be used to enhance the vividness of the visualizations you feel during meditation. For example, if you are led to visualize yourself on a sandy beach, your experience with this visualization will be more authentic if you can actually hear the sound of ocean waves.

In contrast to traditional meditation, in which your goal is to achieve mental calmness through concentration exercises, guided image meditations are based on a living tapestry of visualizations, music, and ambient sounds in order to relax and captivate you. Be careful and immerse yourself in an inner journey. Because this inner journey can be customized to achieve certain results, guided meditation can be even more powerful than traditional passive meditation techniques when it comes to making positive personal changes in your life.

Better Concentration - People who have actually learned to meditate and use guided meditation can continue to focus on the task at hand. You can relax completely and spend the rest of your day with a concentrated being. Guided meditation guides you through focusing on the meditation object, forcing the mind to focus on the goal, not the distractions that are usually present. By using guided meditation, even five or ten minutes a day, the mind gets a break from all the stresses that it endured. It leaves a feeling of peace.

Increase Energy - When you have finished your guided meditation, you should be relaxed and even refreshed. You will feel as if you can manage the rest of the day with confidence and look beyond the source of stress to find a good and reliable solution. Once you have reached the level of meditation guided by consciousness, you can do more and do what is necessary for yourself. You must train your mind from the distracted mind to a focused mind and then to the meditating mind to do this. It takes time to work your way through these three steps, but once you master them, it becomes easier to access the meditating mind.

Reduce negative thoughts - Guided mediation is a great way to improve yourself during the day and reduce the negative aspects of stress. It will only take a few minutes, and you will feel incredibly refreshed and restored. If you have a large meeting that makes you nervous, take time for a short guided meditation, and you'll be able to concentrate on the meeting. It can be used in several ways to calm yourself, and it can be an asset to your life.

First of all, you need to put yourself in the most comfortable position that will allow you to relax. There is no specific position; You can lie down, lie on an armed chair, or even sit on a bed with your legs crossed. You just need to be relaxed, but be careful not to take a position that will put you to sleep.

Then you have to relax. Slow and deep breathing is a good way to relax and prepare well for meditation. Another way to relax is to close your eyes and focus on the stress. Then focus on these limitations and try to drive them out of all parts of your body. Arms, legs, hair, eyes .... etc.

Once you feel relaxed, it's time to start the most important step in your meditation session. The experience outside the body. Close your eyes and imagine how your soul comes out of your body and hovers over your head. This step requires training because you may not be able to do this on the first try. When you feel your soul floating, imagine you are traveling to a place that you feel relaxed.

Guided meditation is an experience outside the body. The relaxing environment differs depending on the person who practices meditation. Some would imagine themselves on a tropical island with an exceptional landscape, while others would instead imagine themselves in a forest amidst flowers and trees. Regardless of your relaxed environment, focus on introducing yourself in the middle.

Guided meditation is about your imaginary sanctuary. Stay in your dreamy relaxation environment for as long as possible. Try to involve all of your senses. Admire the beauty of the landscape, smell the flowers, and enjoy the sounds of birds and running water. After you have finished your journey in your imaginary environment, try to concentrate on imagining that your soul will return from there until it reaches its final destination. When you return, you will feel refreshed and relieved, like coming back from a short break. During a guided meditation, you can use ambient music to help you relax.

Guided meditation is a matter of practice. Every time you do a guided meditation, try to extend your stay in your imaginary sanctuary gradually. In addition, guided meditation with practice will have a greater impact on the intense pressures of life.

PART II

There are many things that you cannot control. You cannot, for instance, determine tomorrow's weather, or derivative prices in the financial markets, or how bad the traffic will be on your way to a weekend picnic. You cannot even control the actions of others, unless through manipulation and force. Your cousin won't stop smoking unless they truly desire to do so and is open to the tools required to help them achieve this goal. In plain terms, much of what goes on in the outside world is out of your control.

On the other hand, there are things you've always had control over. Your habits, belief, emotions, and even your state of health are things you've always been able to take charge of, even if you never realized this. You've always been able to access your subconscious mind to create the peace and calm you've always desired and smoothen out those crooked areas of your life. You have the power and potential to unclutter yourself from within, so you may live a fuller, richer, healthier, more productive life. This is what hypnosis teaches us: That all of the healing begins in the subconscious. Have you ever wondered why even in hospitals with the best of care, some people don't get better even when they could've survived? It's because, on the inside, they had lost all the willpower to live. In the same, by calibrating your subconscious programming and allowing yourself to shift mentally on the inside, you will find that you unlock a new vitality and zest for life.

The conscious mind is where all your logic, willpower, and critical thinking abilities reside. It's the part of your mind to which you're most accustomed. It is where your primary thoughts intertwine and where you access your emotions, thought, and is forced to act. Your subconscious mind encompasses more nuanced elements, such as your imagination, intuition, values, beliefs, habits, and emotions. The interaction between your conscious and subconscious mind is like a one-way street, where your subconscious mind exercises strong influences on your conscious mind but hardly ever the other way round. Self-hypnosis teaches you to reverse this natural rhythm; to reach inside and rewrite the fine prints of your mind. It is only then that you may start to create remarkable changes inside of you that will shine through to the outside world.

Everyone can be hypnotized. It doesn't matter if you think your mind is forged from still, or you regard yourself as ―hyper-analytical,‖ you can reach into your own subconscious. More importantly, everyone can hypnotize themselves, and you will realize this with the techniques that will be shared soon.

Hypnosis is a state of being that's closer to daydreaming than it is to sleep, and it has an incredibly calming effect. True, some people access the hypnotic state more easily than others, but with time and practice, everyone can get it right. Hypnosis is simply meditation with a goal. Most individuals believe that your mind has to be blank for hypnosis to work, but this is not true, especially not for self-hypnosis, where the focus is concentrating on the things that screw you up from the inside and redefining them to suit you and enhance the quality of your life. Just like in meditation where you're simply relaxed physically and mentally while being very much aware of your surroundings, you can get absorbed in the calm, gentle feeling of hypnosis while also polishing your thoughts and working out the kinks of your mind.

Self-hypnosis is a powerful tool that helps you administer your thoughts and desires more effectively. Many people regard self-hypnosis as more difficult than general hypnosis because it requires a significantly higher level of practice, concentration, and discipline to truly reach into your subconscious mind, but you can do it. If you're the kind of person that's constantly plagued with negative thoughts and tendencies for depression, then self-hypnosis is a good panacea for you. It helps you clear your headspace while channeling your energies in a more wholesome and positive direction.

Self-discipline can help address so many issues; from insomnia, to stress, to an inability to concentrate. By opening yourself up to your subconscious mind, you build a bridge to your conscious mind through which you can galvanize all your creative, intuitive, and actionable thoughts in a more rewarding direction.

Self-hypnosis helps you demolish mental blocks. It may fascinate you to know that mental blocks are simply constructions in your conscious mind that reflect your perception of yourself. These mental blocks are a leading cause of your inability to concentrate, your rising stress levels, and your productivity slumps. By changing the fundamental beliefs that hold you back, you inject new life into your dreams and finding yourself feeling better at what you do and fresher all day long. The thing is, your subconscious mind is always great at executing whatever it has been programmed to accomplish, which is why you must take your time to ensure that you're asserting the right things at all times. Self-hypnosis will help you accomplish this.

As you must have already realized, your subconscious mind wields great power. This is why you must learn to master it and use it for your own enhancement. Everything you feel and think is stored in your subconscious. That natural instinct that is sometimes referred to as your ‚gut' finds its root in your subconscious. It is what fuels your active mind and, ultimately, shapes your reality. Most people are confident that they believe in themselves, but they soon find that in their heart of hearts, they are filled with doubts and uncertainties. These doubts can be devastating on so many levels, including physically and psychologically, and severely limiting. The ability to rework your subconscious mind will also prove effective in helping you make these doubts fade away.

One powerful thing about self-hypnosis is how it helps you come to terms with yourself and boost progress on the journey to loving yourself. The way you feel about a particular situation is a powerful indicator of how you'll handle it in the future. Negative feelings can lead to unsavory reactions. Self-hypnosis helps ensure that emotional reactions don't overturn your life by helping you recalibrate your headspace and facilitating your ability to manage those things that trigger you while also balancing your emotions.

Self-hypnosis will help you realize that you always have a choice when it comes to how to act in a given scenario. Whether or not you agree, hard science explicitly proves that as a person, you have power over how you choose to manage every situation. Choosing anger, violent eruptions, and resentment, though you may not realize it, is still a choice that was made somewhere in the vastness of your mind. These actions could reflect badly on you or result in consequences so dire that you find yourself consumed by regret. And if there's one thing about regret, it's how corrosive it can be on your mental health. Self-hypnosis sets you on the path to self-redemption, and reclaiming the power to direct your life on your own terms and with an acute consciousness of the power that you wield.

Stages of Self Hypnosis

Modern hypnotherapists over the years have been very inventive with models of general hypnosis and self-hypnosis alike. While certain hypnosis techniques allow for a great degree of flexibility, care must still be taken to ensure that things don't spiral out of control. Of course, self-hypnosis doesn't always put you in a trance. However, you still shouldn't listen to self-hypnosis audio instruction while driving because who knows how you could react?

Also, hypnosis in all its forms is medically disapproved for use with people who have been diagnosed with schizophrenia. And while you may find yourself gaining so much from self-hypnosis sessions and feel the burning need to share your newfound treasure with friends and loved ones, it is very important that you don't apply the techniques you learn in this book on anyone else but yourself unless you become a certified hypnotherapist because the consequences of wrong use of techniques are less than desirable.

A classical self-hypnosis session is generally divided into three core parts. Usually, in modern practice, one of the stages may be skipped—especially with quick sessions—but it's important that you understand how the process works, as this is critical for you to reap the maximum benefits of the process.

Stage 1: Preparation

A self-hypnosis session shouldn't be complicated, as this will only lead to an unproductive outcome. Simplicity ensures that your goals for the session are as clear as possible and easily achievable. The following factors may be considered and rationalized in the preparation stage:

Location

It's always best for a self-hypnosis session to happen in a closed room. Your location of choice can greatly affect your convenience during the session and determine the session's tone, which is why it's absolutely important. The room should be lukewarm, have soft lighting, and should be free of disturbances. Any slight distraction, like a pet walking across the room, can totally disrupt a self-hypnosis session, especially for beginners.

Solitude

As already established, distractions can adversely impact the success of a self-hypnosis session. Make sure your doors and windows are closed, and phones and alarms are kept silent. If you're expecting an important call, then ensure that you take it before beginning the session. In fact, complete all outstanding work before beginning the session, because nothing should bog down your mind while you're trying to balance it.

Posture

Just like in meditation, your posture can play a big role in the efficacy of your self-hypnosis session. Determine where you'll sit. Your most preferred chair in the room will do just fine. There's also the issue of how to sit. You don't want to finish a self-hypnosis session with a nagging back pain, so avoid slouching and other poor sitting postures. For best results, sit straight and relaxed, with your arms and legs uncrossed.

Outfit

Loose, simple clothes are encouraged. Sweat shorts, for instance, are ideal for a self-hypnosis session. Avoid tight-fitting clothes because they might get very uncomfortable during the session, and when this happens, you'll get distracted.

Goals

Like all important self-help tools, a self-hypnosis session must be engaged with a purpose. You're not just doing it for the activity, you must be focused on the impact. Because of the methodical nature of self hypnosis, it always helps to have a definitive target. It doesn't have to be extraordinary: It may simply be a means to achieve deep relaxation for you, or an exercise to attain mental peace, or a tool to deal with emotional trauma. It could be anything.

The first stage of self-hypnosis is vital, especially the setting of goals. Through it, you become mentally ready to break bad habits, boost your brain function, overcome negativity, and much more.

Stage 2: Induction

Induction symbolizes the functional starting point of self-hypnosis. Induction is what truly opens you up to your subconscious and begins the process of self-healing. It is generally advised, then, that induction shouldn't be launched abruptly, but rather slowly and methodically. You should also consider the following at this stage:

Shut Down Your Thoughts

Thoughts here doesn't refer to the blanket of ideas and information that roam around your mind in every waking moment. It refers to stray thoughts that are completely uncorrelated with the agenda of the session. Some self-hypnosis sessions require you to shelve all thoughts, but others such as emotional hypnotherapy may require you to screen certain thoughts and reactions. Still, it would be generally unhelpful to make dinner plans even while trying to achieve self-hypnosis.

Breathing Technique

The way you breathe can significantly affect the quality of a self-hypnosis session. Good breathing techniques get you relaxed and get you in the right frame of mind. Slow, deep breathing has also been shown to possess significant health benefits.

Close Your Eyes

More than half of the distractions around you can be eliminated by simply closing your eyes. It slows the world around you down and can have a very calming effect. We connect with the world first through our eyes, so by breaking this connection, we find it easier to focus on what's going on inside.

Imagination

For self-hypnosis to work, you need to get to a place of relaxation and pure focus. Make your imagination vivid and colorful and reflective of your deepest desire. If you want to feel grounded, imagine yourself as a mountain. If you want to feel untethered and truly free, visualize yourself as a bird, taking flight in the cloudless sky. The more detailed it is, the easier it'll be for your mind to accept it.

Determine Tension Spots

Over time, tensions begin to gather in different parts of the average person's body. For a self-hypnosis session to be maximally productive, you have to eliminate this tension. Start with your toes and work your way slowly toward your head, feeling, or the tension in each body part. It's helpful to imagine the tension as a clogged dam when you find a spot. Massage the spot slowly and feel the tension dissipate. Imagine it like a stream, flowing gently away.

Statements

This is where the true magic of self-hypnosis begins to take effect. You already have a goal for the session. Select a statement that aligns with it. Make it definitive and straightforward. So, say your goal for the session is reducing stress, say things like ‚I am no longer stressed' or –Stress has vanished from my life.‖ Making the statement firm and unambiguous enables you to reprogram your subconscious and achieve the desired impact.

When you feel yourself starting to feel woozy, try saying the statement in a loop. Begin by saying it slowly, 5 times a minute, with breaks in between for deep breaths. Once you get comfortable with it, increase the rate to 10, then 20, then 30, and beyond.

The induction stage is critical because this is where you work yourself into a state of self-hypnosis. Don't be afraid to delve deep, and be wary of your thoughts.

Stage 3: Consistency

Self-hypnosis is definitely not a one-time wonder. It takes consistent practice and discipline to harness its true benefits. It requires you to seize every opportunity that you have to reiterate the statements that you selected during the induction phase, in the car, at the office, in the restroom, while taking out the trash, and everywhere else when the opportunity presents itself.

You must also realize that it is important to implement lifestyle changes where they are relevant for the accomplishment or the goal(s) for which you took up self-hypnosis. You must abstain from harmful habits and take deliberate steps to manage your anger better. Giving in to the temptations that made you consider self-hypnosis in the first place will only set you back.

You should also work on the following:

Focus

You may initially find it hard to clear out stray thoughts during a self-hypnosis session. It happens to everyone. Select the nearest object and focus on it. Observe the patterns and contours on its surface, then try to phase them out. With a few attempts, you'll find that it becomes easier to blur these patterns from the scope of your vision. This will make it easier for you to banish stray thoughts, in readiness for a self-hypnosis session.

Fix Your Trigger

Fear and doubt are two important triggers that you must dominate to make the most out of self-hypnosis. In the process of self-healing, doubt can be a serious dampener. The more you question your chances of getting better, the harder you will find it to connect with the core of your subconscious mind and put it all together.

Fear can make you undermine your capacity for growth and progress. Negative events can make you indecisive about your abilities and unsure of your potentials. By changing the way you view these events, you may find that they are helpful in that they are opportunities for you to interrogate what you could've done better. Don't shy away from the negativity of events that impacted your self-confidence. Rather, use them as a benchmark to remind yourself of how much you've grown and how much better you are now. You will find that through this, you cure yourself of emotional trauma.

Create Anchor Points

Anchor points are useful because they are an appendage for relaxation but cost nothing. Find an accessible part of your body, say your elbow, and associate it with calm and relaxation. As you do so, think of someone or something that makes you calm and relaxed. Then imagine you're with this person or doing this thing, even as you touch this anchor point. Remember, the more vivid the visualization that more you're assured that your mind will believe it. Reinforce the anchor point anytime you touch it by telling yourself in unequivocal terms that you are now calm.

It is good practice to start and end sessions with your anchor point. At the beginning of the session, close your eyes and touch the anchor point. Inhale, exhale, then slowly count backward from 10. At the end of the session, repeat the same process, opening your eyes only after you're done counting back from 10.

Relieving Stress in 60 Seconds Through Self Hypnosis

Stress is scary and damaging. It poisons moods and cuts productivity in half. When the brain produces too much of the stress hormone cortisol, it begins to operate from a place of fear. As we've already established, fear is problematic because it causes you to question your capacity for growth and really slows down your progress.

Another reason you need to work on chronic stress is how it spreads so much that it clouds other aspects of your life. A wait at the bank isn't intrinsically stressful. It's inconvenient, yes, and maybe at a point frustrating, but not stressful in its own right. Yet, many people in a similar scenario would be quick complaining about how the wait is stressing them out. This is because your brain is churning out cortisol on overdrive. The technique below promises to help detoxify you from the free radicals that clog up your happiness.

Try to read through the directions a few times and internalize the process, especially because glancing at your phone for each step could severely distract you. For now though, the most important thing is that you let your self relax.

Directions

On a scale of 0–10, sincerely determine your actual stress levels, where 0= No stress and 10= Panic attack mode. As you practice self-hypnosis more regularly, you will find yourself scoring a 0. Remember this number that you have determined.

Get yourself comfortable in a silent, closed, moderately lit room.

Select your best chair and place your feet flat on the ground. Position your hands gently in your laps.

Take 4 deep, slow breaths and exhale slowly 4 times for 8 counts. Keep your back straight but comfortable.

With your eyes totally shut, count down from 10 to 1 very slowly. After each number, say -I am delving deeper.‖ As in: Ten, I am delving deeper, Nine, I am delving deeper...

Try Hypno-affirmations. Take another slow, deep breath, and say out loud: I am safe, I am free, I am hereby choice.

Exercise your imagination. With another slow, deep breath, imagine that you're happy for the rest of the day. Make the visual clear, colorful, and convincing. Tell yourself that nothing can stress you today.

After about a minute of imagining a happy rest of the day, open your eyes and let the wave of calm wash over you.

Stretch your arms over the top of your head and say _Yes!'.

Determine your new stress ranking on a scale of 0–10, where 0= No stress, and congratulate yourself for the progress made.

Overcoming Pain With Self Hypnosis

Self-hypnosis can accelerate healing in unimaginable ways. It can help with expediting recovery from nausea in chemotherapy patients and the healing of bones. It can bring comfort and ease to any area of your body that's experiencing pain or discomfort. Extensive conditioning with a certified hypnotherapist can completely replace surgeries and anesthesia, but while that may be out of reach for a individual engaging self-hypnosis, you'll still be able to remedy headaches, body pains, and general aches.

Directions

Get comfortable. Wear loose clothes and find a closed, moderately lit room.

Sincerely, determine your stress ranking on a scale of 0–10, where 0 is the absolute minimum level of stress the most relaxed person can accomplish. Remember this number.

Sit in a comfortable chair and keep your spine straight and comfortable. Ensure your feet are flat on the ground, and your palms are rested on your laps.

Take 4 slow, deep inhales, and 4 corresponding exhales for a count of 8.

Close your eyes and imagine yourself as your favorite plant. Feel your roots spread from your feet and push gently below the Earth's surface, grounding you.

Imagine your favorite color as a light. Let it flow all over you, right from the depths of your roots at the center of the Earth to the tips of your fingers and the crown of your head.

You may begin to feel a tingling sensation, like a heartbeat, in your palms. Concentrate on this feeling. Direct all your attention to the feeling in your palms and get comfortable with it. As you do so, breathe for at least 20 seconds.

With your eyes still closed, count down from 10 to 1, saying, –I am delving deeper.‖ after every number.

Silently, but preferably out loud, say the following Hypno-affirmations 10 times: I am safe, I am improving, I send my _____(name a part of your body)_____love and calm, I feel better already.

Focus on the part(s) of your body that are experiencing pain individually. With expansive breaths, visualize all the pain draining out from that part of your body. Feel the warm, soothing energy of healing caress that spot. Feel and experience the healing sensation wash over you.

After about 2 minutes of visualizing yourself getting healed, imagine that favorite color as a wave of light once again. But this time, let it cascade down from the top of your head to the soles of your feet, and then down to your roots in the center of the Earth.

Exhale and allow yourself to feel relief. Stretch your hands above your head and say, —Yes!‖

Determine your new ranking on the stress scale. Congratulate yourself for your progress with transforming your state positively.

Don't be afraid to let your love wash over you. And you can be flexible with your choice of color during the session on pain reduction. What matters the most is that you don't restrict your mind and that you trust yourself enough to reprogram your mind and heal yourself.

Is Overcoming Anxiety Possible?

Anxiety is a very strong sensation. It's a more advanced form of panic attacks, can completely destabilize you and break your focus. It's erroneous to view anxiety like some alien sensation fashioned to destroy you. Anxiety is very connected to your natural fight or flight tendencies. For instance, if you were walking down a dark alley and heard metal scraping against a wall in the distance, you could conclude that it was a knife and suddenly find yourself overcome with anxiety, adrenaline, and fear. In this scenario, it's perfectly explainable. Psychologists have found that certain stimuli are universal in the way they trigger fight or flight tendencies. In the case of a fear of getting stabbed in a dark alley, this fear makes sense.

Anxiety may be rational or irrational, and irrational anxiety does get problematic, but it isn't possible to be anxious for no reason. If, say, you had an all-important job interview tomorrow, while you may be very prepared for it, it is reasonable to expect that you may wake up sweating by 3 AM, nervous and full of anxiety. And while this is not nearly as rational a reason for anxiety as in the alleyway instance where your life was in danger, it still suffices. Most folk, however, find that they feel anxiety over minute things, such as everyday conversations, going out in public, or going to work.

Overcoming anxiety is very possible. This is because there is always an underlying reason for whatever we feel as individuals. As long as we can narrow down on the source of the anxiety, it becomes easy to eliminate it. However, the real problem for most individuals who suffer from anxiety attacks is that their anxiety comes from a very ambiguous place. They couldn't possibly place it even if they tried.

Some psychologists argue that the ultimate reason for anxiety is to trigger you to take action, especially seeing as it's connected to one of your most fundamental tendencies as an individual. In the interview instance stated earlier, the anxiety could be helpful to the extent where it pushes you to go through your notes again, crosscheck and verify that your clothes are still good to go, and put finishing touches on your presentation. By ensuring that you're at your most prepared, your chances of securing the job and attaining economic security become higher. In this case, the anxiety served in the line of a specific purpose, and, in this scenario, as you begin to realize that you're as prepared as you'll ever be, you'll find that the anxiety vanishes. Have you ever observed your anxiety fading away once you start taking action towards the goal of addressing the anxiety-causing issue?

The most problematic kind of anxiety is that which the roots are ambiguous. This is what we'll focus the bulk of our energy in this section toward eradicating. In English Language, there are over 2500 words describing a vast range of emotions, yet when most people are asked how they feel, they tend to be able to provide only about a dozen words. Even more interestingly, studies have shown that many individuals end up repeating the same dozen words week after week. For this category of people, the mind and body are two separate worlds that don't intersect. As a result of this, they tend to label their emotions rather than truly experience them.

If self-hypnosis teaches anything at all, it's that your strongest internal powers are only unlocked when you become attuned with your mind. All emotions find their roots in the subconscious mind, and the stronger your mind-body connection, the easier you'll find the process of parsing your emotions. Most emotions start off with similar fundamental sensations and maintain this similarity all the way through in many instances. This is why some people find the ambiguous sensation of stage fright terrifying, while others find it exciting and exhilarating. Your reaction to these sensations, hence, is a product if your self-perception.

Thus you will find that positive emotional labeling has a potent therapeutic effect. Overcoming anxiety becomes easily attainable once you learn to truly experience your emotions before attempting to label them and then describe them in a positive light. For instance, based solely on your perspective, a stimulus that was meant to trigger euphoria, excitement, pride in yourself tends to always be summarized as -happiness.‖ In the same vein, a stimulus that was meant to inspire nervousness, excitement, and worry simply becomes −anxiety.‖ As a result, a situation could present a stimulus that is supposed to excite you, but you end up getting anxious because you misinterpreted it.

To see how easily you can set yourself on the path to overcoming anxiety, let's engage this quick exercise. Imagine yourself as a decorator who has been trained to understand the nuances of color. Now, think of your emotions as colors. You may find that primary colors pop up in your mind. That's fine. Concentrate on each color, and then multiply it with at least 4 substitutes. Transform the blues into aquamarine, cyan, teal, and iris. Decompose the reds into pink, ruby, magenta, and sangria.

Now, let us transmit the breakthrough above toward dealing with your emotions. Now, take a moment to recall a vivid memory where you felt what you believed was anxiety. Look for a memory that you can recall in detail, preferably one where the anxiety only seemed to worsen with time. Now, grab a pen and paper. In your own words, describe how you felt at the time. Now, write out 10 words that succinctly and accurately describe your state of mind in that precise moment: you could've said you felt gloomy, even though you were only slightly saddened, or you could've said you were nervous, even if you were actually excited. Use a dictionary or thesaurus to find the words that best describe your emotions at the time, if you need to.

Scrutinize your list of 10 words. Of the ten, which emotions give you the most positive outlook of the situation as compared to the anxiety you thought you were feeling? Write them out separately. As was established previously, most emotions start out with the same sensations and maintain a consistent similarity all through. So, imagine how differently that situation would've turned out if you had labeled your emotions at the time through these positive lenses instead. Does the situation suddenly feel different in your head?

If you were to apply this technique to events that happen in your life daily, you'd find that it suddenly becomes easier to cancel out negative emotions. Repeat this exercise over and over, focusing on a different emotion each time. You'll realize in no time that anxiety will no longer surface, because you have now cultivated the ability to replace it with more desirable emotions.

How Do You Overcome Anxiety?

Your emotions speak to you all the time. There's a robust internal communication system inside of you that is highly developed, but you can only bring out its true potential when you learn the controls of it. In the last exercise, you learned how to cancel out negative emotions of anxiety in memory (and even in concurrent events) by labeling them more positively or replacing them with brighter emotions. In this section, you'll learn even more advanced techniques. Primarily, you'll be exposed to the rudiments of listening to your emotions and how this can help you overcome anxiety. After this, you'll learn how to manipulate the technique of visualization for your emotional advantage. Finally, you'll learn how to use the technique of dissociation with a practical example.

Let's begin with listening to your emotions. At this point, you must have realized the deep relevance of maintaining a strong connection with all facets of your mind, especially your subconscious mind. Your subconscious mind communicates with your body, which is why it makes sense that we're first hit by our feelings before thoughts. It generally works in this way: (1) Your subconscious mind perceives a stimulus and generates some response, which is sometimes referred to as a stress response (2) Your conscious mind scans the environment and tries to attach these stimuli to external objects or concepts, with these attachments manifesting as feelings (3) Having attached the stimulus to your external environment, you are now poised to take action.

If you were camping in the woods and you came across a snake, your fight or flight instincts would kick in instantly. Your heart rate would skyrocket, and your senses would heighten.

Adrenaline would fill you from the inside in a mad rush. In this scenario, you're feeling strong emotions and, more importantly, you know why you're feeling them. Whatever decision you decide to take here—whether to run or stay and confront the snake—is entirely at your discretion and instinct. As you can see, there are multiple possibilities to choose from in terms of your emotions. You could let fear take over, or you could welcome boldness and deep resolve. In the same way, you become more conscious of the stimuli your subconscious mind processes, you will find that you will always have choices rather than anxiety to pick from in every scenario.

Most times, when we feel discomfort, stress, or anxiety, they're actually signals that our subconscious is trying to alert us to a problem. It may be sending you this message because you have left important tasks unresolved, or because you have paused integral plans in your life and ignored them completely. It could be alerting you because your struggles are creating internal friction and destabilizing the alignment of your life. Your subconscious always tries to get across to you, and it's usually for very significant matters.

Have you ever considered that anxiety could simply be your mind's way of motivating you to address an issue or fix a loose end from the past that has been dangling ever since? By learning to listen to your emotions, you can better tell these messages apart and eliminate all ambiguity as regards their roots. We have already examined the tool of elimination. Now, let us consider another tool for overcoming anxiety: acknowledging and labeling emotions.

The process involves asking several questions. The next time you feel anxiety, ask yourself these questions: Why am I feeling anxious? Why do I feel this anxiety now? What is my subconscious trying to tell me?

Listen to your mind as you ask these questions. Really listen for the answer. Write in a journal as many causes as you can rationally come up with, in the context of the situation. Then take time to cross them out in order of improbability, until you arrive at one or two potential causes. What this process does is eliminate all ambiguity, as you now know the exact cause(s) of your anxiety. This newfound clarity enables you to easily tackle the sources of your anxiety quickly and overcome them without any damage to your psychological health.

Alternately if you do not have the time or aren't in the mental state to tackle your anxiety at that moment, this technique helps you to schedule a time for dealing with it in the future while at the same time breaking the hold of stress and anxiety, seeing as your subconscious will stop alerting you because you've already received the message. You want to eliminate any anchors of anxiety before you destroy it.

The second technique you may employ is visualization. Before we delve into the nitty-gritties of this technique, it is essential that we understand the power of imagery. You must have, at least at one point in your life, woken up from a dream with your heart racing. What does this tell you? It reveals that your mind cannot exactly differentiate between what occurs in the outside world and what occurs only in your mind. The point is: images are so powerful that they can convince your mind into believing things that aren't real. This attribute can be a disadvantage or an advantage, depending on how you look at it.

Sometimes an upcoming event can be so insignificant or mellow in its consequences that you can mentally brush it aside, while at other times, the event is so important that it takes up all the space your mind has to give. This is why a Saturday afternoon picnic may not bother you very much if only your family members are in attendance, but can quickly become a source of serious anxiety if, say, your boss or a client decided to join you.

When important events are coming up, the doors fling wide open for anxiety to come in. If you were to give a keynote speech at an international conference, you would definitely be under intense pressure to put your very best foot forward. This scenario provides fertile soil for anxiety to thrive. Your mind may begin to traumatize you with images of things going horribly wrong, of you forgetting your speech, or making a blunder in front of the audience, or spilling coffee on the laptop containing your slides and then having to make an extemporaneous presentation. A thousand and one thoughts may plague your mind. This is a perfect opportunity to engage the time-tested technique of visualization.

In the actual sense, all of us use visualizations, whether consciously or unconsciously. The only difference is that the average person allows the images they create to run wild and morph into negative emotions, while others who learn how to manipulate the images their minds create can control them and strengthen their minds through these images. By engaging the exercise below, you will be in a better position to take charge of the visuals in your mind and eliminate all anxiety.

To begin with, find a quiet place with mild lighting. Lie down and close your eyes. Make sure you're comfortable. Then breathe. Let your inhalations be slow, deep, and wholesome. Now, imagine the event that is causing you anxiety—let's say it's an idea pitching meeting you're having with potential investors in your company—and focus on it. Imagine it going really well. Imagine the awe on the faces of the investors as you wow them with your ideas. Imagine the charisma and finesse with which you deliver all your lines. Imagine your jokes landing perfectly. Play this image over and over in your mind, rewinding, and making each new iteration better than the last. Imagine walking out of the meeting with a look for pride and accomplishment on your face.

Think about it: After engaging this exercise, how do you think you would feel about this hypothetical pitch meeting? You would feel amazing, of course. Even more, you would have a greater chance of succeeding at it, according to several studies. You must never underestimate the power of mental images. They can play a powerful role in shaping your reality. Remember, you can make your mind believe anything. Use this power to your advantage.

Finally, let us consider the technique of mental dissociation. Dissociation is a tremendously powerful exercise that has evolved over the last few decades. It is a highly effective technique that helps catalyze mental shifts and reprogram the subconscious mind.

Dissociation involves a copious amount of visualization, but it is a lot more powerful because it helps you view yourself as others do. You become like an external observer of your own self, giving you a level of fresh insight that was previously inaccessible. You start to see your actions like recorded events and piece them together better.

For this technique to work, you'll have to zone in on a situation that causes you a lot of anxiety. Before you begin the dissociation process, all you need is a rough sketch of the situation in your mind. Don't conjure the full details yet. We will call this situation —the event.‖

Now, sit up tall and straight. Breathe slowly and powerfully until you feel your confidence and strength increase. To facilitate this, cast your mind back to moments when you felt strong and capable. Now, walk through the following steps:

Imagine a cinema. Imagine yourself sitting in the back row and facing the large screen. Don't forget to view this in dissociation (that is like it's all happening outside you). Imagine yourself looking at the screen. On the screen, imagine that the main actor is another dissociation of yourself. Somewhere else in the scene, imagine another relaxed version of you.

Imagine the event as a door at an edge of the screen. Imagine your main-actor self beginning to walk toward the event. Imagine that the frame pauses 20 seconds before you get to the door

Now, imagine that your character in the back row has a laptop. On that laptop, imagine a second screen in which the movie frame is also paused at the same point. With one tap of a button, the movie will continue.

Think of yourself as a movie director, determine what the character does and when and how they do it. The movie's ending is solely at your discretion. Be calm, collected, confident, and in control. Allow yourself to deal with the event that caused you trouble in the past. Make it fun and exciting. Create the best happy ending that you can imagine.

Leave your body and go with the new version of the movie to the back room. Connect the laptop to the projector.

Play the new version of the movie on the big screen and watch it until the end. Allow yourself to feel satisfaction at the fact that things are much better now.

Return to the back row and enter your body on the seat. Ensure that you like what you see with each rewatch until you're fully convinced that you have the best ending you can think of.

By getting back into your body, you switched from dissociation to association. Check your progress by reloading your memories of the anxiety episode and check how you feel about it now. You should definitely feel a lot better than you used to. With more practice, you will feel better and better, and anxiety will become less terrifying.

You may find that certain situations are so grave that you may need to attempt dissociation severally to achieve lasting results, and that's fine. The stronger the internal association you have with the memory, the more times you will have to apply dissociation to weaken the links.

How You Can Overcome Anxiety Naturally

In dealing with anxiety, most individuals have been made to believe that they can only be cured through medication. This is not only totally false, but it exposes them to the vulnerability of addiction, side effects, and chemical-induced reactions. Herbal remedies such as the poplar Kava were discovered with the hope that they would be better synthetic drugs in this regard. However, side effects such as liver damage have been associated with these herbal remedies, making them just as scary.

The good news is, there are very natural, non-drug ways to overcome anxiety. Some major natural methods are described below:

Sleep Habits

The terrible thing about anxiety is not just that it makes it harder for you to sleep; it's also that sleep deprivation fuels anxiety, sticking sufferers in an unending loop of health crises. By devoting yourself to sleeping the recommended 8 hours daily, you give your immune system the needed boost for your body to function optimally, while also equipping yourself with the strength to manage the anxiety that only a proper rest can provide.

If anxiety is making sleep inaccessible for you, you can facilitate sleep by; avoiding phone and computer screens for hours before your bedtime, ensuring that your bed is comfortable, and keeping your room's temperature well regulated.

Keep Tense Muscles in Check

Tension is fodder for anxiety. To eliminate the tension in your body, you may consider progressive muscle relaxation. You can accomplish this by choosing any muscle group of your choice, tighten it for a few seconds, and then letting it go. Do this taking each muscle group in turn.

Identify Triggers

Look for patterns in your anxiety. Are there places or events that always cause you to worry or feel anxious? Note them down and, having identified them, overcome them through self-hypnosis or mindfulness meditation techniques.

Exercise

Exercising boosts your sense of wellbeing, which in turn can help minimize your feelings of anxiety. Don't bombard yourself at the beginning. Begin with 15-minute sessions daily and then work your way up from there.

Avoid Caffeine and Alcohol

Anything with caffeine really should be avoided, from Soda to Tea, to Chocolate, to Diet Pills. Caffeinated substances raise your spirits and can be a severe trigger for anxiety. On the other hand, alcohol is a _downer' which can also exacerbate anxiety issues.

How To Reduce Anxiety Quickly

Anxiety isn't a feeling to give one advanced notice. While you can avoid triggers and employ techniques such as self-hypnosis and visualization to overcome it, you should arm yourself with quick methods for ending unexpected anxiety episodes or panic attacks. At the same time, you work on yourself to get better.

When anxiety hits, it generally helps to find a distraction such as music. Distractions help you take your mind off the anxiousness and gather yourself together. Exercises such as jogging, running, and dancing can be instrumental in equipping you to manage anxiety better and quicker. If you're new to exercising and aren't sure that you'll be able to commit to it, you can find an exercise buddy who will motivate you to meet all your exercise goals.

Eat proper, well-balanced meals, and always have high energy snacks on hand. Managing anxiety requires both physical and mental energy, so starving yourself won't cut it. Try quick meditation techniques such as walking meditation. Also, consider getting a massage or a hot bath. These can be quite therapeutic in helping you manage anxiety. Humor has also been known to nullify the worst effects of anxiety. So, the next time to have that panic attack, try to see if you can remember something that transforms your hyperventilation into laughter.

What is Mindfulness?

Imagine for a moment that you're looking at a painting of a majestic mountain with a thick, white cloud right behind it. Mindfulness involves you seeing both the mountain and the clouds with an equal amount of attention, none surpassing the other. By applying the principle of mindfulness to your life, you're exposed to the full range of your intrinsic abilities, all laid out bare with zero noise. It shifts you from assumptive reality to one with clarity, where you can better assess yourself and track your growth.

Mindfulness entails shifting from an ‚either/or' perspective to an ‚and' perspective. As you make this shift, you'll find that you simultaneously outgrow all the pains—both physical and emotional—that limit you and cause you suffering. Rather than try to -get over it‖ or –buck up,‖ which leaves you feeling minimized and sometimes holding a grudge, you learn true acceptance and gain access to the peace that comes along with it.

Acceptance in the context of mindfulness entails an understanding that unpleasant and unexpected things will happen, but that when they do, you still have to treat yourself with honor and kindness. It employs the principle of dissociation to the extent that it teaches you in those situations to regard yourself like you would a friend suffering. This ability to empathize with your own self makes you somewhat a best friend to yourself and has very therapeutic effects on your ability to overcome all forms of pain.

Mindfulness doubles as both a state of mind and a form of meditation. It puts you in the middle ground, ensuring that you don't deny your pain in the quest to blot out your suffering. It helps you assess all those emotions that poison your attitude to life and weaken your spirit. It further helps you to overcome physical pain and emerge stronger after each moment of peace.

Start from where you are now, even if you've never done meditation before. Pay attention to the fact that you're trying to forge a connection with your mind and remain aware of this goal. You may experience uncomfortable emotions or feel like you aren't making progress at the beginning, but trust that you are. Actively cancel out negativity and always be on the lookout to make the most of every mindfulness session.

Formal and Informal Mindfulness Practice

Meditation is the primary route through which mindfulness is practiced. It's best to have a comfortable cushion or stack of blankets to work with.

Mindfulness practice becomes formal when you dedicate a set amount of time daily toward its practice. It's like exercising; it keeps you fit and ready at all times, so you aren't moved when tricky situations arise. Because you have readied yourself through formal practice, you are equipped to take on any challenges, and your mind and body find it easier to return to equilibrium.

Walking meditation is another type of formal mindfulness practice. It involves taking long walks and taking in nature's sweetest spots, while also applying awareness and acceptance techniques through strategic meditation. Walking meditation is especially powerful because it simultaneously heals the mind and body.

Informal mindfulness practice, also called spontaneous awareness, is a means of extending the lessons from your formal mindfulness practice to the real world. It could range from random acts of kindness to strangers, to a heightened awareness of the impulses and sensations in your body as you wait in line at the coffee shop.

Getting Ready for Mindfulness Practice

One myth you must crush from the get-go is the idea that meditation must be perfect. This idea is far from the truth. It's termed mindfulness ‚practice' because it may not always go a certain way, and that's fine. So, rather than waste time trying to make your sessions perfect, focus more on bringing out the most from every session by letting your internal healing energy invigorate you.

Below are some fundamental tasks that you may want to accomplish to facilitate the effectiveness of your mindfulness meditations when you begin with the techniques in the ‚Guided Meditation' section.

Allocate Your Space

If possible, designate a space for your mindfulness practice. A closed, quiet, dimly lit room free from all distractions is always the way to go. Determining your designated practice space can be a motivation in itself because it ensures that you are constantly reminded of your new regimen and meet up with all your practice goals.

Gather The Necessary Materials

Put together all the props and tools that you need for a successful session and store them in the designated practice space. Writing materials, a straight-backed chair, blankets, or a soft cushion, pen and paper, and other tools you may find necessary should all be put together before you begin.

Silence Phones and Other Potentially Noisy Electronics

Even if you've never done so during waking hours, turn off your phone. If you have to keep time with it, then set it to airplane mode. In this case, do not glance at it any more than is necessary.

Determine Practice Time and Length

Mindfulness practice is known to boost the immune system and purify emotions, so you may want to designate adequate time to it. Your sessions should occur at a particular time daily and should span at least 25 minutes.

Prepare Comfortable Clothes

As much as it is possible, wear loose, comfortable clothing. Meditation gurus also generally advise that people dress in layers during mindfulness practice. Ensure that you don't wear anything that constricts you physically.

Establish Your Posture

Sit with your back straight and let your hands rest naturally on your thighs, palms face down. Ensure that your spine is as elongated as possible by tilting your back, but be careful not to arch your back forward or backward. Relax your jaw, but let the space between your upper and lower teeth be little. Your lips should be parted slightly, while your tongue should simply rest against the upper front row of your teeth. Your legs should be apart, uncrossed, and flat on the floor, with your knees pointed at right angles. If you tend to hunch forward, raise the heart center of your chest slightly to prevent this. Finally, tuck in your chin slightly so that your head feels level.

If you decide to go the way of the traditional masters by sitting cross-legged on the floor, do so over a zafu. If you cannot find one, then you may substitute it with a stack of soft blankets. Rather than restricting yourself to a rigid seat, picture yourself sitting with relaxed dignity. Position your body as in the ‚sitting in a chair' instance in the last paragraph, the only difference should be in the posture of your legs. You may cross your legs in front of you or just above your ankles. You may alternately shift one leg in front of the other so that they remain uncrossed if crossing them will be inconvenient for you. Your hips should be above your knees at all times, and your knees should be on the floor.

It is also important that you note that there is no such thing as a bad meditation. As you're very likely new to this, you may find it to be a bit of a learning curve, especially for the first 8 sessions. However, as you immerse yourself further in mindfulness practice, you'll find that you only get better at it. Also, you may have already picked this up, but it's still important to reiterate that meditation and mindfulness practice doesn't necessarily equate to eradicating all your thoughts. You must realize that there are sessions where you will have to meditate on certain thoughts so you can connect with your subconscious mind.

Mindfulness practice helps you manage emotional fallouts through focused practice. Learn to trust the process and never limit any sensations you feel during guided meditation. You may also find yourself getting sleepy during mindfulness practice. This is bound to happen mostly when you're suffering from insomnia and sleep deprivation. Meditation relaxes you, so you could become so calmed that the tiredness in your body starts to reflect. When this happens, by all means, sleep. It's exactly what you need.

Finally, you must be cautious with your use of meditation in situations of trauma. Mindfulness practice does teach body awareness and emotional awareness, both of which are integral to increasing our innate capacity to handle trauma. However, trauma also brings along with it strong, intrusive images and sometimes auditory hallucinations. In this case, it is risky to attempt healing yourself alone. You should consider working with a trauma-sensitive mindfulness instructor or a therapist, even as you boost your recovery through meditation.

Guided Meditation

Guided meditation helps you achieve mindfulness and internal awareness through structured meditation guidelines. Below are a number of meditation exercises to get you started:

Breathing Exercises

These should take no longer than 10 minutes.

Keep your mouth completely closed but very relaxed. Inhale and exhale through your mouth in a rapid sequence, ensuring that your breathing is equal all through, and the breaths are short. This exercise is rather loud, but you'll get accustomed to it with time.

Work toward a breathing cycle of 3 sharp inhalations and exhalations per second. This will lead to rhythmic movements in your diaphragm. If you find that you're beginning to get fatigued, pause, resume regular breathing for one minute, and then return to the breathing cycle.

Breath Counting

This exercise should last for 10–15 minutes.

Sit in a comfortable position with your back straight.

Inhale slowly and deeply and begin shutting your eyes slowly.

Exhale powerfully but slowly. You want to achieve a consistent rhythm.

Do not restrain your thoughts. Let incoming thoughts flow in, but let them go quickly. Return to your breathing, ensuring that the thoughts don't distract you to the point of breaking your rhythm.

Imagine a wave of light flowing from your head to your feet and back. Watch it pulsate as you breathe.

Be mindful of the sensations that occur in all areas of your body that the light passes through.

Don't change these sensations. Aim instead to recognize them and, the moment you do, let them go. The goal is simply to heighten your awareness of these sensations.

Count to 'five' as you exhale. Be careful to breathe out very slowly. Do this over and over.

Do not count higher than five. Once you go beyond it, note that you have been distracted.

Acceptance and Observation Exercises

This helps you concentrate on accepting your pain and finding mental peace, calm, and relief from pain.

Assume a comfortable position with your back straightened and well supported. You can begin this session seated on a straight-backed chair or lying face-up on your back.

Imagine yourself as a calm, distant observer. Pay attention to how you're feeling at the moment. Don't attempt to change it; simply observe and acknowledge.

Pain management begins with observation. Scan your body and identify where the pain and tension resides. Where is all the pain located? What parts of your body are calm and at ease?

Notice all sensations, subtle and strong, in all areas that you scan.

Take a deep inhaling breath and release it in a long exhale. Keep breathing slowly and calmly. In... Out... In again.

Pay close attention to all the sensations your body is feeling. The cold air flowing in through your nostrils. The smoothness of the floor beneath your feet. Paying attention to all these sensations could easily distract you. Be aware of this and restore your attention the moment you do so. Anchor your focus to your breath, so it always brings you back.

Keep observing everything. Your breaths, as they switch from shallow to deep. Observe where your body is tight and free. Feel the pain stored up across your body. Imagine them as knots and unravel them. Watch the pains flow slowly away. Don't judge them, just accept them and let go.

Internal Healing

You may be seated on the floor or in a chair. Whichever you choose, be sure to relax in a comfortable position.

Allow your thoughts to pass through with calmness and acceptance. Focus on your breath. Take in slow, deliberate streams of air. Exhale slowly and calmly. Do this 5 more times, focusing on your breath all the way.

Begin observing your present thoughts. Pay special attention to the thoughts of pain. You have a strong urge to change these thoughts, don't you? Fight the temptation. Simply understand these thoughts, don't try to change them.

Begin labeling your thoughts. As you do, distance yourself from these thoughts. Aim for an understanding that the thoughts are merely transient. They will not always be here, and they do not define who you truly are.

Inhale and exhale as calmly as you can. Don't break the cycle. Now that you've labeled your thoughts, focus your attention on your breathing.

Focus on the discomfort points in your body. Imagine an alternate sensation. It could be anything, anything other than the sensation of pain. If you feel a tingle in your arms or legs, embrace it. This gives you control over your physical sensations.

Immerse yourself fully in this sensation. Feel it replacing your fears and overriding your feelings of pain. Take it one step at a time and, slowly, watch your pain fade away.

Allow yourself to absorb the energy of passively embracing your feelings and thoughts. Distance yourself from them. Feel the healthy sensation that this distance brings. Let yourself bask in this sensation.

At this juncture, be aware of all the things your senses perceive. Notice each sound that flows into your ear. Observe how your clothes sit on your body. Focus on all the thoughts that this observation brings. Label them.

Mentally scan your body from the top of your head to the sole of your feet. Peacefully move along with your body. Don't judge or excessively moderate the sensations you feel at this point. Simply accept them. When you reach your feet, bring attention back to your breath for a final time. Inhale slowly, then exhale.

Open your eyes.

Chapter Two:
Stories Of The Siberia

NORTHERN LIGHTS

There is something absolutely satisfying about visiting an old place with friends. The pleasure of rediscovering someplace absolutely forgotten, experiencing a sight you once beheld as magical but have now dismissed. It is like finding that old sweater you wore a lot as a child or blowing the dust off a childhood diary and burrowing into the comfort of old thoughts. Except this time, you visit with new eyes and places once forgotten take on new light. There is less this time to see and more to experience with the senses of others, a shared companionship.

And so it is that when your plane touches down in the evening, all of your senses immediately come alive, tingling in anticipation of all the wonders to be beheld and seen. You have just arrived in Siberia, a region in Russia, spanning Eurasia and North Asia and home to long, harsh winters and home right now, of course, to you and your company of traveling friends.

It is a quiet winter, and the air is crisp, still, almost expectant. You are standing on the shores of Russia's heartland, your feet protected from the cold with layers of warm, wool clothing, and thick snug boots. This forgotten northern outpost has lost prominence when easier routes across Siberia opened up. And it is why you have chosen here in Nayan-Mar as the spot from which you and your friends will observe the Aurora Borealis – a little more silence, a little more daring. The treasure of knowing you now walk paths that many have forgotten to tread. With the legends and myths that follow your footsteps, you feel as though all of the universe has ushered you to this moment. You cannot help but want to whistle, a sound you know the mountain's echoes will carry along and bring back to you, a returned gift from nature. But you stop yourself – the majesty of this night begs a reverence, a refusal to stain such with spontaneity. It feels as though if you moved too fast, Nature might startle and move away. And so you swallow your whistle, but your mind carries the tune as far as your head can think it. Ooh-ooh-lah-lah-ooh. The perfect rhythm to a perfect night.

Your hands run along your arms, up and down, up and down as though to warm away from the cold. But you are not cold tonight. Rather, your hands enclave your arms in a warm, loving hug. You wish as you do that, you could trap all of these memories in yourself as your warm wool has trapped all of the heat. It seems as you warm yourself with a hug that you would offer the universe one if you could.

Your eyes should be taking in the beautiful landscape and watching the majestic terrain, but your gaze is fixed firmly above on the inky expanse of a starry midnight sky. Above you, the night skies have transformed the world about you into a fairy-tale. The atmosphere is electric and has taken a hopeful tinge upon them. Anything is possible tonight.

In this wilderness of darkened hue, you sit with your friends and wait. Pause. The sound of your breaths fills up the space between you, but you cannot notice. You are transfixed, your gaze set on the mystic sky above. And then...a flicker. Are you holding your breath now? Tiny disturbances in the earth's cover have held you spellbound.

Is that...? – a friend makes to say.

But your finger moves to his lips to shush him before he can get the word out. You nod. Yes. That is. You stare at the awe in their eyes, and you see mirrored there, the marvel on your own. The northern lights in her vivid electromagnetic charm have held you all, and your eyes follow the path of the luminous green light as it shuffles across the sky. Greens and blues and pinks dance a star's song into being while the sky stretches and wakes up and prepares to host this fit of brilliance. You blink, and the night skies seem to wink back at you. Your hearts sigh, and in awe of the wonder you have just beheld, it seems that the universe sighs as well.

NOMADIC PASTORALS

Winding down from a long day, this will help you, Relaxation will find you as you drift further and further down into a night of restorative and blissful night sleep. Find a cozy, safe place where you may lay down, where you can drift off without distractions and interactions. The most important thing to note right now is how much you deserve this time of rest. You may let go of lingering thoughts and allow yourself to feel the pride that comes with making it through another day. Let go of any concerns you may have about tomorrow, the day after that, or the future.

Imagine that you have squirreled these concerns and worries away into a box and set them on a bedside table where they will await you tomorrow when you are ready and better equipped with an hour of rest to tackle these challenges. This story will take you to the night of a young girl nomad as she lies awake at night, thinking through the journeys she has made.

—Go to Sleep,‖ they said to Arya. But Arya only wanted to stare at the sky through the hole in her tent. Through the hole, she could hear the wind whipping through the land, teasing all who hear and daring any who could catch him. Ooooooooh. Oooooooh. Again, and again, the wind whipped through the land. Oooooooooooooooooooh. Oooooooooooooooooooh. It seemed like it went on for longer this time, as though forcing any who tried to catch him to first catch their own breath.

Beyond the frame of the hearty laughter of the wind, its soft cackles, and its howling, fierce ragings, young Arya tried again to stare at the skies. She had become familiar with the wind and the skies in her many travels. Several rooms zipping through strange lands have taught her to look out for the details that matter. Arya, aged only eleven, had decided that those were the two that did the wind and the skies. No more is needed to tell a story of a land and its people than the winds and the skies, Arya's trusty companions. And tonight, as she listens to the winds tell its secrets of the places he's seen and the people he's met, she needs the skies to nod at the tales. Is that true, she would ask silently? Her ears and eyes darting between both wind and skies. Is that true what the wind says, Sky? Is there truly a man in this land with a farm large as this traveling band. What? – can his entire servanthood dwarf even our herd of cattle? Is that true, Sky? Is that true what the wind says? And in its usual calming, soothing town, the wind whispers back, Ooooooooh, yes.

Tonight, young Arya cannot sleep again and so she asks her dear friends, the wind for a story. There's a strangely comforting smell of sheep poop and fur left behind by the last herd that passed through. This, she can tell. She had time to look around before Papa set up the tent and banished her to bed. There's a small grove of oaks, and it's quiet except the small wet wind you can hear pass you by in the cool autumn night. It's a large vast field and her family, pastoral nomads have brought their herd through this vast agricultural site. Sometimes, at night, she can hear a cow move, the indistinct slug of his body as it takes a drink of his water, and she can imagine the lazy blink of its eyes. She pulls all of these from memory.

Once, aged nine, she had snuck away from her parents to watch nature in its full, untapped glory, and she had been awed. She had found a forest with aged white pines by a hamlet off the path her parents had taken. This special place held her in awe for a while, and the silence of the place made it more enchanting. Away from the marching hooves of her father's cows, this lovely place was a soft respite from the sometimes-marching nomadic life.

A dew forms on the emerald-green form of a lush leaf, and she finds that those of the community have adorned trees with miniature sculptures and pieces of art. She feels the damp earth beneath her sandals and hears a twig occasionally crunch or twitch beneath her feet. She is embraced by the warmth she feels here. Rays of light create prism with the dew that covers the forest floor. The night is golden and warm, like kindness filling the inner forest with a sort of welcoming halo. She studies the earth-brown and leaf-green of her surroundings and, like children often do, lets out a burst of tinkling laughter. She is amazed, pleased to find in the oft-monotony of nature, a sliver of creation that amazes and draws her in.

Are you still with this story? Allow all of your joints to sink into the head. Allow your limbs, hands, and necks to simply feel this relaxation together. Remember to take deep breaths as you do this. Take in air and hold it in, allowing It to fill your lungs. Then, just sigh it out, audibly, if you want. Inhale again for Three, two, one, and then let all this air out. You can repeat this again and again as you desire.

As she stared, Arya wondered what it would be to feel like a century-old tree, rooted and grounded in the earth. And suddenly, she began to feel like she was in the exact right place at the time. The wind whispered, and the skies above her echoed her. And from that day, the world was Arya's friend.

REINDEERS

Allow yourself to fall asleep tonight to the sounds from this beautiful sleep story. Immerse yourself here and choose the experiences you connect to and how far you are willing to go before you settle into dreamland. This may be time for intricate self-care. Go ahead- light that jasmine-scented candle and let the warm glow that fills your room fill your heart also. Inhale. Exhale. Allow yourself time for introspection too – flip through the pages of your mind, of your heart, and accept the memories you find there. Wonder at each one, stare in curiosity, and let your heart take you with these memories where your head would only grudgingly go.

This time is especially for you – for self-care and happy fun. It is the time before you are welcomed into dreaming, restorative sleep, it is your right to take the time for deep rest. You are deserving of it. You may now appreciate the bed beneath you, the softness of your wool blanket, and that humidness to the air as though all of Nature and the angels have held their breath in awe at first and then released a collective exhale. Revel in the fact that you have made it through another day.

As you listen, think about my voice as that of a dear and trusted friend, one who may guide you to a comfortable place to get cozy without distraction and interactions from the outside world. Here, you may just let go and breathe, allow yourself to be authentic. Just real, true to who you are, loving and accepting every facet and tenet of yourself. You have made it through your day and soared through the waves of constant change and transition to show victory. If there are things you wish to change, you know that you can. Nothing lasts forever, and you are capable of changing your story still. You are in charge.

Let go now and allow yourself to be transported to the charming community where my story is set. At any point in this story, you may choose to let go of my voice and find your own story. This story is groomed by your own desires and needs. Take a deep breath. Inhale. Exhale. Let go of your breath, audibly, if you care to. Again, do that. take a deep breath in and allow yourself to savor the feel of the breath in your lungs. Then slowly, slowly, let the air out. Through your nostrils and your mouth, if you want. There? Do you feel yourself becoming grounded and becoming lighter, letting go of your today's worries? Watch yourself gather up the worries and fears like little bits of shredded, white paper and blow them into the air. Watch them in your mind's eye as they fall to the ground like little bits of nothing. Sigh it out and feel the back of your heavy eyelids that press upon your eyes, shutting out the pressures of the outside world.

Watch this enchanting scene unfold before you as though a blackout curtain has been pulled down before you. You are now in the magical theatre where you will watch this story play out. But first, take a deep breath again. You must ground yourself at this moment. Exhale. Let it all out. Can you smell it now? The warmth of ageless pines in a large clearing. Above you, soft snowflakes drop in an endearing fall, as though afraid to bother the world about you. As you stare, the white expanse of land before you seem to stretch for as far as your eyes can see and your head can dare comprehend.

There Is a stillness to the air. No man moves, not even you, and you are entranced by this majestic sight before you. Your feet are snugly wrapped in woolen socks and outlined by your best comfortable boots. You tuck your hands into the knit of your oversized sweater and run your fingers along it. It is comfortable out here – you do not want to leave. Your hands drop to pick up the thermos you have packed to enjoy this view. Your hands clutch around it, and you open it to drink your favorite warm beverage that is much appreciated on this morning. The sun rises higher, and you can feel the warm sliver on your face.

You are at rest, as though the boulder that had been tied to your neck has now been removed. You feel as if you are even floating and drifting, the crisp air around you enveloping you. You cover up all the thermos and savor the memory of that warm drink, its honeylike essence moving down your throat in a liquid embrace. Your eyes close at that. it has been a beautiful morning. You set the thermos back into your bag, settling it against your extra blanket, and then begin to walk. This morning is purely for yourself, so no music accompanies you. Only the soft falls of your footsteps are present in your contemplation.

The road you have chosen this morning is one you have taken before, and so you walk purely by memory. It has been a while since you first walked this path, and your memories threaten to fail you. But you are not panicked – you know that even if you do not find the way, it would be okay. The morning has been a blessing, a gift to you already.

You take a right leading you towards a narrower clearing. You know you have taken the right turn because you can hear the distant moving sounds of a nearby creek. Whoooosh – the sound seems to go right by your ears, and you are comforted by the sound of nature. Soon, you are greeted by the iconic statue of a reindeer, and this heralds your entrance into the park. You sigh and stare in wonder. Whose idea was it, you think, to put this statue up? But it is a question built of awe. You are glad – you would like to thank this person, such a beautiful idea. Now, the statue seems to welcome you into the haven.

You caress the straps of your backpack, which has been lightly packed for this long stroll into the woods. You hoist and re-hoist the shoulder straps, and the symphony of crickets and frogs around you lend a theme song to your otherwise unremarkable entrance. A miniature sculpture of another reindeer graces the gate as you push it open gently. The creaking sound it makes is music to your ears. You begin the walk up the park, and occasional crunch marks your steps as it hits a crackling leaf.

Something about this place is an essence that draws you. You first found this place years ago when you were at a time in your life such as this, and despite your many promises, only now have you found your way back to the place your heart calls sanctuary. The Reindeer Park. Your heart leaps in expectation as you gaze upon nature's canvas of cool browns and exciting greens. You can see what the owners have done to make the place even more comfortable. Tiny bells have been hoisted on trees, and as the wind whispers through the land, the bells let out a soft tinkle. And your whole body vibrates with the pleasure of this sound – it is almost as if the sounds massage your shoulders in a soft caress, allowing the tension in you to fall off.

Being here has made you grounded in yourself – you identify with your uniqueness, and your every step is a meditation about the fact that you are here and alive with days, months, and years ahead of you. And you can make anything of those days, months, and years. Anything really. You sigh at the future you see ahead of you, and you smile. You are not merely a survivor. You thrive. And in the days to come, you will thrive.

Much like the tall pine trees that surround you, your gaze cranes for your first sight of the reindeers in years. As you approach the forward-facing bench at the far end of your lawn, you are glad. You are glad that you have come here to find the benches vacant. But today, you are not content merely to sit and watch one reindeer. You long to see the majestic sight of all the reindeers at once.

And so, you take the long-winding stairs at the base of one tree. Ancient structures dot the park and lend to the already visible charm. Beautiful flowers envelop the railings you grasp for support as you climb patiently, one step at a time. You are not in any hurry. You get to the top of the building and walk to the balcony. There, you sink to the floor and allow yourself to connect to the essence of who you are. A brave and strong person who takes on feats and accomplishes them.

You sit calmly for a while and then get to your feet to take the view. And there, you are so taken by the sight you almost forget to breathe. Inhale. Exhale. It is all you can do not to soba the sight. Your heart is full of gratitude. One reindeer, Two, Three, Four. You count so many of them. And something about seeing such abundance in nature allows you to let a single tear go.

Your scalp begins to tingle, and you must listen as you take in this guide. Whatever it is that has bothered you, you are the answer. The answer has been in you all along – in your bravery, your courage, your ability to love, ability to carry on. You see it so much clearly now – how much of a force you are. How much of a presence you are and how much you will take on.

As you watch one graceful antler after another, you allow yourself to take in a big breath and let it out. You are here now. You are brave. You are strong. You know who you are.

SLED

In this small space, imagine that you are on a sled, a sled crafted to suit your tastes and whims. Your legs straddle both sides, and you anticipate the carefreeness of a joyful ride. It is only dawn, and you enjoy the quiet of the road as it is framed by the lushness and stillness of a snowy morning. Many are wrapped up in their homes at this time, but not you.

You have stepped outside for a time as this, to revel in the deep, orangey sky at this time. You have chosen to set out at this time, and you enjoy the experience of your town as the new day rises. You have the entire day ahead to enjoy this experience, and you smile as you take in the cool, intoxicating atmosphere around you. The gentle hum of a man's shed generator somewhere far away reminds you of Christmas mornings, where it seemed like anything could happen, and an adventure was always on the verge of being discovered. Here, it seems, you are limitless.

Your breath catches in expectance of the awe you are about to experience. What joy! What wonder! As your sled speeds onward, you imagine the footsteps that have once walked this path you now sled down. And you imagine the untold stories of these souls who have once walked this path. You are grateful for this opportunity for self-reflection and aloneness. As you continue in your sled, you pass by a home and stop at the sight of a child, hands cupped around his eyes, squinting through the glass of his living room at you. You are transfixed, such childlike wonder, such innocence. Only what seems like moments ago, you too have sat early on a Christmas morning, awake before your household, hands cupped around eyes and squinting at the world around you. You are transfixed at the sight, and soon, your own hands cup around your eyes, imitating the child before you can help it. You are at peace with yourself, at peace with the world.

You continue on your sledding journey as a foggy mist moves in slowly ahead. The lamp you hold in your arms now holds a dimmer light. A warmer light. You recall the advice of your friend as you set out on this morning – have a fun ride, she had called out. I will – you had returned. But now you find that you have not made this a wild ride. Instead, it has been a peaceful one. You have quietly moved down this town's slope. You feel a sense of inner peace and wisdom, one you haven't felt in a while, and you allow yourself to soak in it. Enjoy it.

Here, the burdens of the past do not matter. They fall away from around you like the shedding of a heavy blanket. You feel freer, lighter like fine gossamer print. You imagine this is what it feels like when honey melts in the mouth. Free. Light. Like the thousand winds that blow beneath the night sky. You are exactly where you need to be right now. Whatever has played out in your life thus far, welcome or unwelcome has led to this place. You are grateful to be here, and you can find acceptance for all that has come before. If one moment in the span of your entire life had played out differently, you would not be here. And you are glad to be here.

This day has given you a chance to begin again and start with a new, clean slate. You begin to feel yourself trust. Letting your inner intuition guide you, you take in the fragrance of the clean air and allow it to lead you. Where you are going, you do not know. The town, sparsely awake when you set out, is beginning to awaken. You pass a woman blowing warm air into her hands. She pauses, rubs her hands together, and blows into them again to stay warm. You had wished not to see anyone on this path, but now you are glad you have.

As you pass by her, she gives out a friendly smile, and your heart spins at the pleasantness of her face. You know that this is as much self-care for her as it is for her. You feel blessed, fortunate to have met another traveler on this self-love journey. You do not know what has brought her here, but you are glad she is here. You are both content and you know that your life is bigger and greater than your attempts to control every part of your day. You feel relief as you surrender to the limitless potential, to the possibilities of the greater good. You surrender to the flow, and in this moment, you feel a fullness of joy.

You stop your sled and bend to allow your fingers to dance through the snow. You let it sift through your hands and experience the coolness in your fingers. You glance around again and the stillness in the air reminds you to get going. You hug your arms around you, enjoying the gentle massage, and get back on the sled. It has been a fulfilling morning for you, a reminder to let go of worries, fears, and concerns, to move on with grace and strength.

You yawn as a wave of tiredness comes upon you. But a peaceful tiredness, a lazy one that does not hold pressure or place a demand on you. You are still and content as you begin your journey home. You remember to stare and notice as you continue home. You notice the contrast of red doors against the white of the snow, and you view with bafflement the swirls of purple, blue, and soft greens that your neighbor has spread on her clothesline.

On the property where you stay, you park the sled outside and walk to the door, climbing up your grey-colored stairs, stopping only to remove articles of clothing originally designed to keep you warm. You cannot suppress the smile that forms on your lips as you take the stairs, two at a time. You feel truly a leap of joy in your heart, a surge of peace. You are overwhelmed by love for yourself and this moment.

On a whim, you walk slowly down the stairs again to observe the sled that has bestowed you this experience. You run your hands along it, feel the chipped paint underneath your hands, and wonder how many other people it has humbled with the gift of a snowy experience. You remind yourself to pick up paint for it the next time you visit the store.

You return to your room, and with a soft drowsy smile, you drop off to sleep.

POLAR BEAR

Tonight, we journey into the lands of the polar bears. You may consider this voice as Cuddle up and find a safe, comfortable place where you may drift away and gradually cross the bridge into dreamland. There may have been times in your life where you imagined how wonderful it would be to journey into an unknown land. A strange place you have never been before now. Tonight, you'll find yourself safely encapsulated in a snow bubble and have a sleep adventure from which you can observe the world of the polar bears.

This is a safe protective bubble. With the walls around you, you are enclosed away from worries, and you are free to let go, right now. You are well. You are loved. And you are free to let go. Inhale deeply as your belly rises, and your lungs expand to take in air. Now, let all the air out in a soft exhalation. You are free to empty out all your fears, just sighing it out, how good it is to release all that tension. You may even allow that sigh turn into a yawn and just enjoy that yawn. You may sigh and yawn all you want, without restraint. Simply give your body all the signs that you are ready to descend into sleep.

Inhale for three, two, and one. And exhale for three, two, and one.

As you do, visualize you are walking along the edge of the road. Inhale the crisp air and exhale that air from your mouth. Watch as the warmth of your mouth releases the air in a cold huff. You can feel the stillness of the town behind you as you walk along this edge of the town. Enjoy the stillness and feel it blossom into deep quiet solitude. The air smells of nothing. As you walk along the shoulder of a barely used street, notice the stark contrast of the townsfolk's colors of magenta, chartreuse as the trees near the readiness of letting go. Just as right now, you are ready to let go of anything that weighs you down. Anything that you do not want to accompany you on this trip you are about to embark on.

Take another deep breath and allow yourself to journey to your childhood, to the first time you ever saw your own breath, how you did it again, and again until you felt like you were smoking. Inhale. Exhale. Inhale. Exhale. You walk this path again and your feet, snuggled in warm socks and boots steps on the clean whiteness of the night snow.

You want to make a return to your cabin but pause. Your inner voice leads you in a different direction. You see the flurries of the snowfall, melting as they kiss the ground, some even melting before they hug the floors. It is an amazing sight. You pass the turn to your house and follow the bend to another turn. It is now damp beneath your boots, and a cooler wind begins to blow as the air changes from crisp to slightly windy.

Warm your hands against the soft flannel of your shirt and let your thoughts wander, not settling on anything. You startle as a family of deer walk across, and your eyes watch them in awe of the simplicity with which you have stumbled on such sight. You note your happiness and is humbled to be considered worthy of viewing such a sight. You know that you are deserving of such beauty. Such beauty.

You walk on for a while, not stopping to check how far you have come. Instead, you focus on the drops of snow lakes, the contrast of your brown boots against the white of the snow and the clarity of your breath as you exhale. Inhale. Exhale.

The polar bear stops, and you are caught in a direct gaze. Slowly, it turns, and you begin to follow slowly, unsure as it winds through the snowy island. You wonder if you have dreamt this up, but the stark whiteness of its fur lends a reality to it that is distinctly un-dreamlike. Its largeness baffles you even as you enjoy its slow gait across the land. One foot in front of the other, you shuffle behind it, following wherever it takes you. The simplicity of it frees you – you have only one job tonight, to follow and it is a pleasant job.

You do not have to think about anything – only to walk slowly behind, and this frees you to follow and explore your thoughts. You examine each one, accepting it, and let it go like the melting of a snowflake. One thought and then another and then another and then another. It is a peaceful evening.

Suddenly, the polar bear stops, and you are brought to a halt as well. It rises on its hind limbs and stops as though to stare at you, and in them, you see the wisdom of your years reflected at you. You remind yourself of how wise you are, how many transitions, and challenges in your life you have forged through and triumphed over. You know of the strength of the polar bear and are convinced in this moment of your strength as well. As you meditate on this, all harmful thoughts that do not serve you are allowed to escape into the night air. Take the time to appreciate the gentle shift in your energy, from just a few minutes ago. How peaceful and calm your mind is now.

Deep within, you feel a grounded stillness – calm at ease. A warm glow of appreciation surrounds you for the bucolic beauty that surrounds you on this journey. You have stopped for a while, but you only now notice, allowing yourself to savor this moment. You feel warm – almost too warm even, and it is all you can do to break out into joyous laughter. Peace surrounds you. Peace encloses you. You are wrapped snuggly in this peace.

You feel the soft fabric of your scarf tickle your face as you continue in the serenity of this night. You inhale the fresh air and cock your ear for any sounds. There are no sounds. It is still and calm in the world tonight. You remember your distant companion, the polar bear, and look up, but he is no longer there. You feel a sense of relief, this solitude is something you have been seeking, and here it is – all for you right now. The air so clean and fresh makes you feel so festive as you inhale and exhale.

You feel the cold wind shifting against your face, and you decide that rather than return to your home, you will continue this invigorating walk for a while. Your lungs fill with the cold air, and you are compelled to run and dance along the way. You focus all of your energy on this mind-tingling energy of being alive, of being present to witness that. you smile in gratitude that this is all yours right now. Laughter escapes your snow-kissed lips, almost shattering the silence. You realize that you could do anything here- you could lay against the down to feel the snow against you, and you could dance and run around in circles.

You are ready to head home now, feeling fulfilled as tiredness takes over. Your body suddenly feels heavy and ready to let go. Your mind counts the steps as you go up to your room. One, two, three, four, five – you turn the knob of your room. There, you take off your winter layers and let your cool toes find warmth within your plush slippers. You sink into your bed, and there you drift away to dreamland where you dream of friendly, companionable polar bears.

SEALS

Fall asleep in this story as you dive under the deep waters of serenity. Like being under a thick blanket, there is a stillness, a solitude that offers you distance from the madness and noise of your waking life. You may go deeper and deeper into this aquatic escape where peace is as abundant as the water itself. There is no room for anything but self-love, self-care, and the nourishing of your body and mind and spirit here before you drift to sleep.

Burrow under the sheets for restoration and a good night's sleep for every night for the rest of your life. Use this time too, with your mind embellish so that these words may take you wherever you want to go. And as you read, you may let go of yourself and fall into sleep. Get comfortable in your bed as you sink deeper and deeper down as you inhale like the crest of a wave.

Notice the feeling of hydration in your own body right now and pay attention to the gentle flow of your life force so that the ocean feels welcoming as it beckons to you. You may visualize the flapping of the waves and the feeling of your feet stepping upon the metallic blue of the ocean's sandy shores. Above you, it is a starry, starry night, and the sky is a cooling shade of velvet black.

The salty seashore reaches your toes as the waves crash again and again over your feet. You realize that this moment, like many other moments in our lives, is only temporary. This place is for tranquillity, and in this moment, you feel a distinct peace so real you feel you could trap it in a bottle. Beyond you, a family of seals play ons hore, and you watch the water glisten on their bodies as they move one, two, three in ocean-like movements.

You pocket this sliver of time as a memory you will remember even in your waking moments. You are entranced by the black of the night, and soon, your eyes begin to droop as you allow the soft sounds of the ocean waves carry you to sleep.

Chapter Three:
Stories Of The Jungle

TROPICAL RAIN FOREST

Nested within a forest, a composition of beautiful scenery, exquisite sounds, and an array of beauty was the habituation of a group of people. People bound by love, connected by blood, and lived based on trust. They can be considered and be said to be living off the grid, completely far from everyone, on the outskirts and away from modern civilization. Choosing to live incommunicado and finding solace in the arms of nature. Tracing the steps back to their primordial roots, they dined and wined with the forces of nature. They lived their lives to the fullest, avoiding the daily grind, the hustle and bustle of the metropolis, the pollution of the urban centers, and the noise of residential areas. The world in the forest is one that is peaceful, indirect contact with nature. And environment where there was an abundance of everything one ever needed. A compendium of symphonies can be heard by day, while soothing, relaxing tones can be heard at night.

The forest, a place of humble abode, a place where one can hear his or her thoughts explicitly. In the middle of all this peace, there dwelled two of the world's most notorious and deviant minds.

They devised a plan to steal the most precious thing belonging to all the forests of the world, the eye of the panther. The eye of the panther is very similar to the heart of any living thing, the life-giving organ, the organ that ensures the continuity of life. The eye of the panther would be expected to be a huge piece of gold, shaped into a ball. Rather, it is a blue-colored jewel with two distinct lines coming from the top to the bottom of it. On it was inscribed the name of the goddess of the forests. Her name no one knew, but often time, prayer and offerings were offered in honor of her. Without the eye of the panther in its rightful position, everything would be in a state... A state no one ever wished would come.

However, these two despite knowing they weren't meant to even conceive such an idea in their hearts at first went to the heart of the jungle, through the streams and the oceans, down the cliffs and around the valleys, riding the waves and flowing along the treacherous rapids plucked out the forest's jewel. They literally removed the heart of the jungle. The life-giving force that was encapsulated in the blue jewel in the eye of the panther, which was located on the ridge of Olympia, had been removed.

They turned the forest to a flaming region; it was as though an apocalypse had begun. Lightning and thunder, earthquakes and tremors, fire and brimstone rained down on the forests of the world. The goddess had unleashed her wrath as her heart had been stolen by some miscreants. Rains seized, and the droughts rolled in majestically. The grains of the fields tuned to ash, and smoke plummeted from within. Jaayla and Markel had done evil. They had awoken the fury of the goddess.

Sipping on coconut juice and enjoying themselves, the two men discussed and rejoiced about the havoc they had caused over the world. They joked and laughed about how they should be recognized as world powers since they held the key to putting an end to the world's misery.

Peace had seized all over the world, and a worldwide manhunt began for the two most wanted criminals in the universe at that time. The forest, which has always been known for its grilling rigidities even without the present chaos and disasters, it's unpredictable, volatile, and dangerous nature has now made everywhere inhabitable, and many people fled to the seas for comfort, with the Sea becoming a haven for people.

A haven that only spans over a particular region and has jurisdiction only within a specific region. It is not an international standard for safety. So if any inhabitants of the safe-haven now the seas should step out, such individuals would be left to face and deal with the impulses and problems that the goddess fires at such person.

This was the case for the two miscreants, Jaayla and Markel, after being drunk with wine and under the influence. They stepped out of their haven, they wanted to see and feel what the new world felt like. Wanting to know what was on the other side of the curtain of peace the experienced in their place of abode, they wanted to explore. Go far, explore the treacherous depths of the world, give meaning to all her dimensions. Little did they know that their past would catch up to them so fast. The grievous thing they had done in times past were just at their heels.

All the havoc caused to nature, the deforestation, global warming, river pollutions, famines, drought, the ravaging plagues, and all evils and putting safe havens, the very element that house nature completely and in her true form all around the globe at risk of extinction. So with these, people who were already on a manhunt for them, found and caught them in the act as they were about robbing another precious jewel.

Upon catching them, they were taken to court, made to present the eye of the panther, and all other precious jewels which were illegally in their possession. So many things was discovered, and they were rightly tried and sentenced to the dungeons of Zeus.

The fruits of our labor of the world soldiers were soon seen. The green leaves of the forests return to their original state, animals exclaiming loudly under the canopy of the trees. We can see a rejuvenation of life in the forest.

How good is the feeling of restoration? The jewel was restored by Amazonia, the leader of the 12Th battalion of conservationists. Equilibrium was reset, and balance is once again restored to the environment. The forest is back on her feet, a safe haven for all.

RIVERS

So many beauties exist in this world of ours, so many things that can bring joy to individuals and organisms living and co-habiting on the surface of the earth. We have several mountains, plateaus, hills, ridges, oceans, and seas. But one that catches the attention strikingly is the river called emerald. Her beauty, the energy, the majesty, and the grace all encapsulated in one body of water, finding her course through the land with confidence.

Roaring and snaking around the hills was the mighty and great river emerald. It was majestic as it was the singular river that gave birth to so many tributaries and also wet the environment. At its peak, her voice can be heard miles away, thrashing and banging into the sides of the rocks that are in her way.

Emerald had a sparkle when called to life could be seen in her. She carried various lives, and so many things depended on River emerald, without her is drought, without her spamming, without her the low Green and beautiful flowers in the valleys would be absent. She was a force to be reckoned with, the great on mighty real.

But soon disaster hits, there is chaos in the land. River emerald is drying up, the rains were held back, the sun increased its intensity, and nothing seemed to be working well. The Waters of the deep was refraining while the oceans were silent. Lush greens of the valleys, the beautiful flowers the majestic trees all became like a skeletal frame of a starved mouse.

The tributaries dried up, emerald grew quiet, farming ceased, and famine took over. Nothing seemed to be in equilibrium; it was as though the world had shifted off its axis, and Earth had been shaken to her very foundation. But as we all know or have experienced time to time, no bad situation lasts forever. Darkness only is for a while; the sun has its appointed time to rise. The moon her time to glow and the stars their time to shine. A friend will always come to our aid. A family will have compassion and run to our rescue. So was the case for emerald. Her glow was missed, her roars cherished, the valleys grew too silent, and the groaning of people excited.

A huge god stooped to meet river emerald. The river, once mighty, pushing through every crevice and opening, now meandered through the sand and dreamt of the sea. The god spoke to her with the voice of the ancients — —Let me help you roar again.‖ The god made it rain endlessly for time. Minutes turned into hours, hours turned into days, days into weeks, and weeks into months till the very last cloud was gone. The river swelled and gained her pride back. But along with the clouds, the god lost his voice.

Months then rolled by. Now the summer scorched. The sun relentlessly beat the river, dried up the deep, and left the hungry sand with no choice but to eat up the dwindling river.

The river didn‘t die, though, a very resilient river. Silently, she found her way and flowed beneath the sand, beneath the rocky mounds, on which she unleashed her fury in past times, in and out of caves where bats slept all day. She birthed millions of ferns, figs, and shrubs that thrived in the dark. The god didn‘t know what to do concerning the issue at hand. But being a very wise god and one desperate to save this river that had captured his heart, he left his throne behind and broke off the crown of a huge iceberg and sent the largest glacier down. It rained ice! The glacier coming down from a height that is indescribable, formed a furious stream. A stream that was never going to be at the mercies of the sun, the scorching heat produced by the sun, or any other force of nature that can threaten her existence.

The glacier could be seen plummeting down with only one purpose; rejuvenation. And it sure did accomplish the purpose for which it was sent.

Nourished forever, the river flourished forever. She flooded the caves with power, wet the valleys with perfection, and restored beauty and balance, the plains were made whole again. She also met the faraway sea. Mangrove forests soon lined her banks. Balance was restored back to the land. River emerald‘s smile every time the sun was overhead was always a sight to behold.

After all the help the god proffered, he went back to his humble abode and smiled constantly as he saw something great that he had been able to achieve. He saw hope, he saw joy, and that made him happy. Also, as a token of appreciation to the god, emerald always gives a tenth of all life in her to the god's court. Fishes, eels, crabs, amongst other things.

PARROTS ECHOED

Chirp! Chirp! The birds sang, their sounds bounced off the walls, echoing with such symphony and grace. Effortless in capturing the attention of the onlookers and drawing them closer. I listened to the blend of sounds and the delivery of such. The sounds spoke to me, sent a message into the depths of my soul, resonating within me, and stirring up passion and excellence. Their echoes soothing and relieving. Also, it was backed with the very essence that eased my stress.

Oh! How splendid these parrots looked, the elegant patterns that spoke with depth. How majestic they are in their own little way. But paying more rapt attention, I could see that the echoes were as a result of a parrot being stuck in a situation, frantically trying to rescue and help one of its own. I watched from a distance, from the window of my little hut on the other end of the jungle. The songs seemed to be fading in and out. Then as I took a deeper look, I saw a sight that made me smile.

A spotted animal, which walked with ease and ran faster than any other animal in the kingdom had witnessed the crimes of one of the tyrannical snakes in the kingdom first hand, was set to stand before the whole jungle as a witness. But he was just a toddler, a young one. Due to the peculiarity and sensitivity of the case, she had to be transported in the best animal convoy ever to where happened to be a fort Knox room. A room that was completely sealed and no slithering, crawling, gnarling, or roaring animal could get into. Moreover, the location is unknown to any soul in the jungle except the top leaders. From the room, a live message was to be broadcast straight to the congress hall. This was done in order to protect the high priced witness. I saw a great number of guard dogs, well-trained horses, and an army of ostriches all for the purpose of protecting —the package.‖   She was very beautiful, majestic, and well looking.

So, the standard procedure is that an animal brings the equipment to be used for the live feed. The elegant couriers in past times are not known by the inhabitants. But we know the animal always happens to be a fast, strong muscular animal, one that would be able to maneuver his way through the jungle with minimal interruptions. The animal that is never challenged to a race, the whispers on the streets said. Their maneuvering skills are top-notch, the accuracy, none can beat, even the beauty, only a few can stand up to it. But little did anyone know amongst the general populace of the jungle that the convoy had been compromised. ADT 1 (Animal Delta Team 1) had been compromised.

On getting to the Haven, ‒Fort Knox,‖ the place for the live transmission, one of the ostrich, the head of the whole operations checked in the courier who brought in the equipment for the broadcast. After the courier was checked and the package delivered, one of the security escorts was asked to lead her out, but upon reaching the door, the fellow pushed the courier into another room. She was searched, and all means by which she could communicate with other animals were seized immediately. She protested, what are you doing? She asked, but she was shot 9 different times. She collapsed to the floor, consequently, the setup for the broadcast is complete, and the process initiated.

The key was slotted into the hole, and the connection was established. Immediately, like lightning and thunder, a green-colored gas filled up the whole room. The gas is called ENXOME. Enxome happens to be a naturally occurring gas in the animal kingdom. A liquid extracted from the leaves and the stalk of the kwayakwaya tree. It is then changed to the gaseous state. The gas was released, and it always has the same effect on everyone, like cyanide to humans. But this has a different effect; it puts them straight into a comatose state. Reason why the gas is usually kept in vaults hidden in the mountains with the elders being the ones to possess the copy of the map per time. The rogue cop then proceeded to get a gas mask to escape since he presumed that everyone in the room was already in the induced comatose state. But little did he know the courier had a kamanon, and this prevented the penetration of the bullets into the heart.

The courier stood up and clawed at the ostrich's face. Stomping and leaving a permanent indentation on the beak. But all this was the beginning of the whole story. Due to compassion, the courier grabbed the witness on his way out. The witness who happened to be in shock due to the fast-paced cataclysmic events that surrounded him momentarily did not want to follow the courier. The courier grabbed him again and said, ‒let's leave! Your life is in danger, and if you do not leave now, something else might happen. The whole team has been compromised, and I'm the only one you can trust.‖

A pure soul, one filled with compassion she backed him, and they flew.

But as they were about exiting the already compromised area, a troop of men was seen opening the gate, and their motives were well written on their faces. Hunt them down, we saw. A full-blown attempted murder was in process.

Wow, what a wonderful story! My name is Adler, a parrot, and my owner has taught me a wide variety of words, phrases. And due to my well-developed brain, I've been able to write books of my own. Surprising right? Yup! Yup!! Yup!!! I also have a parrot voice, so... you can imagine how I'm talking also!

Skrrrrrrrrrrrrrrrrrrrrrrrrrrrrrrrrrrrrrrrrrrrrrrrrrrrrrrrrrrrrrrrrrrrrrrrrrrrrrrrrrrr!

You'll be surprised how much I know about you humans as well. Bye!

BIG TREES

Many years ago, Bambi always thought Himself to be the best because only Him and just a few others had that unique feature that attracted human beings and brought a lot of attention. He would mockingly tell Shifa to add more weight because He was too slim, so he might die soon. —You're a man and men ought to be bigger than this, slim‖ He would always ring daily in his head. At first, Shifa always laughed about it, but when he saw that his brothers were beginning to get bothered and saddened by the mockful assertions, Bambi made to all of them, he cried and condemned himself for being so slim yet so tall. —No one comes close; I rarely get any attention from anyone. Am I really that bad?‖ went through his mind daily. He always blamed the gods for allowing him to have such exquisite height but so bony, hence looking so unattractive.

Many times, because of how He and his family appeared, one of his brothers had been taken away captive to be used in forced labor somewhere unknown to the rest of them. Not only that, his brother, his younger sister, and mum, had to undergo such a difficult situation as well. Therefore, everyone lived in fear of when they would be kidnapped, taken away from their loved ones. So, for Shifa's family, every day was a day they were expecting to be taken away from their loved ones.

Such a life of negative expectations and fear! And Bambi, who on the other end kept reminding him of this predicament, didn't make the matter better at all.

Bambi was a tall, wide, and full green tree that always provided shades for people from sun and rain while Shifa was very tall but was not wide enough to provide any shades for humans.

What the trees used to compete with one another was the amount of attention they got from humans, and so imagine how Shifa and his family always felt all day, all week, all month and all year long! They simply never stood a chance to be outstanding among the trees because virtually no humans came close.

In fact; many times, the government would order that trees of such nature as Shifa be cut down for their industrial use. So, all the wide and tall trees which were referred to as the big trees had all it took; they attracted human attention while the tall and slim trees attracted more eyes of people looking to fell trees for various purposes.

Over the months, Shifa seemed to be among the last survivors. He lived a life of sorrow because he could not predict what would happen tomorrow and could not become like Bambi overnight.

Shifa had made so many prayers such that the gods finally could not stand the bitterness of his heart and for his remaining family. The gods decided to react in a way that would spur equilibrium.

Early the next day, Bambi noticed Shifa looking very different. Shifa was all of a sudden looking as full as the rest.

Obviously, Shifa had just been groomed by the gods, and not only did Shifa escape death, she also attracted much more attention from humans. Therefore, till date, the bambi and Shifa never relate because although Shifa is an open hearted beauty, Bambi did not like the god's idea of making tall and slim trees wide. He did not want so many people to be referred to as big trees. However, having no control over the situation, he struggled for weeks to accept it but later got to.

The most difficult times were when He had to watch his regular visitors stare at Him and then walk right past to Shifa and his family.

Shifa, however, was always good from the onset and never mocked Bambi, knowing and coming to agree that the sky is large enough for everyone to fly!

TRIBU

—Good morning class, we have two new students joining us today,‖ said Mrs. Brad as the students of Hazal college made a noise in their classroom.

–Hi, my name is stresan, I love to put people on the edge and many times I am inconsiderate, but we just might get along. I'm just being honest about how I am!‖ Said the first new student who got booed by the whole class when he gave such an introduction. –Put people on the edge? Inconsiderate? You can't stay in our class then!‖ murmured the students all over the large spaced class, which had just 20 tables and chairs for students studying metaphysics.

After the little uproar Stresan had caused, the second student was asked to introduce herself. It was so obvious she was more of a quiet, calm person. Sweetly, she said, —I'm Yogen, it's nice to meet you, everyone, you'd have delight knowing me better, trust me.‖ Everyone cheered, especially because of that innocent kind of smile she had.

Hazal college was barely five years old existent, so each course had just a little number of students available, and one trend that was noticeable among the students was only new students got along with each other.

One time, a red hair called Steve joined in and actually kept walking alone until a new class member came along six months later. The remaining classmates already created unbreakable groups that they just always frowned at receiving anyone new. The whole students in the school were patterned like that, so if anyone came, they decided to be hostile and just keep to their —groups,‖ that person would have to wait for another newbie student or the person was lucky if a student was to join in at the same time.

This was the case of Stresan and Yogen. Even though Yogen would have preferred to have a female friend, stresan was Male, and she just had to get used to that, so she doesn't walk alone all her years in college.

At lunchtime, Stresan approached Yogen and started a conversation. —Hi,‖ he said, admiring how cute she was. -Hello, can we make proper introductions now, not all that bulldog stuff you said in the class‖ Yogen replied, and Stresan immediately started laughing. –Okay, fine, I am stresan, everyone calls me stress because I actually like to get people on the edge and leave them tired every time I meet them.‖ Stresan said. Yogen looked at the expression on his face and seeing that He actually was not smiling, knew that he was not joking about the introduction. Although she wondered but she just introduced herself in like manner as He did.

—I'm yogen, widely called Yoga, I help people have a touch with their inner mind, and I aid relaxation every time.‖

—Really!‖ Stresan said, —That's like the direct opposite of me, I definitely want to know you better.‖ Yogen replied, —we would know each other better; the next class seems to be canceled, so I actually don't mind talking right now, so tell me all about you!‖

They smiled at each other and sipped some water just before the conversation continued.

—My real name is Stress Nosleep, but because of how people hated me, I had to start calling myself Stresan. I uncontrollably put people under tension, weary them out. Even though I am a normal part of people's lives, many times, I am spoken against by doctors, health workers. People are always advised to get rid of me. I have gone to various schools and tried to make friends but before I know, whoever gets along with me does so for only about two weeks max before they start getting strict advises to stay off me if they don't want to regret it. That's the kind of life I have lived thus far! I've tried to be in a relationship several times, but all have failed. One time, I dated a girl named Anger, and we seemed to be the worst combination just from the third day of dating! Other girls have just outrightly told me no. Finding someone who gets me and can get other people to love me as well has been my greatest desire for so many years now. How about you, tell me about yourself.‖

—That's a lot to be going on with just one person, I am really sorry about all that you've had to go through. I'm yogen, original name is Yoga Relief. People love me and talk to me when they want to get some physical and health well-being. I teach people wellness all round. Everywhere I go, I get introduced, I see people flocking all around me trying to say hi and ask if we could be friends. Truth is I am actually a relief to people who are worked up or have undergone a lot of activities and just need to chill out. I have different ways I do this. Primarily, I teach them to relax their body, relax their mind, understand how their mind works, develop a connection between their body and mind and how to release emotional energy. I teach them various ways they can achieve this. Then, I encourage them to practice all I have thought as often as they can, and because my prescriptions have always worked, more people flock around me and want to talk to me. So, the truth is I can't really relate with how your life has been because mine has been the direct opposite. But, I do think we would be best of friends, we complement one another, and your weakness is my strength. Whatcha think?ǀ

Stresan was speechless; he had never heard or seen someone as delightful as Yogen. He already liked her! He felt there was a connection he had with her that he had never had with anyone. He thought that if perhaps over time he gets her to date him and then marries him, even if people shut him out, his wife would be there to help him get relieved of all that hurt. And oh well, when people shut Him out, He could just as well introduce his wife to them and in that way get to be loved by them since he gave them an easy way out.

Stresan looked forward to spending more time with Yogen. —If only I get her to be mine, then I myself would have a way to relieve myself when I feel bad because of how people treat me.ǁ

While he was lost in his thoughts, Yogen told him it was time for their next class. So, the two new friends picked up their bags and went for their class.

MONKEYS

—I don't know if I really want to go on this trip, I'd just rather stay home and prepare for dad's birthday.‖ Said Charlotte, the daughter of Mr. Sarfs, the wealthiest man in Florida.

—That's a silly excuse, party planners are on the edge for that already. Come on girl, let's go. Remember, it's our last year here, spending any extracurricular time with our friends and classmates wouldn't be bad.‖ Anna persuasively told her best friend since kindergarten.

The medal high school had a camping trip for the finalists, and this especially was a time for various parents and guardians to show off their wealth starting from the Parent-teacher forum meetings to the sports day and then finally to the camp facilities sponsorship.

Charlotte Sarfs's dad was a billionaire, highly reputable for his four-star hotels in strategic places in Florida. Her dad was one to show off his wealth and let everyone know He was proud of his daughter. On the other hand, Charlotte was an indoor kind of person, even though she had all she needed provided for her, she was very weird and loved to keep to herself. Everyone complained about how unpredictable she always was; especially in her reactions, her sense of humor, you just cannot say how she would react to certain things, for this reason, Anna, her best friend, was the only one who stuck around her.

Many students tried to be close to her because of her dad's status, but when they saw she really wasn't that kind of a spoilt brat, show off money kind of fellow, they had rethinks.

One thing that was very noticeable about her was her love for animals. Oh, Charlotte could stay in her room with her dog all day and scarcely speak to any human; she was getting better as she advanced in age anyway. When she was a child, she hated anyone carrying her or too many people around. What a strange little girl she was!

Over the weeks, when the camp trip was announced, she didn't even give it any thoughts; she already made up her mind not to be involved in such activities, more especially since she wasn't allowed to bring her dog because it was a time of human bonding as the principal said. That on its own was a double no for her! Charlotte to be separated from her dog? From her dear Max? No way!

Anna didn't let her be until she agreed to join in for the trip. —You are my best friend, I need you there,‖ she constantly said until she finally got Charlotte to reluctantly agree. —Since you have debunked all my excuses, fine then, I would come, only if you help me pack, I'm lazy.‖ —Of course!!!!,‖ screamed excited Anna. Finally, she got her best friend to agree.

A few days down the line, the morning of the day the medal finalists was to set out finally came. Anna had slept over at Charlotte's and was so excited. The girls got ready and got to school to join the bus, which was going quite some miles away to a resort center.

At about 1 pm, the bus arrived at Malago resort center. Everyone was so excited except Charlotte; she couldn't wait to be given their room keys so she would disappear from everyone's presence. Just as her dream finally came to pass, while she passed by in the lobby, she saw her greatest weakness stare at her from some miles away. It was an animal! Charlotte took steps back to see what animal it was exactly as she leaped for joy within. It was a monkey! —This wouldn't be as bad as I thought, you know.‖ She thought to herself. Just when she was very close to having a closer view of the monkey, she saw the resort center workers come in a haste to take the monkey away, they said the monkeys stayed at the other end of the compound but that Lala which was the monkey's name sort of escaped. Charlotte and the monkey had jammed eyes, and the monkey was already stretching her hands to shake Charlotte. There was no way she would allow them take her back!

As expected, Charlotte pleaded with the workers to please allow the monkey to stay with her the three days they would be guests at their resort center. They disagreed over and over, but after so many pleas and so much convincing, they grudgingly agreed. —You know this is not allowed legally, right?‖ They asked, but she said, —I promise nothing would go wrong.‖

The workers knew they had to keep it a secret from the director who might not notice unless told, so they all agreed to do so.

Just as guessed, everywhere Chatlotte went, her new made friend Lala went with her. Even though Charlotte knew about how it was risky having a monkey as a pet and all that restriction, she couldn't resist Lala. This particular one seemed really calm to her, —what could she possibly do wrong?‖ —Just look at this gorgeous albino‖ constantly ran through her mind, and in three days, she got attached to Lala as a mother gets attached to her child over months.

She had already been telling Anna how she was going to ask to buy Lala to take back home. But Anna, who knew much about animal laws, kept telling her the reality which of course she didn't want to agree to. The truth remained that Lala was a monkey, and these animals are wild and cannot be made domestic pets, but Lala just felt something could be done for her to keep it.

She was well aware of the kind of habitat that they would rather be in, and she was sure her dad could easily ask for that to be built. Rather slowly, the three days finally were spent, and the bus was to leave on the evening of the third day. Knowing the possibility of Lala being dropped, Charlotte went to the director's office early enough in the afternoon and laid out her desires not only putting the workers in trouble because they had actually let a monkey stay in a guest's custody but putting the director off guard as well because it simply wasn't the right time to bring up such —impossible‖ matters.

—First of all, it is banned according to the law; monkeys cannot be domesticated, and then this is the only albino monkey left in this area, there's no way the authority would let her go, no matter what happens. So, young lady quit bothering me.‖ He said. —Do you know whose daughter I am? I am the daughter to Mr. Sarfs! My dad would provide the perfect habitat, every precaution needed to be taken, just please let her go‖ pleaded Charlotte, but when it was obvious, her desires won't be met, she left his office greatly sorrowful, and just about twenty minutes later some of the workers came to take Lala back.

Of course, Charlotte was broken, but she was not one to pour out her emotions so easily. The bus left at about 4:15, and the memories of her moments with Lala stuck on her mind all through.

On getting to school, the next Monday, a finalist had to volunteer to talk to the whole school about their experience at the camp trip. Charlotte raised her hand tall, and of course, everyone was astonished. —What would she possibly say?‖ they all wondered.

—I know for humans' safety, many rules are laid out, but I feel there should always be an exception. Lala was sweet, reasonable, and in no way can cause harm or detrimental effects in a home. I know monkeys are wild, but I wish they would have just given it another thought...‖ Charlotte said and in the middle started sobbing.

The whole students were astonished and felt empathetic because of her passion, while some just felt —all rich kids get spoilt, some just do really stupid things, crying for a monkey barely met three days?‖

Well, one thing was certain, if monkeys actually have emotions, then Lala was definitely as hurt as Charlotte was!

Chapter Four:
Stories of Tropical Islands

ATOLLO

Hello there, my name is John. I used to be a very stressed out person. Ever since the age of nine, my parents decided that I had a multiple personality disorder. They were saying that because I was always moody and tired. It seemed as though something or someone else might have been living inside of me. Little did they know that this was because they were separated. The separation really stressed me out and made me create someone to protect myself from the stress caused by it. However, recently, it had gotten worse now. I am twenty-two years old, in college, and studying for my master's degree in physics.

Yes, it is the time of the year when I have to prepare for my exams. This year was a particularly stressful year for me, especially with the lecturers demanding short deadlines and lots of assignments. This really got me stressed. I was so stressed that I couldn't even sleep at all. Eventually, I was beginning to show signs of insomnia as my stress levels got extremely high. Ultimately, my diverse personalities kicked in. One of my personalities shows evidence of madness while the other shows evidence of anger then one day, my friend, Jane, got really concerned about my multiple personalities resulting from my stress levels, and she suggested I sought help. To do this, I had to go very far, and that's where I met a meditation teacher on a tropical island in the Maldives. The name of the island was Atollo.

This island was very beautiful, and the wind blew all so soft and made me feel life and the reinvigorating aspects of life. The sea shore's water redirected the sun's extraordinary glare at me and is compelled to turn away towards an ever-growing vine jungle, trees, and murkiness. The trees making an overhang of the wilderness concealing what lies underneath. There is no dense of a creepy-crawly, winged animal or reptile, no call of a human voice, just the consistent rhythmical lap of the ocean. The sound of the ocean makes him shudder with dread for what could be lying in the wilderness.

As I stroll through the wilderness, my mental fortitude is raised by the light, which streams through the covering illuminating the wonders of the wilderness and I stopped to smell the blossoms and look at things, which I never thought existed.

I prevent myself from getting occupied and focus on my reason for coming here. I cleared my path through the wilderness, chopping down vines and leaves in my way, attempting to discover a conclusion to this unending wilderness. Similarly, as I was going to abandon my mission, I saw a light not very far up ahead and race for it.

In the evenings, you would see the trees move rhythmically as though the wind was playing a musical tune to them. They danced all so easily and made me also want to dance. And as I continued staring at the beauty of this place, I met the meditation teacher, who then gave me something very simple to do to calm my stress. It was then I realized that the solution to all of life's troubles lies in the simple things of life. The most important things in life are the basic things. He said that every evening, I should go for a walk around the island. He said I should do this every evening around 9:30 for about 3 hours.

Seeing that I work majorly at night, it was quite easy for me to do. So, as I walked around the island and listened to the beautiful gems of the wind, my mind became much calmer, and I became much more mindful.

Doing this the first night, I assumed that I slept more peacefully because I was tired from walking around the island. I continued the next day and the day after and the day after that and then I realized I wasn't tired, I was actually just calm and relaxed from moving around in a calm environment.

I decide to do one more activity. The next time I went, I took my pocket knife along with me on my now regular evening strolls, and I decided to carve and write songs and poems into the trees this was very relaxing. It helped me realize that the little things of life, the things that we seemingly ignore, the beauty of the trees, the wonder of the traffic, the colors of humanity, and things like this. I did this much more regularly, and eventually, my stress levels became very low.

This, new routine, did not only reduce my stress levels but also helped to satisfy my multiple personalities. Each personality came out but was never in a bad mood. They were all happy and satisfied.

Going back to college, I decided to carry out this activity continually. Every evening, by 9:00 pm, I would go to the college fountain and take a stroll imagining myself still in the Atollo island. This tropical island was it for me, it made me very relaxed, and sleep was now much easier to come across.

MY SUMMER WITH PALMS

I remembered when daddy came in with the news about our vacation for the summer. He had prepared our minds so much that we anticipated the travel, as though it was possible to travel ahead of time. We still had 3weeks before the breaks. Our hearts were so fixed on the mountain town of Salento in Central Columbia.

We have had stories about how nature screams in Cocora valley. From the giant palm trees to the hummingbirds and streams that flow through the jungle. A lovely sight to behold.

Daddy told us stories about the memories he had shared with his friends in his high school days when they went for an excursion. He always speaks with this very wild smile on his lips as he says, ‚'these stories are ever fresh like it was yesterday". Daddy was never given opportunities to always go a distance from his parents. When he was in school, he was always under a close watch of his teachers and students rarely played with him because of his health conditions. When his Geography teacher spoke about this excursion, he had seen it as an opportunity to do things he was never opportune to do. He had made plans with his teacher who loves and has always had compassion for him to do anything possible to go on this trip. He had made plans with friends on how they were going to have fun like it was going to be his last. Daddy said he had actually thought that these days might actually be his last because he had always lived with the fear that if he ever stayed far from his parents for days, he might never survive it. He swore to himself that if these days were going to be his last days, he must make it his best last.

Daddy had kept to the promise he had made to himself. He went hiking with friends, had baths on several occasions with friends on the streams. He almost drowned on his first attempt when he dived into the water without any precautions.

Not long now, the long-awaited day is now. We all set out for our summer trip. We sang together, ate together, it was a long trip from QqQqQq to Salento Columbia. It was as though the weather had changed. I can feel the cool breeze. Indeed the sight was one to behold. It feels like we were being featured in the movies. I have never seen trees as tall as this, only in the movies.

The Palms looked evergreen, ever fresh, a beauty to behold. I couldn't take my eyes off it. How they rise triumphantly regardless of what was around them confident in their roots to grow as tall as they are with its peaceful nature as it bends towards the direction of the winds. No wonder the Palms symbolizes great strength, victory, and peace.

We had so much fun at the stream that cool evening, but I barely took my eyes away from the beauty of these palms and the lessons I have learned. I can't wait to share this with my friends, so I nicknamed myself as PALMS.

THE BLUE OCEAN

There are days that seem like it will never be over. Days where it seems like your entire life will end, as every activity done, takes a toll on you, from your annoying boss to some annoying customers.

This has been my daily routine. My nights are no different. My heart burns from the excessive caffeine I take to keep me on the job. Life is not as easy as I thought it would be. I had my entire life planned out with set goals and achievements to acquire. I always strive for the best, but the best never comes easy at all.

Gone are the days when you had someone do all the house chores, prepare your breakfast, and just have you wake up like a queen to the tables. Being an adult is not as easy as I thought. Now I yearn for the days before the ocean, with a cool breeze and the singing waves, the flip flop sound as dolphins delve from one point to the other. Just that sanity, where my head can clear out from all these emotional drama and affairs of life.

These thoughts ran through my head as I walk through the hospital lobby. My youngest son has been diagnosed with cancer of the lungs; we were told he had a few months to live.

Few minutes later, I was in Kanye's ward. His bed was close to the window, where he actually takes a view when he feels like. He basically spends a major part of his day doing that. Today was no different as I met him on his regular wheelchair beside this window; he was being attended to by his nurse.

Kanye is a killer for nature's gentle touch. He is either looking out the window or reading his books. They were always books that talk about nature. Kanye would always ask, Mama, why don't we have a house around an ocean? Have you ever seen a dolphin before? Why is the wind around the ocean cooler than that we have here? Do oceans ever get tired of ever-flowing? Do oceans die? Can they ever dry up?

He would always say, -I want to be like the ocean, when can I see one?"

Lost in my thoughts I heard him call _'mummy."

‚'Your eyes are heavy" he said.

Can I be your Blue Ocean?

I looked deep into his blue eyes. It reminds me of a rhyme from a page in his book. I picked him up and lay him on his bed as he sat up straight, he rests his back on the soft and gentle pillow, picked up his book and searched for that page. He reads;

I hear you call from upon the waters; my heart skips as your voice roars as that of the waves of the ocean. I see your eyes, so blue worthy to look upon. My heavy heart race would need your gentle touch to calm.

My feet are wobbling, and my body is calling. My nights are scary, my eyes are teary and dreary. I need your touch to help calm my storm.

But when my heart rise like the ocean rise, who will calm this storm?

The gentle wind hovers as it spoke, I can't but hear peace. So I'm calm as I rest in its embrace.

As he read, I lay my head beside him as I pictured every word he said and beyond. I could see us holding hands, as Kanye ran towards the ocean just some feet away, he laughed as hard as he placed his feet on the shore. The waves came and splashed the waters on him. For once, I saw my Kanye differently, not as the dying child, but one full of life. Somehow I found peace. Indeed you are my Ocean.

Chapter Five:
Other Stories

THREE SIMPLE RULES

A long time ago in Thailand, there was a wealthy man. His name was Chalong. He was a rich man. However, he needed more wealth, more cash.

One day he was strolling in his nursery. He saw an unusual fledgling in a hedge. It was little. In any case, it had wonderful and beautiful highlights. Its voice was likewise lovely. Chalong had never observed such a winged creature in his life. He gradually went close to the bramble inconspicuous. He got the bird. Now, the fledgling started to talk.

—Why have you gotten me?‖ the feathered creature inquired.

—I need to bring in cash. I can sell you for a major sum,‖ answered Chalong.

—In any case, you are now rich. For what reason do you need more?‖ asked the winged animal.

—Since I need to get more extravagant and more extravagant,‖ answered Chalong.

—Be that as it may, don't fantasy about bringing in cash through me!‖ said the feathered creature. It further included, —You can not sell me. Nobody will get me, because, in detainment, I lose my magnificence and my sweet voice.‖ Then it gradually transformed into a dark winged creature.

The excellent highlights were currently resembling the plumes of a crow.

Chalong, any expectations of bringing in cash, were broken. He said irately, —I will slaughter you, and I will eat your meat.‖

—Eat me! I am so little. You won't get any meat out of me,‖ answered the winged creature.

Chalong couldn't reply. The fledgling at that point recommended, —All around set me free. Consequently, I will show you three simple; however, helpful principles.‖

—What is the use of the principles? I just need cash,‖ said Chalong. He was bothered.

—Be that as it may, these principles can benefit you incredibly,‖ said the flying creature.

—Benefit me! Truly? At that point, I will liberate you. How might I confide in you? You may take off,‖ said Chalong.

—I give you my word. What's more, I generally keep my words,‖ said the flying creature.

Chalong needed to take a risk. He released the feathered creature. It flew up at once. At that point, it sat on the part of a tree. Its shading began evolving. It became wonderful once more.

Chalong asked, —Now, show me the principles.‖

—Unquestionably,‖ said the winged animal.

At that point, it stated, —The main principle is Never Believe all that others state. The subsequent principle is Never tragic about something you don't have. The third principle is Never discard what you have in your grasp.‖

—Your senseless feathered creature,‖ yelled Chalong. What's more, he included, —These three guidelines are known to each one. You have tricked me.‖

The winged animal stated, —Chalong, simply plunk down for some time. Consider every one of your activities today. You had me in your grasp, yet you released me (discharged me). You accepted all that I said. Also, you are dismal about not having me. The principles are simple. In any case, you never tailed them. Presently do you see the estimation of the guidelines?‖ so saying this, the winged animal took off and vanished from his sight.

THE ARROGANT SWANS

In a distant realm, there was a stream. This waterway was home to numerous brilliant swans. The swans invested the greater part of their energy in the banks of the waterway. At regular intervals, the swans would leave a brilliant plume as an expense for using the lake. The fighters of the realm would gather the plumes and store them in the regal treasury.

At some point, a destitute fowl saw the waterway. —The water right now so cool and calming. I will make my home here,‖ thought the fledgling.

When the winged creature settled down close to the stream, the brilliant swans saw her. They came yelling. —This waterway has a place with us. We pay a brilliant quill to the King to use this stream. You can not live here.‖

—I am destitute, siblings. I also will pay the lease. It will be ideal if you give me cover,‖ the fledgling argued. —By what method will you pay the lease? You don't have brilliant quills,‖ said the swans chuckling. They further included –Quit dreaming and leave once.‖ The unassuming winged animal argued commonly. However, the haughty swans drove the winged creature away.

—I will show them a thing or two!‖ said the mortified feathered creature.

She went to the King and stated, -O King! The swans in your stream are discourteous and cruel. I asked for cover, yet they said that they had bought the stream with brilliant plumes.‖

The King was irate with the haughty swans for having offended the destitute fowl. He requested his officers to carry the haughty swans to his court. In a matter of moments, all the brilliant swans were brought to the King's court.

—Do you think the imperial treasury relies on your brilliant plumes? You can not choose who lives by the waterway. Leave the waterway at once, or all of you will be beheaded!‖ yelled the King.

The swans shuddered with dread on hearing the King. They took off never to return. The feathered creature manufactured her home close to the stream and lived there cheerfully until the end of time. The winged animal offered asylum to every other fowl in the waterway.

THE IGNORANT MAN

There was a town in a realm. There was a milkman. His name was Deena. He had fabricated his cottage far away from his town, in the forested areas. He cherished the quietness of the forested areas as opposed to the uproarious air of the town. He lived in his cottage with his two dairy animals. He took care of them well and took appropriate consideration of them. Ordinarily, he took the two dairy animals to a close-by lake to shower them. The two bovines gave more milk.

Deena was a fair man. Even though he was content, on occasion, he would be fretful. -There is such a lot of off-base and evil right now. Is there nobody to direct the individuals?‖ this idea made him pitiful from time to time.

One night, the uninformed man, Deenu was getting back in the wake of selling milk in the town. He saw a holy person sitting under a tree and contemplating. He gradually approached him and trusted that the holy person would open his eyes. He was glad to be with the holy person for quite a while. He chose to hold up there till the holy person opened his eyes.

Sooner or later, the holy person gradually opened his eyes. He was astounded to see a man quietly sitting alongside him.

—What do you need?‖ asked the holy person modestly.

—I need to know what the way to Truth and Piety? Where will I discover Honesty?‖ asked Deena.

The holy person grinned and stated, —Go to the lake close by and ask the fish a similar inquiry. She will offer you the response.‖

At that point, as requested, the oblivious man, Deena went to the close-by lake and posed a similar inquiry to the fish. The fish stated, -O kind man! To start with, present to me some water to drink.‖ Deny was astonished. He stated, —You live in water. However, you, despite everything, need water to drink? How weird!‖

As of now, the fish answered, —You are correct. What's more, that offers you the response to your inquiry also. Truth, Piety, and trustworthiness are inside the core of a man. Be that as it may, being oblivious, he looks for them in the external world. Rather than meandering to a great extent, search inside yourself, and you will discover them.‖

This gave a tremendous fulfillment to Deena. He expressed gratitude toward the fish and strolled home a more astute man. He changed the manner by which he saw this world just like himself. From that day, Deena never felt eager.

He took his best to convey this back rub to the remainder of his kindred individuals. Every one of his companions acknowledged him as their Lord and counseled him to beat their psychological issues. He drove them appropriately.

GRACE AND LOLA

Once upon a time, there was a lord and sovereign, who had a solitary little girl. Her exceptional excellence, sweetness, and insight made her be named Grace. She was her mom's delight. Consistently she had given her an alternate dress, of gold brocade, velvet, or glossy silk; yet she was neither conceited nor bombastic. She used to spend her mornings in the study, and toward the evening, she sat sewing by the sovereign's side. She had, notwithstanding, a lot of play-time, and sweetmeats without end, so she was through and through the most joyful princess alive.

At a similar court was an old youngster named Duchess Grignon, who was the extreme opposite of Grace. Her hair was red hot red, her face fat and spotty, and she had yet one eye. Her mouth was huge to such an extent that you may have figured she could gobble you up, just she had no teeth to do it with; she was also humpbacked and faltering. Obviously, she was unable to support her grotesqueness, and nobody would have disdained her for that, if she had not been of such a disagreeable temper, that she detested everything sweet and lovely, and particularly Grace. She had an excellent assessment of herself also, and when anyone adulated the princess, would state indignantly, —That is an untruth! My little finger merits her entire body.‖

Over time, the sovereign fell ill and died, and her girl was nearly grieved. So was her significant other for a year, and then, he started to comfort himself by chasing. At some point, after a long pursue, he went to a weird mansion, which happened to be that of Duchess Grignon. She, educated regarding his methodology, went out to meet him and got him most consciously. As he was hot with chasing, she brought him into the coolest spot in the royal residence, which was a vaulted cavern, most exquisitely outfitted, where there were 200 barrels masterminded in long columns.

—Madam, are these all yours?‖ asked the ruler.

—Truly, sire, yet I will be generally cheerful if you will agree to taste our wine. Which wine do you like – canary, seclusion, champagne?‖ and she ran over a considerable rundown, out of which his greatness settled on his decision.

Grignon took a little mallet, and struck -toc, toc,‖ on the barrel, from which there revealed a bunch of silver cash. —Nay, what is this?‖ said she, grinning, and gave to the following, from which, when she tapped it, out poured a surge of gold coins. —I never observed the like-what garbage!‖ and she tried the third, out of which came a stack of pearls and precious stones, so the floor of the cavern was strewn with them. —Sire,‖ she shouted, —somebody has denied me of my great wine, and set this trash in its proper place.‖

—Junk, madam! Why such trash would purchase my entire realm.‖

—It is yours, sire,‖ answered the duchess, —if you will make me your sovereign.‖

The lord, who was an incredible admirer of cash, answered energetically, —Definitely, madam, I'll wed you tomorrow, maybe.‖

Grignon, profoundly pleased, made yet one other condition that she ought to have Princess Grace altogether in her own standard and influence, similarly, as though she had been her genuine mother; to which the stupid ruler consented, for he figured considerably more of wealth than he did of his youngster. So he and Grognon withdrew connected at the hip out of the cavern, very much satisfied.

At the point when the lord got back, Grace ran out with bliss to respect her dad and inquired as to whether he had a great game in his chasing.

—Truly, my youngster,‖ said he, —for I have taken a bird alive.‖

—Goodness, give it to me, and I will sustain and value it,‖ cried the princess.

—That is unimaginable, for it is the Duchess Grognon, whom I have vowed to wed.‖

—She a pigeon – she is fairly a bird of prey,‖ murmured the princess hopelessly; yet her dad bade her hold her tongue, and guarantee to adore her stepmother.

The loyal princess went to her condo, where her attendant before long discovered the distress on her face and its motivation.

—My youngster,‖ said old fashioned lady, – princesses should demonstrate a good guide to humbler ladies. Allow me to put forth a valiant effort to satisfy your dad, and to make yourself pleasant to the stepmother he has decided for you. She may not be so terrible after all.‖

Also, the medical caretaker offered such a lot of good guidance, that Grace started to grin, and dressed herself in her best clothing, a green robe weaved with gold; while her reasonable, free-falling hair was embellished, as per the design of the day, with a coronet of jasmine, of which the leaves were made of huge emeralds.

Grignon, on her part, made the best of herself that was conceivable. She put on a high-obeyed shoe to show up less faltering, she cushioned her shoulders, colored her red hair dark, and put in a bogus eye; at that point dressed in a hooped slip of glossy violet silk cut with blue, and an upper outfit of yellow with green ribands. Now, she wished to enter the city riding a horse, as she comprehended the sovereigns were prone to do.

Meanwhile, Grace held up in dread the snapshot of her appearance, and, to take a breakaway, she went isolated into a little wood, where she cried and sobbed covertly, until out of nowhere there showed up before her a youthful page, whom she had never seen.

—Who are you?‖ she asked, —And when did his magnificence bring you into his administration?‖

—I am in nobody's administration yet your own. I am Lola, a sovereign in my own nation, so that there is no imbalance of rank between us. I have cherished you long, and seen you frequently, for I have the pixie endowment of making myself undetectable. I may longer have concealed myself from you, yet for your present distress, wherein, be that as it may, I would like to be of both solace and help – a page but then a ruler, and your unwavering darling.‖

At these words, at once delicate and deferential, the princess, who had since a long time ago knew about the pixie ruler Lola, felt so glad that she dreaded Grognon no more. They talked a short time together and afterward came back to the royal residence, where the page helped her to mount her pony; on which she looked so wonderful, that all the new sovereign's qualities blurred into nothing in correlation, and none of the squires had eyes for any aside from Grace.

When Grognon saw it, —What!‖ she cried, -has this animal, the impudence to be preferably mounted over me! Drop, Miss, and let me try your pony; and your page, whom everybody has a favorable opinion of, offer him come and hold my harness.‖

Ruler Lola, who was the page, cast one look at Grace and complied; however, no sooner had the duchess mounted that the pony fled with her and hauled her over briers, stones, and mud, lastly tossed her into a profound dump. Her head was cut in a few spots, and her arm broken.

They got her in little pieces, similar to a messed up wineglass; never was there a poor lady of the hour in a more terrible predicament. However, regardless of her sufferings, her perniciousness remained. She sent for the ruler:

—This is all Grace's fault; she wished to murder me. I want that your grandness will rebuff her, or leave me to do it – else I will positively be vindicated upon you both.‖

The lord, scared of losing his barrels brimming with gold pieces, consented, and Grace was instructed to show up. The brutal Grognon requested four ladies, terrible as witches, to take her and strip off her fine garments, and whip her with bars till her white shoulders were red with blood. Be that as it may, lo! when the poles contacted her, they transformed into groups of plumes, and the ladies tired themselves to death with whipping, without harming Grace the least on the planet!

—Ok! kind Lola, what do I not owe you? What should I manage without you!‖ moaned the princess when she was reclaimed to her own chamber and her attendant. And afterward, she saw the sovereign remaining before her, in his green dress and his white crest, the most beguiling of pages.

Lola exhorted her to imagine sickness because of the coldblooded treatment she should have gotten, which so pleased Grognon, that she got well all the sooner, and the marriage was praised with extraordinary quality.

Before long, the lord, who realized that his significant other's frail point was her vanity, gave a competition, at which he requested the six most daring knights of the court to declare that Queen Grognon was the most attractive woman alive. No knight dared to debate this reality until there seemed one which conveyed a little box decorated with jewels and declared out loud that Grognon was the ugliest lady known to man, and that the most wonderful was she whose picture was in the case. He opened it, and see the picture of Princess Grace.

The princess sat behind her stepmother, felt sure that the obscure knight was Lola; however, she challenged state nothing. The challenge was fixed for the following day; however, meanwhile, Grognon, wild with outrage, instructed Grace to be taken in the night to a timberland a hundred alliances far off, brimming with wolves, lions, tigers, and bears. Futile the poor lady entreated that the orderlies would murder her at once, as opposed leave her in that appalling summit: the sovereign's requests must have complied; no answer was made to her, yet the workers remounted and rode away. Grace, in isolation and obscurity, grabbed through the timberland, sometimes falling against the trunks of trees, sometimes tearing herself with shrubs and briers; finally, defeat with dread and misery, she sank on the ground, crying out, –Lola, Lola, have you rejected me?‖

While she talked, a splendid light amazed her eyes, and the 12 PM woodland was changed into sparkling rear entryways, toward the end of which seemed a royal residence of the gem, sparkling like the sun. She realized it was the doing of the pixie sovereign who adored her, and felt a delight blended with dread. She went flying, yet observed him remaining before her, more attractive and beguiling than any time in recent memory.

–Princess,‖ said he, –for what reason would you say you fear me? This is the castle of the pixie sovereign, my mom, and the princesses my sisters, who will deal with you, and love you softly. Enter this chariot, and I will take you there.‖

Grace entered, and going through numerous exquisite backwoods dell, where it was clear light, and shepherds and shepherdesses were moving to cheerful music, they arrived at the castle, where the sovereign and her two girls got the pitiful princess with extraordinary generosity, and drove her through numerous rooms of rock-precious stone, sparkling with gems, where, incredibly, Grace saw the history of her own life, even down to this experience in the woods, painted on the dividers.

–How is this?‖ she said. –Sovereign, you know it all about me.‖

–Indeed, and I wish to protect everything concerning you,‖ said he softly, after that Grace cast down her eyes. She was very much cheerful and apprehensive that she ought to figure out how to adore the pixie ruler to an extreme.

She went through eight days in his castle – days brimming with each happiness, and Lola attempted all the contentions he could consider to actuate her to wed him and stay there forever. Be that as it may, the great and delicate Grace recalled her dad, who was once so kind to her, and she favored preferably to endure over to be needing in obligation. She pestered Lola to use his pixie capacity to send her home once more, and meanwhile to mention to her what had happened to her dad.

–Accompany me into the extraordinary pinnacle, and you will see with your own eyes.‖

—She won't be a lot of misfortune, sire; and as, when dead, she was very horrible for you to see, I have offered requests to cover her at once.‖

She may well say that, for she had an enormous faggot placed in a box, and fixed up; the lord and all the country grieved over it, and now, that she was no more, they proclaimed there never was such a sweet animal as the lost princess.

Seeing her dad's misery defeated Grace. —Gracious, Lola!‖ she cried, —my dad thinks am dead. If you love me, take me home.‖

The sovereign asserted, however, tragically, saying that she was as brutal to him as Grognon was to her. As they stopped the yard, they heard an incredible clamor, and Grace saw the royal residence all self-destructing with an extraordinary accident.

—What is this?‖ she cried, frightened.

—Princess, my royal residence, which you neglect, is between the things which are no more, dead and gone. You will not enter it anymore till after your entombment.‖

—Ruler, you are furious with me,‖ said Grace gloomily; just she knew well that she endured very as much as he did in subsequently leaving and stopping him.

Shown up in her dad's essence, she had incredible trouble in convincing him that she was not an apparition until the pine box with the faggot inside was taken up, and Grognon's perniciousness found But still, after all that, the ruler was so frail a man, that the sovereign before long caused him to accept he had been cheated, that the princess was dead, and this was a bogus Grace. Without more ado, he relinquished his girl to her stepmother's will.

Grignon moved with bliss, hauled her to a dull jail, removed her garments, made her dress in clothes, feed on bread and water, and sleep upon straw. Sad, Grace challenged not presently call upon Lola; she questioned if he despite everything adored her enough to go to her guide.

Meantime, Grognon had sent for a pixie, who was barely less pernicious than herself. —I have here,‖ said she, —a little scalawag of a young lady for whom I wish to discover a wide range of troublesome undertakings; help me in giving her another one consistently.‖

The pixie vowed to consider it, and before long brought a skein as thick as four people, yet made out of string so fine, that it broke on the off chance that you just blew upon it, thus tangled that it had neither start nor end. Grignon, charmed, sent for her poor detainee.

—There, miss, show your ungainly fingers to loosen up this skein, and if you break a solitary string, I will excoriate you alive. Start when you like, yet you should complete at dusk, or it will be more regrettable for you.‖ Then she sent her to her hopeless cell and treble-bolted the entryway.

Grace stood terrified, turning the skein again and again, and breaking several strings each time. —Ok! Lola,‖ she cried hopelessly, -come and help me, or possibly get my last goodbye.‖

Promptly Lola remained close to her, having entered the cell as effectively as though he conveyed the key in his pocket. —See me, princess, prepared to serve you, even though you neglected me.‖ He contacted the skein with his wand, and it unraveled itself and wrapped itself up in impeccable request. —Do you wish much else, madam?‖ asked he briskly.

—Lola, Lola, don't censure me; I am very much troubled.‖

—It is your own issue. Accompany me and make us both glad.‖ But she didn't utter a word, and the pixie sovereign vanished.

At nightfall, Grognon enthusiastically went to the jail entryway with her three keys and discovered Grace grinning and reasonable, her undertaking all done. There was no grievance to make, yet Grognon shouted that the skein was messy, and boxed the princess' ears till her ruddy cheeks turned yellow and blue. At that point, she left her and overpowered the pixie with rebukes.

—find me, by to-morrow, something totally inconceivable for her to do.‖

The pixie brought an extraordinary bushel loaded with plumes, culled from each type of fowl — songbirds, canaries, linnets, warblers, pigeons, thrushes, peacocks, ostrich, birds, partridges, jaybirds, falcons — indeed, if I revealed to them all finished, I will never reach a conclusion; and every one of these quills was so mixed up, that they couldn't be recognized.

—See,‖ said the pixie, -even one of ourselves would think that its hard to isolate these, and mastermind them as having a place with each kind of fledgling. Order your detainee to do it; she makes certain to come up short.‖

Grignon bounced for satisfaction, sent for the princess, and requested her to take her errand, and finish it, as in the past, by sunset.

Grace attempted calmly. However, she could see no distinction in the plumes; she tossed them all back again into the container and started to sob harshly. —Allow me to pass on,‖ she said, —for death just will end mine distresses. Lola adores me never again; if he did, he would as of now have been here.

—My princess, I'm here,‖ cried a voice from under the bushel; and the pixie sovereign showed up. He gave the 3 taps with his wand – the plumes flew by millions out of the bushel, and engineered themselves in little loads, each having a place with an alternate feathered creature.

—how do I repay you?‖ cried Grace.

—Love me!‖ addressed the ruler, gently, and said no more.

When Grognon showed up, she found the errand done. She was angry at the pixie, who was a lot more surprised herself at the result of their noxious inventions. However, she vowed to try once more. For a few days, using all her industry in concocting a crate, which, she stated, the detainee won't be able to open. —At that point,‖ included the guile pixie, —obviously, being such an insubordinate and fiendish young lady, as you state, she will open it, and the outcome will fulfill you however much you might want.‖

Grignon took the case, and told Grace to convey it to her château, and set it on a specific table, in a loft she named, yet not upon any record, to open it or inspect its substance.

Grace withdrew. She was dressed like any poor laborer, in a cotton outfit, a woolen hood and wooden shoes; yet, as she strolled along, individuals took her for a sovereign in camouflage, so beautiful were her looks and ways. In any case, being frail with detainment, she before long became tired, and, plunking downward on the edge of a little wood, took the crate upon her lap, out of nowhere a outstanding want held onto her to open it.

—I will take nothing out, I will contact nothing,‖ said she to herself, —yet I should perceive what is inside.‖

Without thinking about the outcomes, she lifted up the top. She quickly there leaped out various little men and little ladies, conveying little tables and seats, little dishes, and minimal instruments. The entire organization was little to such an extent that the greatest monster among them was hardly the stature of a finger. They jumped into the green knoll, isolated into different groups, and started moving and singing, eating and drinking, to Grace's marvel and joy. Yet, when she recalled herself and wished to get them into the crate once more, they all rushed away, played at finding the stowaway in the wood, and in no way, shape or form would she be able to get a single one.

Once more, in her trouble, she called upon Lola, and again he showed up; and, with a single pinch of his wand, sent all the little individuals once more into the container. At that point, in his chariot, drawn by stags, he took her to the mansion, where she did all that she had been told, and returned in wellbeing, to her stepmother, who was angrier than ever in recent memory. If a pixie could be choked, Grognon unquestionably would have done it in her fury. Finally, she made plans to ask help no more, yet to work her own devious will upon Grace.

She caused to dive an enormous gap in the nursery, and taking the princess there, indicated her the stone which secured it.

-Underneath this stone lies an incredible fortune; lift it up, and you will see.‖

Grace complied, and keeping in mind that she was remaining at the edge of the pit. After this, there appeared to be no more trust in the poor princess.

—O Lola,‖ cried she, —you are retaliated for. For what reason did I not return your adoration, and wed you! Passing will be less severe if just you lament me a bit.‖

While she talked, she saw through the clear murkiness a gleam of light; it got through a little entryway. She recollected what Lola had stated: that she could stay away forever to the pixie royal residence, until after she was covered. Maybe this last remorselessness of Grognon would be the end of her distresses. So she took mental fortitude, crawled through the little entryway, and lo! she turned out into an excellent nursery, with extended rear entryways, natural product trees, and blossom beds. Well, she knew it, and well, she knew the sparkle of the stone precious stone dividers. Also, there, at the royal residence entryway, stood Lola, and the sovereign, his mom, and the princesses, his sisters. —Welcome, Grace!‖ cried they all, and Grace, after the entirety of her sufferings, sobbed for euphoria.

The marriage was commended with extraordinary wonder, and all the pixies, for a thousand classes round, went to it. Some came in chariots drawn by mythical serpents, or swans, or peacocks; some were mounted upon drifting mists or globes of fire. Among the rest, showed up the very pixie who had helped Grognon to torment Grace. At the point when she found that Grognon's poor detainee was currently Prince Lola's lady of the hour, she was overpowered with disarray and begged her to overlook all that had passed, in light of the fact that she truly was oblivious who she had been so pitilessly harrowing.

—However, I will present appropriate reparations in light of all the evil that I have done,‖ said the pixie; and, declining to remain for the wedding-supper, she remounted her chariot, drawn by two horrible snakes, and travelled to the royal residence of Grace's dad. There, under the steady gaze of either lord, or squires, or women in-waiting could stop her – she came behind the insidious Grognon, and turned her neck, similarly as a cook does a horse shelter entryway fowl. So Grognon died and was covered, and nobody was especially upset for the equivalent.

THE CLEVER EUNICE

There was a man who had a girl, who was classified —Smart Eunice, and when she was grown up, her dad stated, —We should see about her wedding.‖

—Truly, answered her mom, –at any point, a youngster will show up who is deserving of her.

Finally, a specific youth, by the name Hans, originated from separation to make a proposition of marriage; however, he required one condition, that the Clever Eunice ought to be extremely reasonable.

—Goodness,‖ said her dad, –no dread of that! she has a head loaded with cerebrums; and the mother included, —Ah, she can see the breeze explode the road, and hear the flies hack!‖

—Great,‖ answered Hans; —however, recall, if she isn't exceptionally wise, I won't take her.‖ Soon, they plunked down to supper, and her mom stated, -Eunice, go down into the basement and draw some lager.‖

So Clever Eunice brought the container down from the divider, and went into the basement, jolting the top here and there on her way, to take a break. When she got the first floor, she drew a stool and set it before the container, all together that she probably won't need to stop, for she figured stooping may harm her back, and give it an unwanted twist. Then she put the can before her and turned the tap, and keeping in mind that the brew was running, as she didn't want her eyes to be inactive, she looked about upon the divider above and underneath. Then she saw, after much peeping into every corner, an axe, which the bricklayers had abandoned, standing out of the roof directly over her head. At seeing this Clever Eunice started to cry, saying, —Goodness! in the event that I wed Hans, and we have a kid, and he grows up, and we send him into the basement to draw brew, the axe will fall upon his head and murder him; thus she stayed there sobbing energetically over the looming hardship.

In the end, the great people upstairs were sitting tight for the lager. However as Clever Eunice didn't come, her mom advised the house cleaner to take a quick trip and see what she was halting for. The house cleaner went down into the basement and discovered Eunice sitting before the container crying healthily, and she asked, —Eunice, what are you sobbing about?‖

─Ok,‖ she answered, -have I not cause? If I wed Hans, and we have a youngster, and he grows up, and we send him an errand here to draw lager, that ax will fall upon his head and execute him.‖

─Gracious,‖ said the house cleaner, ─what a cunning Eunice we have!‖ And, plunking down, she started to sob, as well, for the adversity that was to occur.

Inevitably, when the worker didn't return, many people above started to feel parched, so the spouse advised the kid to go down into the basement and see what had happened to Eunice and the housekeeper. The kid went down, and there sat Clever Eunice and the house cleaner both crying, so he asked what happened; and Eunice revealed to him a similar story, of the ax that was to fall on her youngster, if she wedded Hans, and if they had a kid. When she had completed, the kid shouted, ─What a sharp Eunice we have!‖ and fell sobbing and wailing with the others.

Upstairs they were all the while waiting, and the spouse stated, when the kid didn't return, ─Do you go down, wife, into the basement and see why Eunice remains so long.‖ So she went down and discovering every one of the three stayings there crying, asked for an explanation, and Eunice educated her regarding the ax, which should definitely fall upon the head of her child. At that point, the mother in like manner shouted, ─Gracious, what a wise Eunice we have!‖ and, plunking down, started to sob as much as any of the rest.

In the end, the spouse waited for his significant other's arrival; however, finally, he felt so parched, that he stated, ─I should go myself down into the basement and see what is keeping our Eunice.‖ As soon as he entered the basement, where he found the four sitting and crying together, and when he heard the explanation, he also shouted, ─Goodness, what a clever Eunice we have!‖ and plunked down to cry with the whole of his lungs.

This time the groom above sat, waiting, yet when nobody returned, he figured they should be waiting for him. Thus he went down to perceive what was wrong. At the point when he entered, there sat the five crying and moaning, everyone louder than his neighbor.

─What adversity has occurred?‖ he inquired.

─Ok, dear Hans!‖ cried Eunice, ─if you and I wed each other, and have a kid, and he grow up, and we, maybe, send him down to this basement to tap the lager, the ax which has been left standing up there may fall on his head, thus slaughter him: and do you not think this is sufficient to sob about?‖

—Now,‖ said Hans, —more judiciousness than this isn't essential for my housekeeping; since you are such a smart Eunice, I will have you for my better half.‖ And, grasping her hand, he drove her home and commended the wedding legitimately.

After they had been married a short time, Hans said one morning, —Spouse, I will go out to work and win some cash; go into the field and assemble some corn wherewith to make bread.‖

As she went to the field, she said to herself, -What will I do? Will, I cut first, or eat first? Ay, I will eat first!‖ Then she gobbled up the substance of her pot. When it was done, she contemplated internally, —now, will I procure first or sleep first? I figure I will have a snooze!‖ thus, she laid herself down among the corn, and rested.

In the end, Hans got back, yet Eunice didn't come. Thus he stated, —Goodness, what a reasonable Eunice I have! She is innovative to the point that she doesn't get back home to eat anything.‖ Then, the evening came, and still, she didn't return; so Hans went out to see the amount she had harvested; in any case, see, nothing by any means, and there lay Eunice sleeping soundly among the corn! So home, he ran quickly and brought a net with little ringers holding tight it, which he tossed over her head while she, despite everything rested on. When he had done this, he returned again and closed to the house-entryway, and, seating himself on his stool, started working enterprisingly.

Finally, when it was about to dim, the Clever Eunice got up, and when she stood up, the net fell all over her hair, and the chimes jingled at each progression she took. This startled her, and she started to question whether she was an extremely Clever Eunice, and said to herself, —Am I she, or am I not?‖ This was an inquiry she was unable to reply, and she stopped for a drawn-out period of time considering about it. Finally, she figured she would return home and ask whether she was truly herself, assuming somebody would have the option to advise her. At the point when she went to the house-entryway, it was closed, so she tapped at the window, and asked, —Hans, is Eunice inside?‖ —Yes,‖ he answered, —she is.‖ At which answer she turned out to be truly startled, and shouting, —Ah, paradise, at that point, I am not Eunice!‖ she approached another house, expecting to pose a similar inquiry. Be that as it may, when the people inside heard the jingling of the ringers in her net, they wouldn't open their entryways, and nobody would get her. So she fled from the town, and nobody has ever seen her since.

Chapter 6:
Stories of the Countryside

<u>*DOG*</u>

JOSH AND BUDDY, THE FLUPPY PUPPY

Once upon a time, in the country-side suburb lived a young lad, Josh, and his family, which dwelt in their farm-yard. Josh is a boisterous young lad, fair as the sun with blackheads running riots on his face. He wore a yellow curly hair; he was fond of two things in the entire world, his father and pets that were gifted to him by his father. Josh was the first of three; he was popularly called, Josh!!The farm-boy by his peers, this is irrespective of the fact that farming and ranching was a popular enterprise in this settlement his family abodes. Josh seemed emotionally drifted since he lost his dad to an ailment. Josh and his family had since struggled to meet up with the financial quota for the family.

Josh, as every lad of his cadre, always fancied playing with his peers in the fields from mid-afternoon to the evening. As opposed to the parents of his friends, Josh's mom is skeptical about staying out late, and she always warns Josh to make haste to be home before 6'O clock. Josh heeled briskly through the Allen's walk-way en-route his home this very evening. He hast to meet up with curfew this very evening, as he ran through the sand path, his heart raced, and he felt different. Maybe what troubled his mind was how to avoid the constant nagging from his mom. Suddenly he heard a noise from the waste-bins that lay across the path, and he flipped in agitation. He literally skipped a beat; he then halted and walked in stealth fashion. As he drew near, as it was for an exploring lad of such caliber. He beckoned and raised the cans, to his amazement lay a white-furred puppy covered in patched mud. The eyes of this puppy were dark and alluring, and the mild cry aroused pity in the heart of Josh. Compassion filled the heart of Josh, and he picked up the puppy and placed it between its arms. Thoughts raced through his mind, I am definitely keeping this one, whether his mom was going to nag or spank him did not bother him. Since his dad's demise, she suggested he let go of their flamboyant lifestyle and opts for a decent lifestyle. He had to grudging let go of his pet, Nemo the gold-fish and Frankie the Wistar mice.

Josh strolled in gentle strides along the sandy foot-walk with green stout grass at both sides. He pelted the furs of the puppy as he walked and thought of names for his new pet flew across his mind. He said to himself, I should name him Jack, No!! Jack is quite a common name for puppies. I should name him buddy, buddy is nice, he said to himself. He hopped joyfully as he headed home, buddy, my buddy!! He said.

On arrival, Josh snuck to his room and prepared a warm bath and washed off the mud from the body of buddy. Josh, in a long while, seem filled with joy, he raced to show his mom his new friend. Josh's mom, Alexis, was at the dining table, set for supper. Josh raced to din from his room with Buddy, in his arm, and said to his mom, ‚' mom look who I found," his name is buddy. Alexis was furious, as Josh was expected to have arrived earlier to assist prepare for dinner, she replied in harshest of words, ‚Josh would you return that creature from where you picked it from, we have more mouths to feed than hands to work". She continued, ‚you have chosen not to come to terms with reality, stupid child." Josh was crushed to the bones, he always wondered if Alexis was his biological mom. He fled to the farm-yard in resentment.

Josh usually found solace at the porch in the farmyard; he sat there staring to the moon, and his hands were found pelting the furs of buddy. He wondered why his mom complained a lot and why his father had to abandon him and his siblings on earth so early. Josh always felt abandoned and lonely, but on the bright-side maybe Buddy was God-sent to be his company, finally God heard his prayers, he figured. He made that brighten grimace. He refused to eat, but he felt warm because of his newfound company. Josh and buddy slept in the farm-yard that night.

Josh's farm-house was built as a scattered settlement was surrounded by tall trees and bushes, as the trade was farming. Trades also ride along with their hazards. They are like Siamese twins. The local council has put out a warning to locals to deceased from uncontrolled bush burning as it put lives at risk. Many of the locals tend to carry out their evil menace in the dead of night. Unfortunately, that night, a certain farmer indulged in bush burning, and the fire drifted out of control. The fire burned fiercely, and burning down everything and anything that stood its way, it burnt it down into ashes.

The bush continued to burn hesitantly, but as folks would say, sometimes, blessings come in disguise. Buddy woke up and began to bark unceasingly woo!! Woo!! Josh said in a sleepy tone, sleep buddy, you are making a lot of noise. Josh's words seem to be fuel to fire, and Buddy kept on barking. Josh, in annoyance, reluctantly woke up. As Josh stood up from where he laid, he perceived fumes of smoke, he wondered to himself, ‚'who would be cooking at the early hours of the morning." But the fumes seem enormous to be from cooking. Josh and buddy hurried out of the farm-house to investigate, and to his amazement, he saw climbing soot to the clouds, and blazing fire raged through like a horde of horses. Josh immediately, he took to his heels, yelling, ‚'Mom!! Mom!! Wake up, Fire!! Fire!! Alexis woke up like someone experiencing a nightmare. She heeled out and found the same scary sights. Josh headed to his sibling's room and woke them up. The down-size of where Josh resided was that houses were far apart. You would have to walk meters to get to your neighbor. Alexis took her children, the livestock they would gather and buddy and fled for safety. As they walked, Josh recounted the ordeal, and all that Alexis thought was that, ‚'the one thing she feared has befell them" But certainly, buddy is not just a member of the family but he saved their lives today.

The End.

THE PURPLE ALOE

Once upon a time, in a far-away country lived a rich merchant and his family. The merchant had all he desired as pertaining to material acquisitions, but he would bear a seed. Life can be ironical, he wondered. He sought the advice of many wise folks and drank different potions to enable his wife to conceive but all to no avail. One faithful day, he was returning from one of his numerous trading sojourns in his cart. As they rode speedily, he gazed through the window of his cart as he drowned in his own thoughts. Suddenly, he saw an old man, half-naked with bruises and sores plaguing his entire body. He looked like someone who was a victim of snares of the night, which would be referred to as the claws of robbers. The rich merchant was hesitant to highlight as he thought that it would be a trap, but on taking a second consideration on the matter, he signaled his cart-rider to halt. The rich merchant stepped out and approached the old man. The old man narrated his ordeal, how he was ambushed by a band of thieves, and all his belongings and money were carted away. The rich merchant took the old man and headed to an inn where they passed the night. The rich man ensured that the sores and injuries of the old man were tended for, and ointments for healing were administered.

On the departure of the rich merchant, he gifted the old man some pieces of silver as financial assistance. The old man called the rich merchant and thanked him, and in gratitude, gave him seeds of flower called the purple aloe. The old man told him that it was passed unto him by his father, and the fluid that flows out of its nectar is known for its magical and fertility potency. They hugged tightly and bade themselves goodbye. The rich merchant rejoiced as he hurried home, he kept saying to himself, 'the gods have found favor in my sight." On arrival home, he narrated journey tale to his wife, and she rejoiced.

That week, the rich merchant, erected a glasshouse and planted the purple aloe only. The rich merchant and his wife took conscious efforts to make a child as they drank of the potion from the purple aloe regularly. Shortly after, the wife of the rich merchant conceived a child and gave birth to a beautiful girl. The rich merchant named her flower because her birth was miraculously from the potion that runs in the veins of the purple aloe.

Flower was a beauty to behold. As she grew with every increasing inch, her fairness was like that of the sun. Her beauty was insurmountable in comparison with her peers. Her hair was long and white, falling gently off her shoulders. Before she reached the age of marriage, suitors flocked the gates of the rich merchant. These recent happening was a thing of concern for the rich merchant, his daughter was precious to him and didn't wish any harm should beset her as a result of a wrong spouse. Sometimes the rich merchant wondered if his affection for his daughter must be birth out of their long wait for her conception, fifteen long years.

When flower was of age, her father, the rich merchant, took her for a stroll around their castle. He took time to explain how much she meant to him and how her mother and him had to wait for fifteen years to conceive her. The rich merchant also told flower about the importance of the purple aloe to their family.

Men from far away countries and countries near trooped in numbers for the hand in marriage of the rich merchant's daughter, Flower. They were men of different sizes, caliber: some were sons of war-lords, princes of kingdoms and even men known for their resounding wisdom made appearance in the bit to make a bride and wife from Flower. Every suitor had their sessions with Flower, they had their opportunities to woo, some came in wearing the regalia of the wealth of their father, some came with promises that Flower would not lift a finger to carry out a core in her life. Flower was a child groomed in wisdom and seemed to be indifferent about these promises as they emanated from the mouth of a spoilt brat.

But to her amazement, there was young prince Williams who seemed different. He was tall and handsome with a charming aura. She had a lengthy conversation, and he was thoughtful to really make efforts to know her, what she likes, and her ideals. They both began to have regular walks where they talked, chatted, and laughed. She grew so fond of Williams as grew from the skin of their parent's riches to genuine relationship of simple girl meets a young boy, and they both fell in love. Just one thing seems to fall-out for Flower, concerning Williams that his country was always at war against a rival country and the kings are always short-lived as the hazard of the battles they engaged in regularly. In the case of Williams, his father and grandfather's reign was short-lived. Flower feared this gravely.

Shortly after Flower grew fond of Williams, war between his country and their rivals became eminent. She was gravely scared, but like her father told her that since her birth, their heritage seemed to be tied to the purple aloe. Before Williams headed for battle, she prepared the potion and was put into a bottle and handed it over to him. She cried and kiss him goodbye, but Williams promised Flower that he was coming back for her.

With his army, he rode into battle, and days drifted into weeks and weeks into months. With every passing day, the chances Williams was returning from the battle diminished, but Flower kept on praying relentlessly every day. This very cold evening, as Flower prayed in the purple aloe glasshouse, then she heard the whining of a galloping horse and a fair young man rode it and behold to her greatest surprise, it was Williams, her heart leaped for joy. They hugged each other tightly, and Williams recounted the stories of their victory in battle and how the potency of the purple aloe was indeed a magical and lifesaving potion. Finally, Flower and Williams got married and lived happily ever after.

The End.

DUCKS

ZACH, THE FOGGILY DUCK

Once upon a time, Papa Gander and Mama Goose were expecting their first set of off-springs. It is basically a thing of great joy for the new couple. As the culture, Gander accompanied his wife, Goose, for the routine ante-natal checks at the ducks and duckling general hospital. During the last check-up, the Doctor duck examined Goose. He noticed a discrepancy during the ultra-sound. Doctor duck made his observations know to the couples immediately. He invited the couples to his office and he said to them, 'good morning," during the ultra-sound, I noticed an anomaly likely to affect one of your fetus but this usual occurrence in multiple pregnancies. Goose exclaimed in a sad tone, oh God!! What can be done to redeem this scenario, Doc, she said as her husband wrapped his arms around her in an attempt to console her? Doc responded, nodding his head in negation, 'I am sorry, we cannot really do much than believe the best of outcomes." The couple left the hospital sad but kept their torch of hope burning irrespective of the news they received that morning.

Shortly after, just a few months, Goose was due for delivery, with the build-up of bouts of labor contraction that evening just a few minutes past six; she yelled her husband pet name incessantly, Hun!! I am having contractions. He immediately rushed to her aid, packed all that was required for delivery, and they headed for the hospital. Just a few minutes past eleven that night, she was delivered of five ducklings. Two ducklings were of female gender and the last three of male gender. But of the male gender, one seem special and different. He was an albino-white breed (he had no black patches), and his feet were not properly webbed, unlike his siblings who had black spots or patches littered across their white skin with normal webbed feet. He was quite small but cute and beautiful in his own way, Mama Goose called him Zach.

Zach was indeed different; he was more like a white square amongst a lot of black squares. He was spotted among the horde for his uniqueness. His peers and his siblings referred to Zach as a freak or a weirdo. Hence they nicknamed him, albino Zach, or foggily duck, and he always raced to his mum who consoled and kept ringing this words to his eardrums, 'Zach my boy, you are a special one." Zach sometimes felt some truth in the words of his Mama Goose, as he has a very sensitive nostril, he would trail a duck from miles away as his nostrils pick duck scents. Zach was slow-paced, more like he did things at his own pace, he was last to swim amongst his siblings, made his first utterance (by that I mean the quack!!Quack!! Vocals) last in relation to his peers plus his distinct body features and the fact that he barely was able to make friends.

This year seems different in duck town, the month which the rain was expected to begin to grace the dry and patchy lands was far gone yet no single drop descended from the heavens. As every day passed, it seems imminent that famine was upon duck town. The famine came without any prior notification, the river began to dry up, food barns gradually emptied, and the death toll of ducks was on the rise due to diseases associated with poor nutrition and food shortage. Town meetings were called to ascertain the right step to make to curtail this disaster that has befallen duck town. The gods were consulted, but no answer or solution was obtained. Emissaries were sent out by the town council, but none returned. Most families had lost hope and prepared for the worst possible outcome, which was death.

Zach was always accustomed to always being alone, always found solace in his long and aimless strolls. As Zach strolled through a foot-path in the woods this faithful afternoon as he wondered on what has befallen his town, he perceived an unfamiliar duck scent. He was initially reluctant, yet he followed the trail, and with every step, the scent seems stronger. Somewhere in his mind, he reasoned that it was surely the emissary en-route back to duck town, finally a solution was feasible, he thought. As she got much closer, he was taken his aback by the sight, a gorgeous duck singing melodiously. From the prints on her feathers, she was obviously of a different tribe.

Zach was quite shy; he had never had a proper conversation with female counter-part. He wondered what he would say, or how he was going to introduce himself. He pondered for a while, after which he braced himself to trust his gut despite his assurance that his goofy personality might betray him.

Zach walked up to her and taps her, sorry!! He said, hello dear and he introduces himself, and he asked why she was found in the woods alone. She told him that this was her spot of solitude and that it was a regular habit of hers and in-turn she introduced her, my name is Sally, it turns out that her father was a chief of a town called Gander and Goose harbor. They both got chatty, and Zach explained the challenges that Duck town was experiencing and how they sought different option, but no positive result seem forthcoming. Sally felt sorry for Zach and promised him that she would be of assistance as it turns out that famine was just regional after-all and not global.

Zach fled home with the good news, when got to duck town, he relayed his findings to the council of chiefs. It was no news that they were going to doubt Zach, but he mightily convinced them, and they were clueless, any suggestion was an option to be explored. Some chiefs and emissaries set out for Gander and Goose harbor for answers to their woes. To their great amazement, they found Gander and Goose harbor, and all Zach said was indeed true. The folks of harbor were entertaining and warm; the chiefs of duck town were able to strike a fair deal that would ensure that the food in abundance was made available for their people. Zach was special after all, his art of adventure and uniqueness saved duck town.

The End.

THE STORY OF FORTE THE CAT.

This is a story of Forte the Cat. It's Forte's first day in school, and Forte felt very uneasy, as his mum woke him up. Forte tried to lift up his closing eyelids with all the strength he could muster, he stood up, stretched and yawned before he finally looked at his mum.

—Cats are hardworking, despite being slow and lovely,‖ said his mum. —This is six A.M Forte. It's time to wake up.

—But mum, I still want to sleep some more, I took milk and cheese in the night, and I am still giddy mum will you allow me for thirty more minutes?‖

His mum went to the bathroom, brought his towel and soap, and flung at him. —As I said, Forte, it's time to wake up‖ other cats are already on their way to Winsophia, the Cat school. Please get up and freshen up, and we will be on our way‖ .

Forte slowly got up from the bed, picking up his towel and soap and swaggered to the bathroom, his body slowing this way and that.

When he popped out of the bathroom, his mum had already prepared carrots and juice for breakfast, he ate, and soon enough, they were on their way to school.

It was Forte's first day in school, and he felt so uneasy, he wasn't accustomed to the classroom.

He missed home, where he would be playing with his friends Rob and Wilson and chasing rats and basking in the river.

Now he was here, so slow and lethargic, but he was determined to make something out of school, he needed to make his mum proud and be bright like his mates in school, how was Forte planning to do this? Forte decided he will pay attention in class and make friends with the most intelligent cats in class. His mother complained this morning about his laziness, he didn't like that, and he vowed not to continue like that.

Kathy appeared in front of the class, she started with —cats are nice and are lovely, this is the best cat school in Creston, and you cats here must count yourselves privileged, because many cats will want to be here but cannot because they are less privileged. So you need to make the most of this opportunity cats‖ . —Yes, aunty Kathy‖ the cats echoed, and their voices reverberated in the room.

Forte was mute, he was ruminating on aunty Kathy's words, allowing each sentence to sift into his ears and Bones and marrows, passing into his soul and finding roots in his heart. He kept those words in his heart, and he was going to make the best of the opportunity in school.

He sat near Fred, a shrewd and gentle cat with nice and fresh furs, Fred was keen for knowledge. Throughout the day, Fred paid attention in class and answered questions in class. Milk and chocolates during break, and throughout this time, Forte watched him with keen interest. Fort was determined to be friends with Fred, he was convinced that friendship with Fred was going to be a very fruitful one and one that would help fuel his ambition in school, and he will make his mum proud, and aunty Kathy would be happy with him.

The bell for dismissal rang, and Fred was tidying his box when Forte appeared beside him with a bright smile. —You are a wonderful cat, Fred, and I want to be your friend, hope you don't mind.‖ —Not at all,‖ Fred said, making forward and kissing Forte, Forte was delighted.

And they turned and began to walk home, as they walked they talked about aunty Kathy, about winsophia, about what their parents expect from them in school. About how they would leave up to fulfilling this demands.

Fred said his mum promised to buy him a bicycle and a box of chocolates and cakes if he does well. While Forte retorted that his mum has made no promises but that he would love to make his mum proud, and he was going to do it at all costs.

They kissed each other and vowed to live to their dreams no matter what happened.

When Forte got home, his mum hugged him. —Mum school was very good today, I am getting inspired, and I will try to make the most of my time at Winsophia‖ his mum was so happy to hear this.‖ Did you make any friends?‖ —Yes!‖ Forte screamed triumphantly, his lungs reverberating under his throat.

His mum reached out and hugged him so passionately, gently touching his furs, Forte was smiling, and that reassured him of his stance. Tomorrow, he will tell Fred to introduce him to other bright students in class, and he will keep on paying attention in school and pleasing his mum.

The next day in school was sports day, and the cats were all dressed in their sports wears, they were all out in the field and waited for aunty Kathy to give them instructions on how the sports day would go. Forte was with Fred at the rear of the school field.

—I would love to make more friends with the other bright students like you in class Fred,‖ Forte said, his eyes dimming and revealing the depth of the graveness of what he said.

—It's alright, Forte, but you must know that no one was made bright. We are just a group of cats who told ourselves we were smart, and we started working as though we were, and we became that way.‖ Forte's face tightened to a grimace, he was shocked at the words of Fred, – but my mum says, I am lazy, and I sleep too much.‖ - That's because you think you do, and so you always catch yourself sleeping because you really think so‖ Forte's face lit up, and he was momentarily too stunned to speak as the reality of Fred's words, dawned on him. —Okay, how Fred, I am smart,‖ he shouted. —That's it,‖ Fred screamed and hugged him.‖

As they went home that day, Forte was so ecstatic, he had found a new light, —it doesn't take so much to be amazing after all‖ Forte muttered to himself under his breath. - I am a smart cat, I am so amazing.‖

He was so happy and was willing to share this new light with his mum.

 Her face tore into a wide smile when Forte told him how smart he was, she hugged her kit and licked her furs. Forte was becoming a cat, a fantastic cat.

This is the end of the story of Forte the cat.

THE STORY OF THE GREAT IROKO TREE

In the hills of Normandy, there was once a selfish Iroko tree. It was so big and so luscious, it's leaves sparkled and danced. Its bark was fresh and kinky. Its root, strong and stern. But the Iroko tree lived in solitude, it made sure it's leaves dried up before it fell, it didn't provide its fruit for the animals nor did it provide shades for other trees and shrubs and animals.

Virtually, every living and non-living thing in the hills of Normandy was sore at this tree.

Its gigantic nature didn't offer anything to them, and they had pleaded severally with mother Earth to take him away. But mother Earth kept asking them one question, —what have you done for the big Iroko‖ ? So each time the animals come to plead with mother Earth to kill off the Iroko, they all went home sullen and angry with mother Earth.

They all knew they couldn't do anything to the big Iroko, because one branch of the big Iroko would wipe out all of them. So they all resorted to sulking, they always gathered together to insult and ridicule the Iroko, but all that didn't change anything.

They keep making several plans weaving and weaving and looking for ways to take down the big Iroko.

One day, they planned to set the Iroko on fire. As they were about to carry this out when the king of rats came pleading that the sort of fire that will destroy the Iroko will also burn it's kind and that their children will die. When the other animals thought about this, they decided against the plan and didn't set the Iroko on fire.

The Iroko continued to live In its solitude, rendering no one any helps and getting no helps from anyone, and the animals kept on sulking, each time they stare at the great Iroko tree, a monsoon of bitterness welled up within them. And so, on another day, they came up with the plan to cut the tree.

But they can't get anywhere near the great Iroko, it would use it's branches and destroy all of them and so that was going to be a futile journey.

However, the fox suggested that they can make use of a hook. The plan was nice, so they planned to plant a hook on the big Iroko tree in the night while it slept and attach a very long rope, with which they will pull it down in the morning.

Three nights had passed, and they were done with the plans of hooking the great Iroko tree, they had the hook and the rope. But argued fruitlessly about who will hook the great Iroko tree.

The tortoise suggested that the lions were brave, and this was a matter that required bravery, so the Lions should not have any problems hooking the Iroko tree.

The lions complained that the noise they make would wake up the Iroko, and their plans would crumble.

The other animals reasoned that it was true, and the elephant was asked to walk slowly and attach the hook,but the elephant deferred, saying that it was difficult to do that, because they won't be swift with it.

Every animal kept on coming up with one reason or the other why they can't hook the great Iroko tree until the bull volunteered to do that.

He did that on one condition that the animals would take care of his children if he didn't survive the escapade and the other animals agreed.

So on that faithful night, the bull walked briskly, tiptoeing to where the Iroko tree was situated, it was midnight. So the Iroko tree was deep in sleep. The bull was fearless and so didn't want to make mistakes, so he rounded the Iroko tree seven times, wrapping the great Iroko tree with a rope before finally planting the hook at the bark of the stem of the Iroko tree. As soon as the hook penetrated the Iroko tree, it roused and it's branches came alive, whirling around in a circle very fiercely, and as the bull made to run away, one of the rear branches bent over and swept it off its foot, and it landed with its horn and the horn bent, as it struggled to limp away before the branch makes a fatal move on it. And so the bull escaped by a hair breadth. And the great Iroko tree struggled in futility to set itself free, but the hook remained steadfast on it. And when it found it couldn't do much about unhooking itself, it rested.

In the morning all the animals ate well and were strong and ready to pull down the great Iroko tree, they lined up on a straight file and pulled and pulled, but the Iroko tree stood strong, rooted to its spot. All the veins in all the animals were out as they pulled with all their strength, but they were all sprawling on the grass as the Iroko tree remained unmoved. They all went home, grumbling and sulking at their failed efforts.

While the earth, they complained to mother Earth, asking her why she held the root of the great iroko tree so strongly, but mother Earth greeted their complaints with derisive laughter, they were all pained, and each one went to their houses despondent.

One day, it was very cold and dry, and the leaves of the iroko tree were dry, it was so cold, and the great iroko tree was dying. The animal kingdom felt like heaven on Earth as they watched keenly waiting for when the great iroko tree would drop dead. As they watched on delight, a fair, beautiful girl emerged and looked with pity at the great iroko tree, and so she decided to protect the iroko tree, she used her big blanket to cover the great iroko tree. And the great Iroko tree survived.

The next day was sunny and hot, and the great Iroko was lush and green. It shielded the young Fair Lady from the sun, it bent over and covered her. And mother Earth called all the other animals and when they saw it, they didn't believe what they saw, and mother Earth told them that the great Iroko tree has discovered that it cannot survive on its own. And encouraged them to go and find shield under it's shadow, and they went. The Iroko tree was happy to offer then shield, and they were happy to be shielded. They all lived happily ever after.

THE GRASS STORY

This is a bedtime story that captures the adventures of the elephant grass, spear grass, and carpet grass.

The Elephant grass, Spear grass, and Carpet grass once lived together in the hills of Bentis, and they were discontent with their place of abode, in Bentis, because they didn't like how the place looked.

—We are all alone in this place, and it's so lonely and serene, we can't even play with other plants, I hate this place so much‖ the Elephant grass fussed, and the Spear grass would normally nod in agreement to whatever the elephant grass said.

But the carpet grass would look at them and smile —you should be thankful for what you have, some other grasses wish to exist, but they no longer do because of one tragedy or the other. But you are still alive, you have water, and you can absorb it, the sun shines on you daily, the wind isn't very cruel to you, you basically have everything you need, so why do you whine and fuss about being lonely?‖

Whenever the carpet grass stopped speaking, the elephant grass would look at it with horror and derision, and the Spear grass would also move away from the carpet grass.

They both treated the carpet grass with cruelty because the carpet grass believes that one should be content with what one has, and the elephant grass and spear grass always kept wanting more out of life.

So the Elephant grass and spear grass continued to nurse their hefty dreams, and the carpet grass, lowly and timid, was happy in its little space. It wished for somewhere better, somewhere it would have so many beautiful children, and its owners will take care of it, and its children. However, even as it craved for all this, it was content.

On the other hand, the Elephant grass and spear grass craved earnestly for the worldly pomp and power, they dreamt of being set up in a great hill, where many other plants will surround and respect them.

One day, a couple walked along the hills of Bentis, pushing their trolley and looking around to harvest species of grasses.

They dressed brightly colored cloths, the woman wore a golden earring and bangles, and the man wore a golden wristwatch and shoes.

The elephant grass drew closer to them bending over to get a better look, Its eyes lit up, it was engrossed in the grandiosity of the couple, this was what it had been hoping to get all its life.

And when the spear grass made to get closer, the Elephant grass kicked it away and remained steadfastly and conspicuously positioned, waiting earnestly for the couple to come and get it.

And when the couple finally arrived where the elephant grass was, it leaped for joy and swung itself into their trolley as the woman uprooted and made to cast it into the trolley.

They carted it way, and it danced and bounced along joyfully inside the trolley as the couple rode along.

Soon enough, the butterfly brought the news of the fate of the elephant grass to the spear grass and the carpet grass.

—The elephant grass, was planted in the valleys of kush and it was pruned and made to multiply in abundance, however when it began to multiply, the couple sent their cows to eat up all the elephant grass. And the cows are now eating all the elephant grass and defecating on all its children. The elephant grass cries all day and all night. It murmurs daily, and it agrees that the hills of Bentis was heaven, compared to where it has found itself.

As the butterfly finished and made to go away, the spear grass started to laugh derisively, —I knew the Elephant grass would end badly, I knew it, after bragging about going to a better place and living a good life, it has ended in the bellies of the dirty cows of kush‖ the spear grass said.

The spear grass began to spread it's stems and brag to the carpet grass about how well it would end up.

—I will be taken to the Beverly Hills, and I will be surrounded by many expensive plants, and animals will worship me.‖

—You shouldn't mock the carpet grass, you should try to learn for its ordeal, and not laugh at it, let's keep our calm and composure, spear grass, everything good will come.‖

The spear grass looked at the carpet grass proudly, sighed, and moved away.

One day, a woman dressed in a luxuriant gown, walked past the Bentis hills, her gown was laced with silver linings and many expensive stones. The spear grass was ecstatic, —this is my time,‖ it thought to itself, I have finally made it out of dry and drooly hill it shouted, gladly.

As the woman approached, it bent over spreading its stems to make sure the woman harvests it, when the woman came closer, she hesitated a little and finally harvested the spear grass.

The spear grass was so happy, this was the day it had been hoping for all these while, and its joy could not contain its heart.

After a couple of days, the butterfly brought the news of the fate of the spear grass to the carpet grass, —the spear grass and her children are being fed to the fodders,‖ it said, —they eat and poop on it all day, and the spear grass wished it had remained at Bentis‖ .

The carpet grass felt sorry for the spear grass, it wished the spear grass and the elephant grass had found a better new home than what they have.

One day a woman walked past the Bentis hill, she wore a purple chemise and leather sandals, she sang aloud as he walked, she saw the carpet grass and liked it, she uprooted the carpet grass and took it to her home, in Beverly hills.

She treated the carpet grass well, and she planted the carpet grass at Beverly hills, alongside with other precious plants. She pruned the carpet grass, the carpet grass was the lawn, her children played on the carpet lawn happily. The carpet grass interacted with other plants, the carpet grass was happy ever after.

The butterfly took the news of the carpet grass to the Elephant grass and spear grass. It kept telling the story everywhere it went to everyone who would pay attention.

Conclusion

CONCLUSION: HOW TO IMPROVE ONESELF AND OVERCOMING STRESS

We all face different challenges and hurdles at some point or the other in the course of our lives, and sometimes the pressure might just be overwhelming and hard to handle. When we feel overwhelmed, when we feel unsure about how to meet the demands and cope with the pressures placed on us, we experience stress. In little portions, stress can be a good thing. It can enact the push you need, a little motivating factor to strife for the best, and also to stay focused and alert. Stress is the factor that keeps you on your toes during a presentation in school or that force that drives you to study for your exam when you'd rather be in the cinemas. But when the going gets too tough, and life's demands exceed your natural ability to cope, stress immediately becomes a threat to both your physical and emotional well-being.

There's a biological stress response, a natural one that is meant to protect and support us. It is what helped our ancestors survive the dangerous situations they faced frequently. But in the modern world, most of the stress we feel is a response to psychological rather than physical threats. It's either we're stressed over a looming deadline, assignments, projects, work presentations, an argument with a friend, or a warehouse full of bills, the warning bells ring. And just like a caveman confronting a sabretooth tiger, we go into an automatic overdrive.

Stress is known to be a psychological and physiological response to events that upset our personal balance. When faced with a threat, whether to our physical safety or emotional equilibrium, the body's defenses kick into high gear in a rapid, automatic process known as the -fight-or-flight response. We all know what this stress response feels like, heart pounding in the chest, muscles tensing up, breath coming faster, and every sense on red alert.

If stress were to be a disease, it would be considered a world pandemic. Stress has so much adverse effect on the human body when it's consistently experienced. In this age of technology, coupled with the fast-paced growth of all industries and sectors, we tend to push our bodies to the limits. There's the strife to achieve another milestone, another noble laureate, there's just that one more bound we want to break. And as much as this is very good and healthy for the growth of the society as a whole, so much -evil is being done to our bodies.

We in this modern times have become masters and professionals at maintaining bad, terrible and horrible sleeping patterns, masters at unhealthy eating, we also in recent times have mastered how not to care so much about our health. Good health is very much underrated. All these form a composite of well-balanced ingredients for a meal of stress. Stress has become opium for those wanting to achieve landmarks in their lifetime.

If you have a lot of responsibilities and worries, like a demanding work, the banking sector, for instance, you may be running on stress a good portion of the time—launching into an emergency mode with every traffic jam, phone call from the office, or every shout in the neighborhood. But the problem with the stress response is that the more it is activated, the harder and harder it is to shut off. Instead of the body system to level off once the crisis has passed, the stress hormones, heart rate, and blood pressure remain elevated, all red flags. Furthermore, repeated activation of the stress response takes a heavy toll on the body. The body always needs a certain amount of time to recuperate. Just like a machine needs to be serviced from time to time to keep the systems in check and to avoid breakdown. Prolonged exposure to stress increases your risk of everything from heart disease, obesity, and infection to anxiety, depression, and memory problems. Because of the widespread damage it can cause, it's essential to learn how to deal with stress more positively and reduce its impact on your daily life.

Stress affects virtually every aspect of the human body, the mental health, the psychological health, the total well-being of the person. It affects the total output of the person. The person slowly dissipates, and if conscious efforts are not taken to check the levels of stress, such persons will fade out and eventually burn out. If, for instance, their mental health is impaired, and such a person works in a field of constant logical thinking and loads of mental processes, the person cannot function. For instance, in the battlefront, soldiers have been diagnosed with suffering from Post -Traumatic Stress Disorder upon leaving the war field. Extreme stress reactions can be birthed from sudden and catastrophic events or traumatic experiences such as natural disasters(hurricanes, tornadoes, tsunamis amongst others), sexual assaults(molestation, rape, trafficked victims), life-threatening accident(survivors of shipwrecks, like the survivors from Titanic, survivors from plane crashes) or participation in combat. After the initial shock and emotional crisis, many trauma victims gradually begin to recover from its effects. But as we know that for every case there are always exceptions, in some people, the stress symptoms never go away, the body is not able to regain its equilibrium, the distortion caused by the trauma is so great that the effect remains permanent, and life doesn't return to normal. This severe and persisting reaction to trauma is known as post-traumatic stress disorder (PTSD).

Common symptoms of PTSD include:

Intrusive thoughts, or nightmares about the trauma

Avoidance of places associated with the trauma

Hyper-vigilance for signs of danger

Chronic irritability and tension

Depression.

PTSD is a serious disorder that requires professional intervention.

Chronic stress plunges it's fangs into your mental health, causing emotional damage in addition to physical ailments. People who have experienced varying levels of stress have been seen to have mouth ulcers, stomach ulcers amongst other ailments. Long-term stress can even rewire the brain. One might begin to act off as the mind is being consistently hammered and reshaped by stress. Over time, stress can lead to mental health problems, such as:

Anxiety

Depression

Eating disorders, and

Substance abuse.

The Body's Stress Response

The -fight-or-flight‖ stress response involves a cascade of biological changes that prepare us for emergency action. When our senses are alerted to danger, a small part of the brain called the hypothalamus sets off a chemical alarm. Epinephrine races through the bloodstream, readying us to either flee the scene or battle it out, and in some cases, freeze.

Heart rate and blood flow to the larger muscles increase so we can run faster and fight harder. Blood vessels which lie under the skin constrict to prevent blood loss in case of unintended injury, pupils dilate—they get bigger, so we can see better, and our blood sugar spikes, giving us an energy boost and speeding up reaction time. At the same time, processes in the body that do not aid the whole -flight-or-fight‖ event are suppressed, the digestive and reproductive systems, growth hormones, and the immune response are put on hold.

To get a handle on stress, one needs to learn first how to recognize it in oneself. Stress affects the mind, body, and behavior in many ways. The specific signs and symptoms of stress vary widely from person to person. Some people primarily experience physical symptoms, such as low back pain, stomach problems, and skin outbreaks. In others, the stress pattern is centered on emotional symptoms, such as crying. For some others, change in the way they think or behave predominates. It is very important to identify the symptoms one typically experiences when under stress. If the red flags are known, one can take early steps to deal with the stressful situation before it—or your emotions—spiral out of control to other complications.

After the first stage of identifying stressors, one can move to the next stage. Tackle the stress agents. Learning to be kinder to yourself, in general, can help you control the amount of pressure you feel in different situations, which can help you feel less stressed.

Learning to reward yourself for achievements – even small things. Like completing a piece of work or making a decision (even if its small). You could take a walk, read a book, and treat yourself to the food you enjoy.

Get a change of environment temporarily. You might want to go outside, or even visit a friend's place or go to a café for a break.

Take a break or holiday, sometimes away from routine work can do a lot of work in relieving stress. You'll feel less stressed when there is dynamism in one's life. Also, learn to forgive yourself when you make a mistake or when you don't achieve something you hoped for. Always have it at the back of your mind that nobody is perfect, and putting extra pressure on yourself doesn't help.

Use help from people around you. Remember that whatever you're going through that's causing you stress, you don't have to cope with it alone.

Friends and family: Sometimes talking to people close to you about how you're feeling can have a tremendous impact on stress relief.

You can also get support at work. For example, your line manager, human resources (HR) department e.t.c Do not worry that talking to your manager or colleagues about stress will be seen as a sign of weakness.

Support at university or college, such as your lecturers, student union, or student services.

The is also the online peer support. Sometimes sharing ones experience with people who have been through something similar can really go a long way in helping one to feel less alone.

The International Stress Management Association, an organization established to help those dealing with stress at various levels and degrees, can help find a specialist stress practitioner in your local area.

What treatments are there for stress?

Stress is not medically diagnosed, so there is no specific treatment for it. However, if you are finding it hard to cope with day to day activities because paranoia and one's senses are always at alert for danger and there's also a need to make everything perfect, thus heightening the stress levels a person experiences, treatment can come into play.

Talking treatments

Speaking and dialoguing with trained personnel about stress can help in stress relief therapies. One connects with his thoughts and emotions and can see things more plainly. Some talking therapies include:

Cognitive-behavioral therapy (CBT). This helps to understand one's thought patterns, recognize various trigger points, and identify positive actions that can be taken to combat stress at various degrees.

<u>Mindfulness based stress reduction (MBSR).</u> This combines mindfulness, meditation and yoga with a particular focus on reducing stress. This tries to cover the overall wellness of the person.

Medication

Since stress in itself is not a mental problem, there's no specific drug to use. However, your doctor might offer to prescribe:

Sleeping pills or minor tranquilizers if you're having trouble sleeping

Antidepressants if you're experiencing depression or anxiety

Medication to treat any physical symptoms of stress, such as irritable bowel syndrome (IBS), or high blood pressure.

Eco-therapy

Eco-therapy is a way of improving your wellbeing and self-esteem by spending time in nature. This can include physical exercise in green spaces or taking part in a gardening or conservation project.

Complementary and alternative therapies. Asides the therapies and various ways of relieving stress named above, one can also find certain alternative therapies to help you manage feelings of stress. These might include acupuncture, aromatherapy, massage, or traditional Chinese Medicine.

The complete wellness of the body is paramount as that in itself aggregates to the total wellbeing of the society. Stress has killed people, burnt them out, and it's still doing so. But with proper knowledge on how to manage and efficiently have a balanced life amidst all the stress that we have today, one can survive for years to come.

Made in the USA
Monee, IL
05 May 2021